CULTURE
STORM

H. L. NIEBURG

State University of New York at Binghamton

CULTURE STORM

Politics & the Ritual Order

ST. MARTIN'S PRESS *New York*

Library of Congress Catalog Card Number: 72-91276
Copyright © 1973 by St. Martin's Press, Inc.
All Rights Reserved.
Manufactured in the United States of America.
For information, write: St. Martin's Press, Inc.
175 Fifth Avenue, New York, N.Y. 10010

Affiliated publishers: Macmillan & Company, Limited, London—
also at Bombay, Calcutta, Madras, and Melbourne—
The Macmillan Company of Canada, Limited, Toronto.

. . . singing, "This will be the day that I die . . . ."
Instead, I write this book,
and dedicate it to all the days and works
that survive the storm.

CONTENTS

1 | INTRO & APOLOGIA

The violent revolutionists secretly are in love with the establishment. They believe the establishment is strong, is suffocating them; and so they want to destroy it. But when you do that, you become the establishment yourself. You don't have to kill it or fight it. If you want to change the world, you do it through Art. Art changes values; you don't even have to touch anything, just change values so much that the establishment doesn't mean anything anymore. (Yoko Ono, 1971)[1]

We have witnessed a major storm in the 1960's, a storm whose ravages of wind and wave have transformed the shape of our values and thoroughly battered all the comfortable landmarks of our civilization. In the morning of a new decade we wake up drained of the past. The brightest slogans of the 1950's are now vulgarized by popular acceptance, caricatured by the grab for power of new constituencies. Both the sacred and profane of our mental universe are destroyed; our obscenities have been rendered pallid by overuse; the mysteries of sex have been stripped away; the demands of national security no longer provide goals for organized activity; production and consumption as social imperatives are inverted by an ethos that apparently demands neither work nor discipline. Productivity is to be looted for its high-performance cars, high-fidelity audio, and highs of drugs and sensuality. Looting and vandalism are the order of the day, not only in public parks and school bathrooms, but everywhere that old values and institutions are found to be loose and undefended. This is the age that made the journey to the moon and found it dull and pointless. The age whose counter-culture soon became an over-the-counter-culture. The age whose revolutionary youth descended to "ripping off" cherry trees and park benches in Washington, D.C.

All the highly developed nations find their citizens acting as though they had been defeated in war and as if foreign armies were approaching from all sides; the home bastions disintegrating as a hundred new regimes are proclaimed over the ruins of the shattered state. Whether it was a plague, a revolution, or a storm, the period of excoriation and razing is now receding behind us. As John Lennon said, "The dream is over. I am not just talking about the Beatles, I am talking about the generation thing. It's over, and we gotta—I have to personally—get down to so-called reality."[2]

The "sorry about that" decade like a fierce scythe laid waste throughout the world. From the Chinese cultural revolution through the sequence of U.S. assassinations, from passive resistance to ambushes of policemen, from trashing to bombing, the storm has crested and now begins to fade. Finally, with the turn of the new decade comes the new morning of which Bob Dylan sings.

Has a decade of cultural search-and-destroy created a wave of tolerance based on exhaustion? Now a thousand flowers may truly bloom, but does anyone care? Recession and retrenchment mark this new morning—the surfeit of educated unemployables, the collapse of an economy generated and sustained by war and diplomacy, the general dispirit and fatigue of culture. We wake up with the taste of pennies on the tongue and a stumbling sense of purpose that springs from the compelling requirements of a spent body and a racking headache, like a hangover following an excess of festival.

As a nation we have lost faith. We have become self-conscious and self-critical as a whole people. No longer the exclusive province of the intellectual, the moral decrepitude of the nation is taken for granted even by the plastic middle Americans. Horrors! What is left for Billy Graham and young professors? This crisis in the soul of America provides a great opportunity. It is not enough to attack moribund universities and curricula, to check the military-industrial complex, to point out the inequities and brutalities of our times; rather, we must discover what we want to live for and how to live for it. For thirty years that great positive goal "Stop Communism" has directed our lives. Now we may have to live for a lot of different things—not grand designs, not great world responsibilities—but a lot of different things that people want to do and should be left alone to do. This is a time when we have to liberate ourselves and our energies and permit a period of testing. This is a time for openness and imagination! It is not enough to blame agitators or the Pentagon. To do so is to escape from the responsibility of our time, which is to discover and remake ourselves.

MILIEU THERAPY

The "culture storm" of the last decade constituted the first all-consuming wave of social change to strike the Western world since the period of the 1920's. Nothing has been left untouched—manners, dress, the arts, morals, education, all public priorities. In this book we attempt to assay the nature of that storm, especially as it shaped and modified repertoires of political behavior. We want to look beneath the surface of politics—into the germinal sources of values, behaviors, loyalties, groups, symbols, organizations, and strategies. Specifically, we are concerned with values manifested as behavior forms.

We will attempt to look at the rituals of society, from occasions like elections, law-making, and the judicial process, to the more informal manifestations of generational and seasonal passage that occur in the media of pop culture and the arts, in order to discover how new values are translated into behavior forms. Our approach will be that of "milieu therapy," an attempt to conceptualize and open for analysis the shadowy and ambiguous substrata of the culture process that give rise to all the abstract solidity of political and social systems.

Culture is the precursor of political and institutional change. Values change first; then everything else becomes possible.

Where does culture come from? It arises from the reciprocal exchange of values that goes on simultaneously at all levels of social organization; it involves all values and resources in a web of interpersonal and intergroup transactions, the sum of whose outcomes at any moment is embodied in values that continue to be subject to challenge and further change. Culture, in short, arises from a vast and ever-changing network—a network that is structured by the balance of constituencies and the priorities of social purpose posed by the events of a particular time. The sudden liquidation of structural limits, such as occurred during the last decade, is a periodic feature. Such structural deterioration does not necessarily recur at rhythmic intervals; it, too, is subject to the outcomes of human interaction and natural events.

The political order rests on a culture base. The old political science reflected a period in which culture control was subordinated to national security, war, and diplomacy. Its viewpoint is now a relic of the days of Cold War and national planning. In these days of culture storm and multiple inputs, political analysts must discount old assumptions about interest groups, political parties, and private and public agencies, for the dynamics of culture change are laying the groundwork for a new balance of competing values and constituencies.

In a previous work,[3] I sought to analyze violent behavior and extreme political tactics as instrumental or "rational" methods of gaining objectives. In terms of my own values and the stage of the black revolution and other social causes, this seemed an adequate approach to political behavior. But the use and misuse of extreme tactics by all kinds of claimants for influence has raised with great force the question of whether these tactics are not now examples of noninstrumental and "irrational" behavior. We have become more keenly aware of the process by which goal-directed behavior may be imitated and distorted by every conceivable kind of discontented group.

A few years ago it was commonplace to recognize the efficacy of extreme political tactics while at the same time cautioning against their ambiguity and possible counter-effects. Extreme tactics were justified by the unresponsiveness of policy-makers and the desperateness of conditions. These claims have been exploded by all kinds of crazies on the fringes of social movements, grasping, vulgarizing, and ultimately discrediting the most powerful causes. Each new triumph of direct-action tactics invited a thousand imitators, who ultimately generated more resistance to the causes they intended to further than they broke down, and who splintered the constituencies involved. Tactics that in the past served political purposes became stylized and self-indulgent, quite separate from a concern for practical achievements. Innovative behavior became an art form for its own sake, and it contended with other behavioral inventions and corruptions in search of legitimacy, reinforcement, and ultimate embodiment in a stable culture form.

The concepts of *ritual* and *ritualization* provide a structure in which phenomena of this kind may be analyzed. My first approach was to consider that "unworthy claimants for power," those who imitated otherwise worthy tactics for the wrong reasons, were not "political realists" but rather "ritualists." This view is like that which traditionally surrounds the concept of ritual: a value judgment is made by the analyst separating "reality" (which appeals to his values) from "ritual" (which represents, in the analyst's view, *dubious* reality). But looking at ritual as a kind of hysterical behavior (which seeks to reenact an old success but in an inappropriate context) does not work. We can adhere to such a notion of ritual only if, like Immanuel Kant, who posited a reality independent of his own consciousness, we accept an arbitrary and limited definition of reality.

Definitions of reality are saturated with values. In fact, these definitions raise the underlying issue of legitimacy. Ritualized behavior that works is legitimate for the actor and is therefore considered by him to coincide with reality. But the same behavior may be unrealistic to others for whom it has no acceptable purpose and who deny the legitimacy of the acts themselves. Behavior may be learned not only through direct experience, but also through acculturation, imitation of prescribed actions for which the original instrumental incentives may have changed or become obscure but that possess social legitimacy for a wide variety of reasons. Now, a more general concept of ritual recommends itself, one that views ritual as secondary learning with strong secondary incentives.

Secularization and science put self-righteous blinders on modern man. We view the rituals of primitive societies and of the unwashed and uneducated as expressions of a belief in magic and superstition. But we disguise the pervasive and inescapable sacred dimension of our own lives, which continues unabated even in a highly industrialized and sophisticated society. Our sacred beliefs are obscured by our myths of objectivity and science, yet expressed in the rituals of "news," the conventions of entertainment and art, the rubric of our political lives and ideologies, and the omnipresent network of electronic communications. We live in a sea of sacred mental images and ritual practices, including the magical prescriptions on pill bottles and the demanding fads of language, dress, and manners. Yet our myths require that we think of ourselves as secular and hard-headed types. The rapidity and universality of change in our culture tends to dim the mystical qualities inherent in many forms of behavior. But we need only to look at behavior itself, rather than at the conceits of language, to discover how little human nature has changed.

The tendency of modern man to be blinded by words like *rationality, reason, objectivity, truth,* and so forth, and to equate these uniquely with science is comparable to the way in which untutored and primitive man seeks to control nature through prayers and incantations. Words are important because they carry an operational code about the nature of reality. If you can give a thing the "right" name, you know what to do about it; you are putting it in a frame of reference based on some consensus about the nature of the world. In addition, since words and thoughts do influence the relations of men to one another, it is but a short jump to the conclusion that the physical world will likewise respond to words and thoughts.

Modern man seeks to deal with the world through rationalization. Rationality is not an absolute. In symbolic terms, it is the structure of language—a set of rules governing a sequence of propositions based on irreducible axioms, principles, and definitions. *Rational* merely means uniform, continuous, sequential, capable of being weighed or measured. The syllogism is the basic unit of symbolic rationality; through it anything can be rationalized, that is, made to appear rationally sequential.

In political terms, one may define rationality, as does the economist, as the optimizing of choices and rewards. Such a concept is value-neutral and can be mated to any given set of values. Obviously, this use of the word *rationality* has little to do with its use in formal logic. One can be completely rational, in the sense of maximizing one's bargaining position, without relying on a web of logical symbols and verbal discourse. This is surely the sense in which animals, children, and inarticulate persons use rationality. And much that passes for symbolic rationality on the part of the articulate person is merely *post hoc* rationalization or part of the bargaining process itself (not necessarily the most important part).

It is not unusual for behavioral rationality (optimizing choices and rewards) to constitute a distinct dimension quite apart from symbolic rationality (logical consistency). To achieve the logical consistency, it is often necessary constantly to refine and qualify a verbal bargaining position in order to make it accord with the contradictions and reversals that are inherent in behavioral rationality under conditions of bargaining. In the context of bargaining, rationality is a synonym for pragmatic success: rational behavior is behavior that works; irrational behavior does not work. As students of political behavior, we must avoid the fallacy of assuming that "my values, which work for me, are rational; yours, *which do not work for me,* are irrational."

BEYOND PAIN AND PLEASURE

Simple pragmatism and rationalism contain a vast amount of metaphysics, mysticism, and faith. As a result of the work of Alfred North Whitehead, Bertrand Russell, Rudolph Karnap, I. A. Richards, Ronald D. Laing, Noam Chomsky, and many others, we have grown self-conscious about our paradigms. We recognize the metaphorical nature of all intellectual imagery and conceptual material.

We have learned that "we hold these truths to be self-evident" still provides the touchstone of reality for all creeds, political and physical. We escape the tautologies of language only by taking for granted the self-evident values of language and culture and the equities of interpersonal communication. In all things, beginnings and ends are clouded in mist. The first principle of all logic is the drive, the wish, the preference, the self-evident truth—embattled, defended, or merely passively taken for granted.

Simple pragmatism will no longer serve to describe human behavior. Its foundation is crumbling. The Skinnerian shibboleth of operant conditioning depends on a metaphysic of pain and pleasure and assumes some irreducible hard core in experience that communicates itself by inflicting rewards and punishments on the actor. The flesh adapts itself to "reality" by counting its pains and pleasures and learning to minimize the former while maximizing the latter. This scheme lies at the heart of all modern-day scientific ideologies, behaviorist and behavioral, and has provided the matrix of legitimacy for respectable culture and public systems of education until recent times.

Like all paradigms, those of simple pragmatism can be patched up and made serviceable. But our faith is already irremediably shaken. We are discovering (what we already knew!) that pain and pleasure are indeed reducible. Cultural values, love and legitimacy, human purposes and strategies, may make certain "pains" not only bearable but coveted and cherished. The pinch or the bite of a stranger is loathsome and painful, but those of a lover will give sweet accent and poignancy to ecstasy. The flash of anger from a legitimate leader leads to soul searching and renewed loyalty; the flash of anger from the illegitimate boss leads to revolt. The difficulty of defining and classifying pains and pleasures quickly convinces us to abandon the task. We soon realize that the definitions are tautologies: what we seek, we call *pleasure;* what we avoid, we call *pain.* It is not the other way around, and "there is no disputing tastes."[4] The ways in which we identify and perceive pain and pleasure are dependent upon values, purposes, strategies, and culture. The young James Joyce mortified himself by saturating his nostrils in a putrid urinal; young acolytes glory in leprous pus and filthy feet; St. Theresa found exultation and a rapturous transport (including pelvic ejaculation) by physical contact with every kind of affliction. If values, rather than arising from pain and pleasure, determine what is painful and what is pleasurable, are we enmeshed in an endless circle?

It may be more useful to see values as arising from culture and ritual. Many values represent the collective experience and social invention of the group. They are then transmitted through second-hand learning based on faith and legitimacy. Scientific-industrial man has never for an instant escaped this fact. His denials are based upon the conceits of scientific-industrial culture, which castigate and denigrate faith and legitimacy except as they may be earned or demonstrated through processes of trial-and-error inquiry. Learning occurs through a positive sensitivity among people who serve each other's needs. In short, behavior tends to be ritualized, separated from its instrumental purposes, and learned and transmitted mostly second-hand among people whose relationships are bonded by legitimacy and love.

Culture, defined as ways of doing and making, is the subjective aspect of the social system; ritual expresses and gives content to that aspect and functions as the indirect process by which a society can assimilate isolated experiences and generalize them into cultural values and social policies. Ritual is conditioned learning in which the operant factor is secondary and social rather than primary and physical. The child learns to respect highway traffic not by being struck by a car but by observing the example of others; in the process, he may be struck by his mother's hand. He learns to avoid his mother's blow by not stepping in front of a car. Why does he not run from his mother's hand, which he knows *by experience* will hurt him, into the street, which he does not know from experience will hurt him? What is the reality principle that leads him to remain in the proximity of his mother's hand while attempting to keep from an hypothetical oncoming vehicle? This is the key to the reality frame of cultural learning which reflects not direct physical experience, but rather symbolic learning and political legitimacy.

Culture then, is the storehouse of social learning maintained and transmitted by the ritual process, which facilitates certain kinds of individual behavior while inhibiting other kinds.

In the political arena the fact that greater legitimacy arises from second-hand experience is even more evident. Writing in 1932, Harold D. Lasswell noted that most of mankind is in no position "to know many relevant facts about the men whom it trusts, who may, to all intents and purposes, be as remote as God." Mankind is therefore compelled "to project its loyalty by a simple act of faith, if it would escape the barely tolerable state of suspended judgment or a bitter skepticism." Lasswell finds few characteristics of behavior "so obvious" as man's capacity to attach "strong emotional attachments and aversions in respect to a handful of public characters."[5]

One purpose of ritual is to insulate the individual and the group against new experience. An individual amid the swirl of experience is constantly in danger of overload and disorientation. Learning occurs only when the experience itself can be abstracted by an act of will on the part of the learner. An absence of preconceived cognitive structures (which the individual acquires from culture) would render one defenseless before a flood of meaningless data. The arbitrary constructs of culture (and the secondarily learned behavior that they involve) insulate the individual from this undifferentiated onslaught. These learned responses receive their legitimacy through faith and through their efficacy in dealing with a blind and angry reality.

Ritual behavior reverses the dynamics of pragmatism; it enables us to assert the reality of our arbitrary paradigms by means of our behavior, rather than justifying our actions as the results of some objective force or physical truth. Simple pragmatic behavior may be formulated thusly: If such and such were true, then my actions would be justified. Ritual action, in contrast, may be formulated in the following proposition: My action is justified, therefore such and such is true. In other words, ritualized action may be defined as behavior that argues the truth of the assumption on which the action is based. The legitimacy of culture, the fact that mankind accepts learned responses by faith, provides a basis for a more complex pragmatism in which rituals and self-evident paradigms control behavior, maintaining a minimal degree of openness and adaptability while at the same time conserving the main structure and flow of energy and resources.

PARADIGMS AND REALITY

Thomas S. Kuhn, a philosopher of science, marked the current trend in his *Structure of Scientific Revolutions* (1962). In it, he stepped away from the positivism that has dominated scientific writing for two generations. He recognized that scientific theories are metaphors ("paradigms" in Kuhn's language) with no inevitable or necessary correspondence to any objective universe. Paradigms are seen as cultural inventions, "universally recognizable scientific achievements that for a time provide model problems and solutions to a community of practitioners."[6] The metaphor constitutes "truth" about the nature of reality by definition and consensus. It may provide the inspiration for several bodies of theory and is never completely formulated or spelled out in all of its implications. Its underlying character is "metaphysical."

At any given time "normal science" consists of working within and in the light of the prevailing paradigm, making it more specific and precise "by extending the knowledge of those facts that the paradigm displays as particularly revealing, by increasing the extent of the match between those facts and the paradigm's predictions, and by further articulation of the paradigm itself."[7] Anomalies exist in any theoretical material. When a motive to challenge the prevailing legitimacy of the paradigm or its practitioners arises (from whatever incentives), such anomalies are given emphasis by young and critical scientists making their own reputations and building their careers on the shoulders of the past. Scientific revolution occurs when the existing paradigms lose legitimacy, not necessarily because they cannot deal with the anomalies (if there is a will, there is a way), but because they have been challenged by a new metaphor which represents new activity, new personnel, and new culture forms. Kuhn emphasizes that scientific revolutions are "non-cumulative developmental episodes in which an older paradigm is replaced in whole or in part by an incompatible new one."[8]

Exactly the same process occurs in all aspects of culture. If you were to turn the process of technological growth backwards and remove the extensions of man layer by layer, then the operationally true description of reality would likewise regress, and all the things that contemporary science takes for granted would become mad and meaningless dreams. A modern man living in remote Amazonian jungles experiences this regression of reality as his radio batteries die and are not replaced, his modern tools are lost or broken, the ammunition for his rifle is exhausted, his machine-woven clothes disintegrate, and his last can of corned-beef hash is traded to the native chief for a clay pot and a spear. Should this unfortunate traveler cling to his modern technological knowledge, he may not survive. He would be well advised to adopt the reality theory of his native hosts, accepting as well the rituals and incantations that go with the hunting of game or the planting of seed. Their "superstitious" behavior embodies a rich store of pragmatic experience and observation as to how best to use the resources available at their own level of technology. They have proven their ability to survive.

In effect, the whole vision of truth is a paradigm based on a myth of legitimacy; its continuation or decline depends upon a political process. All truth has a provisional and a political basis. There is no absolute sense in which one theory is more or less true than another. *Something is true because people are disposed to act as though it were.* Elaborate rituals of action are created to substantiate a "truth," just as a bereaved widow achieves the sense of her husband's presence by acting as though he were there, or as an assassinated political leader is elevated to a legend, continuing to serve the magical function of symbolizing the body politic and the legitimacy of commitments undertaken during his actual rule. A truth is only "absolute" among believers who share the same values, and who deem the "truth" so obvious as to be beyond challenge. We become aware of this relative or transitory nature only when a "truth" is already dead or dying.[9]

The consensus of scientific theory at any given time is therefore not an inexorable approximation of reality. It contains an arbitrary and imaginative element that is more or less the result of a historical and social process. The old notion that scientific laws contain an element of necessity and represent an approach to "things in themselves" is no longer considered a necessary supposition. So-called laws of nature are a figurative shorthand that should be extended only tentatively beyond the specified conditions of the observations they contain, subject to the test of new experiments and observations. The fact that some theories are richer and have greater integrating power is due to their symbolic economy and evocative potential. It is more important, writes England's Nobelist Paul Dirac, the predictor of antiparticles, "to have beauty in one's equation than to have them [equations] fit experiments."[10]

Scientific theories that endure represent a felicitous selection among many possible ways of symbolizing events. Any construct, no matter how primitive, can be qualified with enough variables to express man's experiences and his capability for predicting and controlling phenomena. When scientists "discover" theories, they are in fact inventing them, for, in the words of Simon Kuznets, "the order which they bring into the structure of the universe is of their own contriving even though the test lies in an agreement between theoretical conclusions and operational data mirroring the real world."[11] Theory may suggest new experiments; out of these may come new discoveries. But to suppose that theory ever has more than a formalistic and conditional correspondence to environment is unnecessary and unsophisticated. Theory does not really anticipate future discovery, but merely offers elaborations and extensions as the bases for future research.

Reality and truth are the product of social invention, fantasy, and ritual. So-called scientific theory is an improvisation and contrivance of the mind of man. Occam's Razor holds that the truth of scientific theory arises from economy and grace. It also complies with the ethos of the age. Philosophers of science recognize that it is quite feasible to build into any kind of conceptual material an operational code for manipulating the levers and indicators of technology and the physical world. By postulating enough variables and rationalizing the experimental and laboratory results ("saving the appearances"), one might compose an operations manual for nuclear reactors based on the metaphors of extrasensory perception and prayer, with all the proper qualifications and exceptions. There is nothing inevitable in any scientific theory; indeed, contradictory theories can and have coexisted in time, and drastic revisions of theory are always possible.

The mythical and the magical are part of the total vision of what is real, what has authority, what has legitimacy, and what can be confidently used as the basis for planning future actions, for rationalizing and excusing past actions, for communicating about common enterprises.

The fads and styles of "scientific method" are a search for authority and legitimacy. Society craves science as a prophetic magic. The legitimacy of "truth" derives from its success in helping man deal with his world, whether in scientific or in prescientific systems of authority. Successful prophecy includes the delineation of future trends along fashionable lines, a prediction that can be identified with a successful emerging culture form or political group. The success of quantitative behavioralism and survey research, the tremendous funding of operations research during and after the Second World War, and the later application of the new computer technology brought honor and riches to the quantitative methodology which thereby acquired legitimacy and a host of imitators.

Hans Morgenthau dismisses the doctrinaire elevation of quantification: "The only question that counts is whether you are right or wrong. If you are right, it is irrelevant that the proposition you propound falls behind or goes beyond the emotional expectations of your contemporaries."[12] The claims and promises of quantitative methodology have not been "equivalent to the delivery of the goods." Prophecy is what matters. The ultimate prestige and authority of the practitioner must stand upon the judicious way in which he hedges his bets, conserves and expends his prestige, and takes courageous positions when to do otherwise is to fail. Prophecy is a ritual art and entails the same pitfalls of nuance and creative invention as does any kind of behavior. The process is ultimately political; its object is to win and maintain legitimacy, that is, social truth and authority.

The quantitative methodology is not an isolated example; all methods are essentially the same. They are formed by self-correcting trial and error rationalized within certain systematic conceptual material. Since operational codes can be worked into virtually any such materials, the success of the theory itself is not strictly dependent on how well it operates but rather on whether it attains legitimacy.

Old myths of authority begin to dissipate as the decades revolve and the counter-culture challenges all things. So-called quantifiers turn out to be no more empirical than anyone else and probably more baroque and metaphysical than many traditional social scientists. Daily events are the arbiters of the legitimacy of current myths. No scientific method rises above this process to attain an absolute status; everything is transformed by ritual into magic-wonder fairy tales. Every researcher starts with his own experience and his own self-discovered truths, the values that represent the accumulated grievances of his life and all of his current alibis for himself. Every researcher gains his insights from attempts to build legitimacy on the wreckage of himself. Data and methods are props and incantations. "Professionalism" and "the scientific method" are the Better Business Bureau driving out the most transparent schlock dealers, lest the audience discover that unprincipled merchandise is sometimes just as good as the official stuff.

As social inventions, reality and truth are imbued with rituals of all kinds, serving a wide variety of functions apart from the instrumental manipulation of the environment. The arts, the media, abstract symbols, daydreaming, subjective fantasy—all are part of a process by which reality is invented, challenged, and confirmed. Fantasy is part of a continuous process by which all of the options of behavior at any time are reviewed and edited. Human actions and the verbal representations are in effect the result of an elaborate filtering and editing of the vast reservoir of fantasy that surges both above and below the limits of consciousness.

The description of reality and right conduct was primarily intended to support political authority and the social order. In Somalia the world is believed to be the center of the universe and saucer-shaped. This is not an empirical belief but an ethical and political one (to assert it is round is to defy the established order). The flatness of the world is an institutional truth, as is the Newtonian formulation; each in their own place and time serve different societies. Indeed, the flatness of the world is true in Somalia in every sense in which it is false in scientifically advanced societies, and for the same reasons. Having no experience in circumnavigation and no access to telescopes and accurate tools for studying the motions of the planets, Somalians find no useful purpose to be served by challenging the assumption. All abstractions are "myths" in the sense that they provide a concise and instant concept of a complex process; no generalization completely accords with particular and unique events and experiences. All generalities are verbal tautologies, cultural artifacts whose practical value lies in the social experience and prescribed activities they contain.

The tendency of a society founded on social and technological change is to separate its myths of moral action (involving the human and social order) from those of physical action (involving animals and objects of nature). However, from its beginning, the scientific distinction between the physical and the social broke down. The success of technology in dealing with the physical environment tempts men to couch their moral actions in the same conceptual material. The breakdown has also gone in the opposite direction, that is, the schema of impersonal physical action is extended to the treatment of men in the social order. Both kinds of transfer involve science in an ideological role not unlike that served by religion. Science has become a contemporary "myth of legitimacy," associated with all things that are good, true, and beneficial.

For the average man (and most scientists themselves are average men) science is a revealed faith, an invisible world. Mathematical formulae are its sacred texts whose meaning must be adumbrated by the Initiated Ones, whose miracles in agriculture, medicine, transportation, and weaponry are a source of constant awe and astonishment. The scientists and doctors mediate between the aches of self and an implacable eternity much as priests and shamans did at a more primitive state of the arts.

Books and reading are rituals that support the authority of learning. The Bible or Mao's Little Red Book are talismans for conjuring spirits and putting oneself in closer contact with the demiurges of life. How insular and glowing with salvation is the student who carries a book! Like the Sunday School Bible scholar, what a sense of beatitude transforms the bookly! Like prayer, books and reading are forms of ritual with a sacred aura. The political scientist in his carrel hunched over the dusty pages of forgotten books acquires the mystery and the priestliness that may make him a confidante of presidential candidates.

In modern societies intellectuals are ritual figures. Their primary role is in the elaboration and supply of authoritative symbolic material. Intellectuals express the symbolic dimension of social life in much the same way as the organized priesthood did in Medieval Europe. All specialists and experts compete in maintaining authority. One of the specialties apparently still in vogue, although mainly in certain middle- and upper-class income groups, is the psychiatrists, especially those with Jewish names and foreign accents. Now their credibility is beginning to be challenged, and the professionals themselves question the value-oriented role of their authority. Seymour C. Halleck, in *The Politics of Therapy,* notes, "Just about anything a psychiatrist says publicly can be used for moral or political purposes; in fact, he makes certain pronouncements for their political effect. . . . Groups advocating a particular political or moral position will use any kind of psychiatric statement, written or spoken, to support their point."[13]

The sociology of religion has experienced a decline in recent decades as the institutions of traditional religion have themselves lost their pertinency. But modern man is immersed in a universe of magic and ritual that he ethnocentrically considers "scientific" and "rational." He thinks himself the most advanced product of human history standing at a pinnacle of self-understanding, mastery of his environment, and freedom from delusion and superstition. This pose has always been characteristic of man whatever his condition. Advanced civilization is greatly augmented by technology and large-scale organization, but it remains as saturated with ritual as any primitive society. Magic, faith, and arbitrary mental constructs encompass the needs of modern man.

Modern man has not freed himself from the fact that all culture is the product of the social process. The role of social contrivance in creating reality has become better appreciated as the bastions of tradition have crumbled. Rationality has lost much of its authority and aplomb, and we have seen a resurgence of ritual invention borrowed from prescientific epochs. With Freud, Jung, and Adler the ground was laid for greater attention and respect to the imaginative and emotional nature of man. Fantasy is no longer dismissed as lying outside of significant experience. The ambiguities of dream imagery, the dynamics of wit and cunning, the baffling utterances of psychotics are analyzed to discover clues to the structure of society and the normal psyche. Anthropologist Claude Levi-Strauss detects in preliterate myths and rituals intellectual structures common to the work of modern philosophy. Ronald Laing and Victor Turner have in very recent times made an important contribution, carrying forward the work of Tylor, Robertson-Smith, Durkheim, Mauss, Levy-Bruhl, Hubert, Herz, van Gennep, Max Weber, Boas, Lowie, Malinowski, Radcliffe-Brown, Griaulle, Dieterlen, and a host of successors. The literature of premodern ritual has become massive, including meticulous and exacting observations of hundreds of performances, vernacular texts of myths and prayers, gathered with loving care and with scientific rigor.[14]

Social policies, political organizations, laws, and institutions are imperfect attempts to maintain currency between the substrata of individual and group bargaining and the institutions above the threshold of organized social life. The ritual process is primarily political and reflects a changing balance of constituencies as well as environmental and intergroup relations. In the following chapters we will develop paradigms in an attempt to explain irrational and nonrational behavior, the cycles of values as they arise and decline over time, what determines which cultural inputs will become permanent features of organized group life, and the mechanism of reciprocal schooling among individuals and groups that maintains continuity and stability in the face of adaptation, conflict, and change.

All culture forms including the political are, in a sense, works of art; when we achieve a better understanding of how works of art penetrate to our bones and move our hearts, we will be approaching an understanding of political behavior. In the pages ahead, we seek to expand the once rigid and sterile boundaries of political inquiry, to appreciate the role of imagination and invention in the making of values that underlie the workings of politics.

NOTES

1. *Village Voice*, July 8, 1971, p. 47.
2. John Lennon, *Rolling Stone*, January 7, 1971, p. 4.
3. H. L. Nieburg, *Political Violence: The Behavioral Process* (New York: St. Martin's Press, 1969).
4. See Michel Cabanac, "Physiological Role of Pleasure," *Science*, September 17, 1971, pp. 1103–07.
5. Harold D. Lasswell, "The Triple Appeal Principle: A Contribution of Psychoanalysis to Political and Social Science," *The American Journal of Sociology*, January 1932, pp. 5–26.
6. Thomas S. Kuhn, *The Structure of Scientific Revolutions* (Chicago: University of Chicago Press, 1970), p. x.
7. *Ibid.*, p. 24; see also pp. 17, 42, 102.
8. *Ibid.*, p. 91; see also C. G. Jung, *Psyche and Symbol* (Garden City, N.Y.: Doubleday, 1958).
9. In this regard, see Alvin W. Gouldner, *The Coming Crisis of Western Sociology* (New York: Basic Books, 1970).
10. Quoted in Jacob Schmookler, *Invention and Economic Growth* (Cambridge, Mass.: Harvard University Press, 1966), p. 19.
11. *Ibid.*, p. 22.
12. Quoted in James C. Charlesworth, ed., "Conference Discussion on Objectives," *A Design for Political Science: Scope Objectives and Methods* (Philadelphia: American Academy of Political and Social Science, 1966), p. 133.
13. Seymour C. Halleck, *The Politics of Therapy* (New York: Science House, 1971), pp. 114–15.
14. Victor W. Turner, *The Ritual Process: Structure and Anti-Structure* (Chicago: Aldine, 1969), p. 3.

2 | FORMS & FUNCTIONS

. . . the uniqueness of man cannot be seen in all its imposing grandeur unless it is set off against the background of those ancient historical characteristics which man still shares with the higher forms of animal life today. (Konrad Lorenz)[1]

One usage of the term *ritual* defines it as "any expression of cultural form." Another would limit it to the performance of religious acts. Psychoanalytic theory uses the term for repetitive, involuntary sequences of behavior stemming from compulsion, while most anthropologists think of ritual as any prescribed form of behavior that is not essential to technical and practical affairs. Malinowski, Redfield, and others have demonstrated that ritual cannot be separated from nonritual experience.

All of the forms of ritual behavior are parts or dimensions of culture; they are expressions, often nonverbal, of the values, attitudes, theories, interpretations, potential actions, and expectations of individuals in a community. Fairkind provides the classic formulation of ritual as "the collective representation" of the group, which he divides between "sacred" and "profane."[2]

The ritualization of behavior is a process by which values are embodied in behavior, by which the results of search behavior and social invention are transmitted to and assimilated by the whole society. Lewis Mumford and others suggest that the primary task of human groups is the elaborating of the social order; the most elemental human drive toward creativity, ritual, and play gives rise to manners, ceremony, social systems, inventions, and technologies.[3]

The ritual dimension of behavior is described by anthropologist Max Gluckman as "the mystical form of the political system," that which reflects the common interests of all members of the society and the interconnected rights, duties, and sentiments that make it a single community. Ritual embodies the general interest in fertility and prosperity, the need to respond to changes in the physical environment and technology, and the need to adjust to internal and external conflict. In addition to supplying such needs as food, commodities, affection, and reproduction, every action has, in Gluckman's terms, a "moral aspect" expressing sentiments, mobilizing social relationships, expressing claims and anticipated responses, confirming or altering social relationships, and maintaining a reciprocal and mutually balancing system.[4] Ritual is the uniquely "social" aspect of behavior. Pseudo-events, such as elaborate ceremonials and works of art, can be significant events which affirm and perpetuate the social group. "West Side Story" shown to a national TV audience of 65 million people can be a more powerful and consequential event than the Florida presidential primary of the same week.

All behavior is social communication as well as goal-directed activity. That is why men conduct themselves differently depending on the audience for the performance. Even when alone, fantasy conjures up various audiences for every act, even those acts deliberately shrouded in secrecy and darkness.[5]

Every act has multiple levels of meaning whether confirming, influencing, or challenging the expectations of others to respond to or repeat the act. Any act that does not conform to the appropriate social code that governs it makes news because, in Erving Goffman's words, it "disconfirms the selves of the participants."[6] Man is a social being, living in man-made culture; therefore all actions, inactions, and reactions express social values and communicate a highly significant symbolism. Every movement for accomplishing a given act, even one of simple physical manipulation, has social meaning. The fact that the act is done, the way in which it is done, its timing in relation to sequences of acts by oneself and others, are pertinent dimensions that communicate something. The act may become pure ritual in that the dominant intention of the actor is the communication and not the physical outcome.

Whether a person is alone, in a small group, or in front of a television camera, the social dimension of his actions can become dominant, either confirming or challenging values and social groupings. In all of their actions, persons "must sense that they are close enough to be perceived in whatever they are doing, including their experiencing of others, and close enough to be perceived in this sensing of being perceived."[7] All behavior changes its social meaning, though its physical form be the same, depending on its setting, its intended audience, and its intended effect. The level and scope of "mutual monitoring" is what defines a "gathering," in which loosely organized group behavior occurs, having a social meaning distinct and distinguishable from that which the same sequence of actions might have in a different gathering.

However defined, ritual is a powerful force in the shaping and maintaining of a culture. What are some of the functions of ritual? Gluckman states, "The distribution of ritual power helps achieve a balance against competing secular interests." This is true not only of organized religions, where the role of the chaplain and the sanctity of the church are emphasized, but also of spontaneous secular rituals of all kinds and of all degrees of permanence and substance. Gluckman concludes that ritual develops most strongly in those situations where moral judgments on actions affect many social relationships.[8]

Ritual action can be a redressive, reconciling mechanism for re-affirming, testing, and, at times, changing loyalties for new ones, the process being carried out in a kind of muted symbolic display with a symbolic response which changes attitudes and values without major and unlimited conflict, and without the necessity for total and simultaneous involvement in the new value systems by all members of the society. In other words, ritual controls and effects revolution with the least amount of disturbance. The potential for disruptive revolutionary change by escalated violence and internal warfare is always present, unpredictable in its outcome, costly in its logistics, dangerous in the secondary conflicts that may be engendered; ritual controls and moderates these undesirable tendencies by providing for change through less upsetting methods.

Ritual behavior is not habit. The latter may be defined as an automatic response to stimuli through repetition and without necessary cultural significance. Habit allows only fixed responses to stimuli, while ritualized behavior never loses its optional and creative element. Though sometimes performed in a dreamlike way, ritual communicates social meanings from a repertoire of options. It contains strategic and purposeful elements that automatic actions do not.

Ritualized behavior is the general class; formal ceremonial behaviors and manners are subclasses. Ceremonials, whether public or private, large or small, are highly structured performances of collective action that serve to mobilize public opinion. They are a form of ritualized behavior carried to the highest state of exact observance.[9]

Search behavior that is successful tends to be reinforced and imitated and eventually becomes a conventionalized performance. However, few patterns of routinized and repetitive activity remain stable. Behavior is continually modified by imaginative invention, new situations, adjustment and readjustment, and so forth.[10] The reason for this is that the effects of certain actions become well-known and are assimilated into the behavior of others. Once a pattern of action has lost its novelty, surprise, charm, and innocence, it is discounted in advance by its audience and robbed of effect. In terms of group behavior, ritual undergoes the same process of change and adjustment. Every group in some implicit and unconscious way seeks to preserve strategically the purposes of its actions, and this necessitates continuous invention, improvisation, experimentation, and discovery in order to effectively encircle these purposes in behavior patterns. Whatever is successful in terms of individual and social values is reinforced and transmitted to serve purposes other than those contained in the simple acts themselves.

Another function of ritual is its tendency to assimilate the unfamiliar. Its ultimate bases are events that have not yet been discounted by the social system and may cause serious disturbance. Such events bring crisis. Like religious conversion, ritual comes after the fact. The original action or series of actions is spontaneous, reactive, composed of a wild multiplex of suggestions and sources, generated, combined, and recombined by the fantasy process. Whatever its inspiration and source, a successful event suddenly commands repetition and imitation. It has become a ritual. Its meaning has already changed and will change more drastically with each repetition in new situations, involving new actors, reactors, onlookers, and participants. In ritual, as in psychotherapy or conversion, the significant act is the first act, the act of choice, the decision to reenact or repeat. Psychotherapy has its greatest effect prior to the course of treatment; it is contained in the act of choice to submit rather than in the subsequent ritual. In much the same way, religious conversion, being "born again," is a spontaneous act of choice, while the religious instruction and ritual repetitions that follow are secondary. The psychiatrist may tell a patient he is not ready for treatment just as a religious teacher explains his failure to achieve dramatic results. A clairvoyant blames his failure to properly read the signs on the client's skepticism; the client has not made the act of choice.

Similarly, a shift in the social status of groups occurs long before the adjustment to the shift is underway. A revolution in the status of blacks in American society occurred through a series of ritual encounters during the early 1960's. The whole world was witness to the presentations of Sheriff Bull Connor and the Reverend Martin Luther King, Jr., in Selma, Alabama. The passage of civil-rights legislation and the subsequent period of urban rioting were ritual affirmations of the change, rather than sources of the change. The surprising lack of backlash that followed the riot syndrome is evidence of this point. It was almost as if the prevailing power groups of American society, by and large, took the view that all of the hostility and rhetoric of revolution was not going to prevent American society from continuing the incremental process of dismantling racist values and institutions, slow though the process might be.

Certain types of ritual behavior serve as a source of reassurance to mankind. Anthropologists report that the ceremonial occasion in which all the prescriptions of behavior, constraints, and requirements of self-discipline are set aside for a certain period is a common feature of every culture. These occasions have been described as "rituals of rebellion" whose purpose is to release tension while confirming the basic unity and stability of the group. Puritanical societies may approve harvest rituals in which lewd songs and sexual displays are permitted even by staid matrons. Many cultures provide occasions on which ceremonial participants go into a mystic trance during which they are expected to do unmentionable and forbidden things. Western culture has long smiled with tolerance and a knowing wink on Saturday night and special holidays that unleash a wild set of provocative conventions; some examples include New Year's Eve, the end of Lent, the Christmas office party, V-E Day, and the celebration in New York City following the Mets' victory in the World Series. Alcohol, cocaine, costumes, dances, mummery, mimicry, love-making and outragious flirtations, intimate encounters with strangers in dark alleys or side streets—all may be involved in such mass Saturnalias of sexuality and exhibitionism that can be found in every culture as part of a ceremonial occasion or as a spontaneous reaction to a happy or terrible event.

Rituals of rebellion suggest the chaos and outer darkness of the universe, held in check only by the arbitrary meanings of group life; the discipline and order of social life provides the context in which Dionysian revelry gains place, form, and cathartic meaning. Fear and trembling on the brink of disorder and death becomes, from the safe vantage of normative society, a delightful and fulfilling fantasy acted out with temporary abandon. Only the certainty of an early return to sobriety and order facilitates the yielding to mock chaos; like the pseudo-perils of a carnival ride or a horror film, much of the pleasure lies in the return and the confirmation of order and safety. This return to ego-control reestablishes and legitimizes the existing moral order.

In the same way, the profanation of ritual or the development of counter-rituals (Black Masses, witches' rites, and so forth) are methods of safely challenging the legitimacy of the political system. Ceremonial behavior creates a "power of the weak" allowing the expression of the emerging influence of new groups in the informal political systems, thus providing a check on the power of the strong. Power that rests on the formal institutional structure (property, law, and the monopoly of legality and police power of the state) may be offset and limited by informal ritual practices, including claims of special knowledge and power deriving from the practices themselves. A study of African micropolitics[11] describes a society in which the father has almost absolute power, while the mother has control of religious ritual in the family and is able to check, if not overcome, the formal system. This type of countervailing power actually strengthens the political system by allowing for the expression of dissent without the necessity of overthrowing the system.

The ancient Greeks had a holiday in which the slave-master relationship was reversed and the slaves were served by their masters, the regular order reverting on the morrow. This is not unlike a ritual practiced in the United States one day a year when school children reverse roles with teachers and principals, and sometimes with mayors and governors. This is a form of ritual rebellion which has not been given much attention by social scientists. In a recent study of drunken comportment, two sociologists conclude that most behavior supposed to result from alcohol is rather conventionalized ritual for whose performance little alcohol is necessary, which cannot be performed at all if too much alcohol is imbibed. Drunkenness is seen as ritualized behavior which is "time out" from the normal discipline of life. Under the role of drunkenness, all kinds of behavior are excusable, even charming, though they would not be tolerated under the conventions of sobriety.[12]

In primitive societies, ritual aims at dramatizing the critical turning points in the life histories of individuals, the turning of the seasons, major historical events of the group, as well as current crises. Ritual, according to Gluckman, functions "to release beneficent power" and is effective because "it exhibits all the tensions and strife inherent in social life itself." All the threatening disturbances of the natural world, including the transformation of an individual from child to youth to adult, transferring land, moving a village, reorganizing activities, and so forth, are amended and assimilated through a process of ritualistic pseudo-events.

In summary, the functions of ritual include 1) a means of low-risk testing in the continuing conflict for precedence among rising and declining social groups and values; 2) the transmutation of events into knowledge, learning, and consensus that modify the behavior of those involved and others who are affected; 3) the concentration of social meaning of events in ceremonies in order that the power of the original event may be invoked and mobilized to serve social purposes; 4) the provision of a continuous source of experimentation and culture inputs; 5) a means of buffering the group against crises and threatening disturbances by assimilating the unfamiliar into a familiar process; 6) a means of confirming and maintaining social groups and culture forms; 7) the organization of mass ceremonials and demonstration as a display of force, a threat to others, and a source of reassurance and manifest power for those directly involved;[13] 8) a method that is conflict-moderating and behavior-facilitating; and 9) the affirmation and clarification of the reality paradigms of the culture or of a subculture.

THE WEB OF LIFE

Watching his crested grebes, Sir Julian Huxley was struck by the theatrical effect, the stylized "mimic exaggeration" of their movements. Animal behavior patterns, he noted, tend to become highly ritualized, acquiring entirely new functions including learning, communication, social coordination, and integration. Konrad Lorenz observed that "the primary function may still be performed, but it often recedes more and more into the background and may disappear completely so that a typical change of function is achieved."[14]

Over several generations, Robert A. Hinde reports, behavior tends to evolve "to improve its adaptive value and the functional context in which it appears." Rituals of display and presentation have the principal function of "communication with other individuals." Such behavior, whatever its origins, tends to become modified to serve this purpose (although in some cases there is a "need for crypticity," that is, disguise of the behavior and/or the communication in order to protect against predators or for other purposes).[15] Ritualization includes changes in the display movement itself and the development of conspicuous physical structures by which the movement is enhanced. Actual physical changes respond to this behavior pressure.[16]

During ritualization, some behavior takes on a "typical intensity" that makes it distinctive from otherwise similar behavior. Motivational changes control the action, governed by causal factors quite different from those that motivated the behavior in its original simple reflex or trial-and-error forms. For example, the purpose of a specific act of feeding may be not to gain nourishment but to display a nonchalance in another animal's presence as part of an encounter or confrontation.[17]

Virtually all forms of life have some power of intellectual abstraction—a power that used to be thought unique to man (as Socrates said, "Man is a thinking animal"). Display, symbolic behavior, and mimicry are all forms of abstraction and widely characteristic of animal interaction.[18] Gestures of aggression or courtship, nest site displays, nest building displays, greeting ceremonies, conventionalized movements and postures eliciting conventional responses, ritual dances, festivals, and elaborate group ceremonies are not unique to man. Furthermore, laboratory experiments can teach animal subjects to discern abstract qualities. A chicken in a Skinner Box is taught to peck a triangle: *not a certain triangle.* "The animal does more than that. It grasps the idea of *triangleness:* it knows a triangle when it sees one, no matter what the size, position, or background."[19] The power of abstraction has been demonstrated even by fish and insects.[20]

The communicative function of ritualized behavior is a factor in the evolutionary pressure of natural selection. Animals that communicate most effectively tend to survive and multiply; therefore any chance change in form, such as coloring or muscle balance, that improves the ability of the individual to overcome background noise in his own signals will be adaptive and tend to be perpetuated in the genetic material. Ritual overcomes the chance of ambiguity by welding into one obligatory sequence of behavior a long series of independent variable patterns. Lorenz says,

The deans of the university walk into the hall with a measured step; pitch, rhythm, and the loudness of the Catholic priest chanting during mass are all strictly regulated by liturgic prescription. The unambiguity of the communication is also increased by frequent repetition. Rhythmical repetition of the same movement is characteristic . . . the communicative effect of the ritualized movements is further increased by exaggerating all those elements which, in the unritualized prototype, produce visual or auditory stimulation, while those of its parts that were originally effective in some other mechanical way, are greatly reduced or completely eliminated.[21]

A paradoxical impact arises from animal ritual. That which is cultural and learned in its origins may be translated into genetic material through the pressure of natural selection. Form and color accompany both "phyletic and cultural rituals," such as the plumage of the bird of paradise, the peacock's tail, the colors of the Siamese fighting fish, the astonishing beauty that marks the backside of the Mandrill baboon, all of which evolved as an enhancement of particular ritualized movements. It has been suggested that ritual leads to organic changes in humans as well. Irenaeus Eibl-Eibesteldt says that eyebrows have survived on the human face not only to protect the eyes from sweat but also "as a means of emphasizing the optical greeting." Women paint and trace their eyebrows in order "to enhance their signaling powers." The wrinkling of the brow is likewise a form of ritual expression.[22]

Symbolic behavior is more than a means of communication; it is also a learned response that gives a sense of identity and a confirmation of social meaning to the actor. Whether learned by imitation or as an instrumental response to direct experience, symbolic behavior tends to develop an independent dynamic. Pigeons peck a response disc to gain access to grain rewards even while identical grain is freely available within reach. Rats press a lever for food pellets while free pellets are present. It is not necessary to deprive animals of food before they will engage in instrumental food responses. Such responses serve as their own motivation and reward.[23] Monkeys will perform laboratory tests for raisin or peanut rewards or for plastic tokens that can be placed into slot machines, but it was soon found that this was unnecessary. The monkeys would work for no reward at all, enjoying the repetitive ritual for its own sake or, possibly, recapturing the ego state of an earlier situation in which the reward was adequate compensation.[24]

In these experiments with pigeons, rats, and monkeys, the action had lost its instrumental character and had become symbolic. Both work and reward had been ritualized to become something quite different. A number of experiments with rats suggests that exploratory behavior as well becomes independent of the physical environment, a ritualized component of the behavioral repertoire. The presence of new stimuli may follow the exploratory pattern rather than trigger it; in other words, the innovated behavior itself constitutes the new stimuli.[25]

Animal culture serves the same functions as human culture. Energy must be conserved. Ecological spacing must be achieved by symbolic threat displays, rather than by continuous physical interactions that waste energy and upset the priority of values involved in social behavior. Tear away the stylized insulation and stability of culturally ritualized behavior, convert the organism into a continuously sentient creature that responds randomly and totally to his environment, and a bottomless sinkhole of energy loss is created. Behavior that is excessively open-ended transmits entropy. It is like a nervous system without a skin, on fire with sensation. However arbitrary (and even instrumentally effective) the conventions of abstracted culture may be, they contain and protect the organism, enabling a selection of stimuli out of which structured learning is possible. A behavioral pattern that has structure, however ineffective it may be, is more adaptive than fully randomized behavior.

When an animal is subjected to a new or unusual form of stimulation, it shows an "orientation response" in which its sensitivity to stimulation, and especially to the stimulus in question, is enhanced and its readiness for action increased. A process of selective attention then brings somatic changes (such as eye and body movements) as the sense organs and the motor systems are organized around the source of the stimulus. The *generalized* orienting response changes to a *localized* orienting response which reduces specifically the features of the stimulating situation, either insulating the organism against similar stimuli or providing the triggering of the adaptive response. When exposed to the same stimulation thereafter, the animal responds with indifference or the proper adaptive response without first exhibiting an orientation response. The animal has assimilated the stimulus under existing or modified rituals and can now deal with it economically, without the same investment of energy required originally at the stage of general orientation anxiety.[26]

Ritual also reserves adaptability and integrity. Chimpanzees reared in a rich social environment show a high level of adaptability to new situations. They have learned patterns of behavior that allay panic and provide a sequence of adaptive probes as they transfer and test old rituals for relevance in a new situation. But chimpanzees reared in a moderately restrictive environment show reduced adaptability and marked avoidance of novel objects, especially at about two years of age. Rhesus monkeys reared in total isolation for six months or a year have been denied the opportunity of ritual learning by imitation of the example of parents and peers. When first released, they freeze in terror, panic before every unknown, and show profound disturbances in every aspect of behavior. They never develop normal social behavior.[27]

There is considerable basis for the functional superiority and preference of both humans and animals for symbolic and ritualized action as compared with direct learning. Experiments with rats, designed to break down conditioned patterns of behavior, create a high level of "emotional reactivity" which, rather than facilitating exploratory behavior, actually inhibits it. Rats that experience many shocks as a result of exploratory learning tend to lose some of their future learning capacity, while observer rats that assimilate the response by imitation retain greater adaptability for future crises.[28] *The signal has much greater efficacy than the actual experience that the signal represents.* Monkeys subjected to a signal that was followed by a delayed shock developed ulcers; those who were merely given the shock without the signal did not.[29]

Increasing the intensity of shock in negative conditioning increases the rate of learning up to a certain point after which it has the opposite effect. Too much electro-convulsive shock produces retrograde amnesia, disrupts memory trace consolidation and seriously degrades learning ability.[30] Small hints of pain help to maintain a higher degree of sensitivity and responsiveness, leaving intact the available energy of the organism and the integrity of its organization. As pain increases, the threshold of sensitivity rises accordingly, absorbing more energy for the purposes of defense and jeopardizing the organism's structure. At this level, the ability of the organism to respond by assimilating the experience and translating it into purposeful behavior is weakened. Beyond this point, entropic consequences may disorient and destroy the organism. Raw experience is most effective in mobilizing the learning resources of the organism when the indicator and sensory clues are deliberately kept at a low level stimulating the pattern of distance and caution that characterizes exploration. Because of this imperative the discipline of cultural abstraction and ritualization is universally characteristic of the acquired behavior of both animals and man.[31]

EXPRESSIVE RANGE AND MIMICRY

Ritual action is problem-solving. It tends to be more highly developed and explicit when the underlying purpose and strategy of the behavior must overcome the most formidable obstacles. The ritual movements tend to be more embellished, elaborate, and artificial under three conditions: 1) the signal function of the behavior must overcome considerable background noise; 2) the behavior response that is elicited is technically awkward or difficult and thus requires more vivid provocation; 3) competing symbols or signals resemble or mimic the original and thereby jeopardize its efficacy.[32] For example, the requirements of politeness and correctness are most strenuously and extravagantly applied between enemies or during a hostile encounter. Similarly, animal courtship patterns become elaborate and fantastic in response to the physical difficulties and time-space requirements that have to be overcome for a successful mating to occur.

All symbols tend to acquire double, and opposite, meanings, a form of natural irony, humor, and cost-saving. Aggressive and romantic behavior are often identical in their symbolic phases. Ritual marks of laughing and crying are physically similar. Many rituals are ambivalent. It is logical that an animal should conceal its own aggression-eliciting characteristics from potential adversaries, if only to allay aggression in others. For example, the conspicuous black head of laughing gulls provokes aggression among its own species; consequently, in the mating ceremony the gull averts its head in a strange form of friendship signal. Storks, Hans Haas reports, swivel their heads in greeting in order to differentiate the aggressive presentation of the beak from its opposite meaning. Horses greet each other by opening their muzzles and baring their teeth, a procedure identical to the one they perform as a warning; the differentiating factor is the ears, which are pricked in greeting or flattened back in a meaner mood. As the most powerful weapon of the horse is its kick, leaving back the ears is a ritualized form of threat arising from the instrumental concentration of the horse's attention on the area within the range of this weapon.[33] Lorenz holds that the human smile came into being in an analogous way, as a redirected baring of the teeth.

The energy-saving function of signals arises from the large significance elicited by a small effort. It becomes a substitute for a more complex or energetic one and may in fact make the more complex action unnecessary entirely. The asseveration of the signal at the lowest gain level commensurate with successful communication leads to embellishment, adornment, and differentiation. As mentioned above, the most elaborate courtship patterns occur in situations where the highest level of interfering factors exist. Rituals of courtship can be shown to be more closely related to interfering factors than to the sexual functions themselves. There is considerable evidence that precopulatory displays of many birds (such as the yellowhammer and the house sparrow) are sporadic and may be omitted. The inexperienced young engage in the most elaborate displays; these tend to fade from use as the individuals gain experience in consummating sexual contact. Domestic cockerels in home pens display less frequently than cocks in strange pens, although they mate just as often. Margaret Bastock concludes: "Omissions or abbreviations of courtship are associated with situations where sexual responsiveness is high in both partners and opposing factors low."[34]

A ritualized act may shift or be freed from its original set of controlling factors and be transferred to another. The action is displaced from its original stimulus or objective. This phenomenon is known as *displacement* or *emancipation*. Another transformation that occurs in ritual behavior is *condensation;* a set of elaborate symbolic actions becomes concentrated in one of their components, becoming a shorthand symbol for the entire sequence or series that effectively replaces the more formidable array.

As a response to interference or a means of overcoming competitive signals or background noise, behavior rituals become highly specialized. In the continuing process of strategic interaction among individuals of the same species or among different species, a strong pattern of mimicry arises in response to the evolutionary pressure of natural selection. "Aggressive" mimicry is employed by hunters to fool their prey. Australian aborigines put kangaroo pelts on their backs, copy the kangaroo hop with long reflective pauses, pretending to groom themselves or to graze, sprinkling in magical appeals to the kangaroo totem.[35] The zonetailed hawk has evolved a vulturelike look and glides in the company of vultures because small animals have no fear of these carrion-eaters. This pattern has been called "aggressive" mimicry. On the other hand, "defensive" mimicry is a species form or behavior pattern in which the organism imitates nonedible creatures or inanimate objects, thus inhibiting the attack of potential predators.

Mimicry is widespread in nature because the process of natural selection tends to retain and propagate forms that endow their possessors with competitive advantages in the struggle for survival. Even if embodied in a physical rather than a behavioral form, mimicry depends on the ritual significance of signals as behavioral cues. A one-sided interest can lead to the specialization of the signal-receiver, where a predator adapts to recognize its prey as rapidly as possible. A one-sided interest can also lead to a dismantling of the signal, for example, where a predator is adapted to approach its prey unnoticed, or where the prey is adapted to remain as inconspicuous as possible.[36] When the receiver has learned the signal, the model undergoes compensatory evolution to alter its signal in order to shake off the irksome mimic and the predator.

Advantages incorporated in the phylogenic estate for the benefit of the organism are drawn on for purposes of mimicry. A good example of the process is found among Old World monkeys whose females show conspicuous oestrous swellings on their posteriors.

Females develop special color signals on their rears to accentuate the presentation gesture during heat. The similar swellings and red marks on the rear end of the males has nothing to do with glandular conditions but constitutes mimicry to accentuate the presentation gestures and social functions of the males in their agonistic relations with one another.[37]

The study of mimicry raises in a different form the issue of the reality principle of social ritual. Which is the model and which is the mimic? The mimic is that one of the two signal transmitters to which the receiver directs a response that is not of advantage to the receiver himself. As for the model, its signal serves the interest of the receiver. The mimic exploits this fact unilaterally for his own purposes. Similarly, the reality defined by ritual practices in human culture reflects the value positions of those whose interests are served by actions based on the assumption of reality. Once again, the issue of legitimacy raises its hoary head. Where a common interest ceases to exist, the reality of the ritual form is at once under challenge.

"THE WORD MADE FLESH"

Ritual is the acting out of the subjective content of culture. It is the word made flesh. It is not dependent on instrumentality, as a procedure for making or doing, although it has these characteristics. Rather it becomes imbued, immersed, and surrounded with social meaning for the individual. It provides linkage between subjective image and social milieu. For the group, it tests and confirms a web of interrelated roles, interdependencies, past, present, and future exchanges of values.

The analysis of political tactics as rational and instrumental reflects a mechanistic approach to behavior. Such an approach belongs to the scientific world picture of post-Newtonian physics, characterized by assumptions, so well-worn as to be unconscious, of linearity, uniform causality, logic and determinancy. The mechanistic view is clearly inadequate. It is everywhere confounded by the simplest observations. In contrast, the study of ritual reaches all content and action; it provides an approach to the total personality of individuals and the creative principle of social innovation. Through ritualized action, the inner becomes outer, and the subjective world picture becomes a social reality. The study of ritual makes concrete and accessible the most critical part of man's nature, the subjective flux, experienced in floating imagery, dreams, bodily impulses, projections, inventions, and so on. Ritual behavior encompasses the whole range of collective human experience. It places fantasy in its proper role as a set of cultural capabilities and artifacts.

Revaluation of the role of fantasy may lead us to a more balanced view of our own rationality, its nature, and its limits. In the words of Lewis Mumford, it is "the first move toward redeeming for human use the mechanized and electrified wasteland that is now being constructed, at man's expense and to his permanent loss, for the benefit of the megamachine."[38]

Different fantasies represent the hopes and fears of different groups and individuals. The edited result is real action, social forms, allocation of resources, and organized activity—in effect the political process. All fantasy is in a sense "potential public policy." What becomes actual public policy depends on the structure of bargaining relationships, the relative influence and control that groups exercise over resources, differential access and skill available to implement factional values and demands, and other such variables. It may be said that architecture, priorities, zoning and land use, the form and design of products, styles of dress, styles of music and the arts, the allocation of space and resources for this or that activity, all represent political outcomes. Definitions of significant "news" and scientific discoveries arise from the interests and values of the prevailing culture. As Tom Wolfe points out, the sudden emergence of vulgar activities, like stock car racing, car customizing, discotheque dancing, surfing, drug taking, motorcycling, have become major culture forms and have become respectable for other groups because "here was this incredible combination of form plus money in a place nobody ever thought about finding it, namely, among teenagers." Practically every style recorded in art history, Wolfe notes, is the result of the same thing, "a lot of attention to form, plus the money to make monuments to it."

The Second World War liberated energy, activity, and money. Classes of people whose styles of life had been practically invisible built monuments to themselves, their fantasies, their own styles. Wolfe says,

Among teenagers, this took the form of custom cars, the twist, the jerk, the monkey, the shake, rock music generally, stretch pants, decal eyes—and all these things, these teenage styles of life, . . . started having an influence on the life of the whole country. . . . All the prols, peasants, and petty burgers suddenly got enough money to start up their incredible car world. . . . Stock racing, custom cars . . . still seemed beneath serious consideration, still the preserve of ratty people with ratty hair . . . yet all these rancid people are creating new styles all the time and changing the life of the whole country in ways that nobody even seems to bother to record, much less analyze.[39]

The portable apocalypse of the rock festival represents the actualization of fantasies of the newly enfranchised and affluent young who are engaged in creating culture forms.

Like all culture forms, the ritual cycle is accelerated in a mass society. Each episode goes from input to implementation to decline at a rapid pace. Ours is an era marked by tremendous input overload. Technology and the media, the breakdown of the old priorities and systems of organization, the dying fantasies of the Cold War generation, have liberated tremendous energy now available for redirection. The decade of the 1960's experienced a collapse of legitimacy of global dimensions. All of the organizing structures and priorities lost their authority and were no longer available to direct and discipline human energy and values. All of the values of the past therefore came into question, including the cult of efficiency and power, rationality, ethical relativism, egalitarianism, the work ethic, and discipline and restraint in personal behavior. All the energy once disciplined by industrial production and the tasks of warfare and diplomacy has been suddenly liberated and floats like a dangerous vapor over the land, searching and destroying, forming eddies and vortexes of new culture forms, testing both old and new systems for valid, sustainable, and satisfying styles, activities, objectives, and outcomes.

This study will seek to develop a metaphor of social reality based on the ritual process. A study of the ritual process is appropriate for a student of politics. A new culture form would be doomed unless its impulses found a corporeal form in thousands of personalities. It is by a general readiness to adopt a new ritual form "that the formative idea can imprint itself by direct contact and stimulation on a sufficient body of disciples and followers before the idea itself in more purely verbal form can be understood." Walt Whitman spoke of this process: "I and mine do not convince by arguments: We convince by our presence." One comes to know the doctrine by living the life the doctrine implies and by performing actions it prescribes. Mumford says, "By first taking bodily shape, the idea begins to spread throughout the community by bodily imitation before it can be more effectively defined by word of mouth and an intellectual formulation."[40]

It is through ritual that the gaps between apparitions, intuitions, and the realities of social life are bridged. The Confucian Analects, Plato's Dialogues, the Christian Gospels, Mao's Red Book, are meaningless except as incarnated in kinds of concrete behavior. These kinds of behavior become conventionalized performances which are eventually integrated into tradition, a system of education, and a whole surrounding ethos that is retested by fresh experience from generation to generation. Ritual gives institutional extension to subjective impulses that thereby cease to be private, willful, contradictory, and ineffectual, and so become capable of bringing about large scale social coordination and change. The Sayings of Chairman Mao, and all the attendant rites, express an intense will to consolidate the inchoate giant of Chinese feudalism. Unification and discipline against U.S. imperialism and "foreign devils" embody the incomplete birth throes of nation-building and modernization.

The search behaviors of disoriented individuals become the future probes of the whole society. Cults of all kinds, subcultures of youth, minority political movements, the intense and dramatic passion of a single individual, are multiple inputs of adaptation available to society, offering a broad base of options for institutional realignments and new values. Some of these options align themselves with established forms, some threaten and challenge established forms, some induce accommodation, some succumb and disappear, some coexist harmlessly in limited niches, some provide the poetry and dreams of a rising generation, some become the prevailing culture of the future. Ritualization is the process by which all of these options can be generalized for the whole society, providing the creative process by which the social group lives and grows, adapts and learns, suffers and destroys, searches and dies. Like all growth, the cycle of culture forms is often painful and disquieting. No one can judge how the future will use today's tremendously diverse and energetic melange of proffered values.

The ritual process is the primary source of behavior reduction. Out of the vast fluidity of informal transactions in the polity, a solid culture form is precipitated here and there, available for generalized use and part of an emerging consensus of values. Legitimacy makes the individual receptive to a new culture form. Anthropologists Godfrey and Monica Wilson, who did intensive field work on the Nyakyusa of Tanzania, have written, "Rituals reveal values at their deepest level . . . men express in ritual what moves them most, and since the form of expression is conventionalized and obligatory, it is the values of the group that are revealed. I see in the study of rituals the key to an understanding of the essential constitution of human societies."[41]

The mysterious process by which living organisms adapt to their environment, not passively but creatively, owes much to the existence of stable ritualized patterns of behavior. Socially dominant individuals occupy optimum habitats, forcing subordinate, chiefly young, animals to pioneer new kinds of habitats where they may be prospective founders of new evolutionary lineages, while the original population preserves the status quo. This polymorphic dispersionary system provides a continuous mechanism that modifies life forms creatively as a kind of strategic interaction between the organic and the physical environment.[42]

The ritual forms in any particular instance may or may not hold positive survival value. Not all behavior forms prove adaptive. Ritualized behavior and embellishments of physical form, like peacock tails and stag antlers, are exaggerated means of social signaling, but may become so burdensome or conspicuous as to unbalance their positive attributes. No life form is immune from the continued process of strategic interaction and competition. The very invention that gives advantages may also be too highly stylized and specialized to adapt to future challenges. The process of energy-saving accomplished by symbolization and ritualization may in some instances divert too much energy from other kinds of activity essential for life and growth. There is no escape from chance and risk. But the pattern of managing innovation within a framework of stability and continuity embodies a positive survival value for life processes per se, demonstrating the vitality and power of life in all living things.

NOTES

1. Quoted in Hans Hass, *The Human Animal: The Mystery of Mans' Behavior* (New York: Putnam's, 1970), p. 5.

2. Quoted in Paul Friedrich, "Revolutionary Politics and Communal Ritual," in Marc J. Swartz, Victor W. Turner, and Arthur Tuden, eds., *Political Anthropology* (Chicago: Aldine, 1966), pp. 191–93.

3. Lewis Mumford, *The Myth of the Machine: Technics and Human Development* (New York: Harcourt Brace Jovanovich, 1967), p. 3.

4. Max Gluckman, *Politics, Law and Ritual in Tribal Society* (New York: New American Library, 1965), p. 280.

5. See Robert C. Carson, *Interaction Concepts of Personality* (Chicago: Aldine, 1969; also Eric Berne, *Transactional Analysis in Psychotherapy* (New York: Grove Press, 1961).

6. Erving Goffman, *Interaction Ritual: Essays on Face-to-Face Behavior* (Garden City, N.Y.: Doubleday, 1967), p. 51.

7. Erving Goffman, *Behavior in Public Places: Notes on the Social Organization of Gatherings* (New York: Free Press, 1963), p. 17.

8. Gluckman, 1965, pp. 281–300.

9. See Victor W. Turner, *The Ritual Process: Structure and Anti-Structure* (Chicago: Aldine, 1969).

10. See Erving Goffman, *Strategic Interaction* (Philadelphia: University of Pennsylvania Press, 1969).

11. See Friedrich, 1966, pp. 187–219; and Victor W. Turner, "Ritual Aspects of Conflict Control in African Micropolitics," in Swartz, Turner, and Tuden, 1966, pp. 239–46.

12. Craig MacAndrew and Robert B. Edgerton, *Drunken Comportment: A Social Explanation* (Chicago: Aldine, 1969).

13. Parades, marches, mass meetings, and so forth, whatever their avowed purpose, demonstrate commitment, solidarity, and strength, and thereby have great political potency, influence, and deterrent power arising from the mere fact that they occur, quite apart from the rhetoric or declaratory threats of the leaders. Military displays, fly-bys, troop manuevers, draft-eligibles by the thousands singing "Alice's Restaurant," all are mass ceremonials whose main effect is a show of force.

14. Konrad Lorenz, *On Aggression* (New York: Grosset & Dunlap, 1967), p. 72.

15. Robert A. Hinde, *Animal Behavior: A Synthesis of Ethology and Comparative Psychology*, 2nd ed. (New York: McGraw-Hill, 1970), p. 432.

16. See Nicolas Timbergen, "Derived Activities: Their Causation, Biological Significance, Origin and Emancipation During Evolution," *Quarterly Review of Biology*, 1957, pp. 1–32; and A. D. Blest, "The Concept of Ritualisation," in W. H. Thorpe and O. L. Zangwill, eds., *Current Problems in Animal Behavior* (Cambridge, Eng.: Cambridge University Press, 1961).

17. See P. McKinney, "An Analysis of the Displays of the European Eider and The Pacific Eider," in *Behaviour, Supplement No. 7*, cited in Hinde, 1970, p. 433.

18. Margaret Bastock, *Courtship: An Ethological Study* (Chicago: Aldine, 1967), p. 1.

19. Elizabeth Mann Borgese, *The Language Barrier: Beasts and Man* (New York: Holt, Rinehart and Winston, 1968), p. 23.

20. See Richard Hernstein, "In Defense of Bird Brains," *The Atlantic Monthly*, October 1965, pp. 34–43.

21. Lorenz, 1967, p. 73.

22. Quoted in Hass, 1970, pp. 116–17.

23. Allan J. Neringer, Research Report, *Science*, October 17, 1969, pp. 399–401.

24. P. L. Broadhurst, *The Science of Animal Behavior* (Baltimore: Penguin Books, 1963), pp. 100–01.

25. See John Paul Scott and John L. Fuller, *Genetics and the Social Behavior of the Dog* (Chicago: University of Chicago Press, 1965); Hinde, 1970, p. 355; Desmond Morris, ed., *Primate Ethology* (Chicago: Aldine, 1967); Lorus and Margery Milne, *Patterns of Survival* (Englewood Cliffs, N.J.: Prentice-Hall, 1967); S. A. Barnett, *The Rat: A Study in Behavior* (Chicago: Aldine, 1963); and others.

26. See Hinde, 1970. pp. 131–33.

27. *Ibid.*, pp. 532–33.

28. *Ibid.*, p. 352.

29. Broadhurst, 1963, p. 123.

30. See Ronald G. Dawson and James L. McGaugh, Research Report, *Science*, October 24, 1969, pp. 525–27.

31. A ritualized behavior unit has been dubbed a "biogram" by

Chance and Jolly. They theorize that the social structure is the underlying pattern of "attention" that holds together all of the behavior units of a group. The biogram requires for its implementation group patterns of "attention-orientation," which may be classified as *centripical* or *acentric*. The former is characterized by attention-demanding displays that center on the "male cohort," which directs all group activities and movements. Such a structure imposes a high level of ritualized aggressiveness and rank ordering. Under predator attack, threatened animals flee toward the dominant male around whom the adult males mass while the females and immatures follow. In times of low excitement, attention-orientation remains centralized; in this way, the capability for policy-making and coordinated action is at readiness. An *acentric* society is one characterized by "segmented" attention-mobilizing components. Under predator attack, adult males engage in diversionary displays at the perimeter of the group while other members disperse. The "structure of attention" is the core that maintains the activity systems of the group. Ritualized behavior functions as a passive low-energy system that maintains in latency all the capabilities of group activity in routinized and crisis circumstances. (Michael R. A. Chance and Clifford J. Jolly, *Social Groups of Monkeys, Apes, and Men* [New York: Dutton, 1970], pp. 16, 160.)

32. Hinde, 1970, pp. 311–15.

33. See Hass, 1970, p. 124.

34. Bastock, 1967, p. 119.

35. Wolfgang Wickler, *Mimicry in Plants and Animals* (New York: McGraw-Hill, 1968), p. 227.

36. *Ibid.*, p. 228.

37. *Ibid.*, p. 231.

38. Mumford, 1967, p. 76.

39. Tom Wolfe, *The Kandy-Kolored Tangerine-Flake Streamline Baby* (New York: Simon and Shuster, 1966), pp. xiv, xv.

40. Mumford, 1967, p. 360.

41. Godfrey and Monica Wilson, "Ritual in Local Politics," in Marc J Swartz, ed., *Local Level Politics: Social and Cultural Prospectives* (Chicago: Aldine, 1968).

42. See N. D. Eudvardy, *Dynamic Zoogeography* (New York: Van Nostrand Reinhold, 1969); and J. J. Christian, Research Report, *Science*, December 14, 1970, p. 84.

3 | APOTHEOSIS OF THE ACT

After World War II, our scarecrows were grim and military.
Many wore steel helmets and discarded uniforms. Then came an
American period—mechanized scarecrows with waving arms affixed
to crude clockwork. Now that Japan is more affluent, scarecrows
are more elaborate. Some wear business suits; others, inspired
by TV films, simulate fierce samurai warriors and angry student
demonstrators. (Senji Kataoka, 1970)[1]

Human culture, in the words of William James, is "the selection, the rearrangement, the tracing of patterns upon, and the stylizing of the random irradiations and resettlements of our ideas."[2] Culture is man's most important instrument of adaptation, made up of energy systems, objective and specific artifacts, organizations and structures of social relations, projective modes of thought, and the total range of customary behavior transmitted from one generation to another by the social group.[3] All aspects of a group's culture —aesthetics, law, language, religion, personality patterns, therapeutics, kinship, attitudes toward equality and change, and the like— are closely interwoven into a pattern that is unique. Cultures change as a result of contact between groups and of forces within a group (such as technological innovations) that create new challenges and problems.

Every culture is a set of symbols and symbolic practices; therefore culture is capable of stockpiling learned responses for situations not yet encountered. The crux of symbolic learning is the omission of the original situation. In social learning, the individual perceives a person encountering and responding to a stimulus. In symbolic learning, the stimulus is represented by a symbol. The symbol may be a fairly complex bit of representational behavior, but most symbols are relatively simple, highly concentrated substitutes for the originals. Social symbols are cues and labels for ritualized practices, for modal behavior patterns. Culture may be viewed as the totality of conventional behavioral responses acquired primarily by symbolic learning.

We are the beneficiaries of the cultural revolution of the 1960's; accordingly we glimpse chaos through the veil of culture. We behold an interregnum period in the balance of the social groups, values, and purposes of the whole Western world. We see enacted in the abstractions of ideology, art, life styles, and political tactics all the fundamental conflicts about the nature of the world and its problems. In time new culture forms will redefine the reality of that world, its social structure and priorities. Culture is indeed an abstraction, as are all of its parts; but abstractions are tools that man grasps in dealing with his life and time. Therefore, culture embodies a strong reality principle that endows whatever passes for truth with the incandescence of significance and legitimacy.

PRIMACY OF CULTURE

Everything in man that is biological, even his patterns of breathing and sleeping, is always culturalized, suffused with symbolism and culturally approved ways of acting. The first exposure an infant has to the culture of his society concerns the gratification or the frustration of his biological needs. The socially patterned ways of treating these needs supply the foundations for all subsequent social learning.

The reverse is also true: everything that is cultural is part of man's biological adaptation. All adaptations—modes of acquiring a livelihood, family organization, social control, settlement patterns and the use of space, and religion—refer to complex group relationships, even though they are acted out by individuals. No man in any society provides for his family independently of intricate patterns of cooperation and mutual assistance, and these relationships are highly formalized. A youngster taught how to hunt or fish or work a machine is taught not only the mechanical skills but also how to conduct these activities in cooperation with others. All cultural phenomena are made up of socially shared activities and must be regarded as properties of the group and not of individuals alone.[4]

For this reason, culture cannot be separated from the political order. The underlying legitimacy of behavior patterns and values exists in and responds to political bargaining relationships; and the latter are steeped in culture and ritualized practices. A nation's political culture includes traditions and heroes, the spirit of public institutions, the political passions of the citizenry, goals articulated by the political ideology, and both formal and informal rules of the political game. It includes other real, but elusive, factors such as political stereotypes, political styles, political moods, the tone of political exchanges, and some sense of what is appropriately political and what is not.

Gabriel A. Almond points out that "every political system is embedded in a particular pattern of orientations to political actions."[5] Lucian W. Pye has referred to the political culture as "the ordered subjective realm of politics."[6] Sidney Verba writes that the political culture "refers not to what is happening in the world of politics, but what people believe about those happenings. And these beliefs can be of several kinds: they can be empirical beliefs about what the actual state of political life is; they can be beliefs as to the goals or values that ought to be pursued in political life; and these beliefs may have an important expressive or emotional dimension."[7]

Socialization shapes and transmits a nation's political culture. More specifically, political socialization *maintains* a nation's political culture insofar as it transmits that culture from old to new constituents. It *transforms* the political culture insofar as it leads the population, or parts of it, to view and experience politics differently from the way in which it did previously.

The concepts of "political culture" and "political socialization" attempt to isolate acts representing the spheres of government and social policy from the behavioral repertoires of other spheres. This distinction reflects the bias of the period of Cold-War diplomacy and international crisis that has now ended, a period of cultural stability that endowed a centralized government with a high degree of legitimacy. Today, however, modern nations have confronted the tearing apart of the cultural fabric and have lost some of their self-righteous innocence. The notion that the newly independent nations in Asia and Africa are "politically" unstable because of "the crucial socialization tasks of leadership" that must be learned from the advanced nations is now laughable. We can no longer take for granted the political superiority and stability of the West. We have witnessed a total wave of culture change overwhelming "political culture" and thus we are forced to abandon the nice distinctions of the recent past. It becomes clear that political culture is but an outcome of the far deeper realm of total culture where underlying values, behavior, and legitimacy are born.[8]

A related misconception about culture deserves comment. In the classical literature of the social sciences (Frazer, Malinowski, and Sumner, for example) one finds a subtle variety of ethnocentrism. Though the writers take pains to treat the cultures of primitive peoples with respect and seriousness, they share the assumption that primitive man, close to the state of nature, is harassed and driven by environmental forces, fear, and superstitions. They trivialize the imaginative metaphors of reality defined by primitive cultures, holding them to be impoverished by the physical impotence of man overwhelmed by nature. They assume that "progress" is enshrined in human history and that passage up the ladder of technology, self-consciousness, and mastery of nature brings with it a diminution of fantasy and an increase in objectivity. This view is contradicted by two observations that can be made.

First, the images and metaphors that embody cultural reality in our own time are no less fantastic and inventive than were those of simpler folk. Fantasy and arbitrary paradigms create reality for us in much the same manner as do the personalized demons and morality tales of other cultures. It is true that modern sciences attempt to purge themselves of personalized and moral dimensions by developing operational codes for manipulating the technological environment. However, they do not wholly succeed. Even in a scientific culture, manipulative rules become infused with a personal and moral dimension, especially for those practitioners who accept the behavioral routines as a form of ritual and symbolic learning based on the authority of the teacher.

Second, recent studies have shown that primitive man did not necessarily live a life of harried and overwhelmed necessity. Simple subsistence economies based on gathering, hunting, fishing, and rudimentary agriculture appear to have provided a considerable amount of leisure.[9] Ethnologists in the past emphasized the importance of the environment in the molding of culture. They therefore used examples that supported their cultural bias.

A recent study of the Hadza peoples shows how easy it is to believe that the tribe was continually on the brink of starvation. Such great emphasis is placed on meat as proper food that the Hadza describe themselves as hungry when they have less meat than they would like. James Woodburn comments; "In fact, there is never any general shortage of food, even in time of drought. The range of foods in the bush is so great . . . that if weather conditions should cause the failure of some type of root or berry, or the migration of some of the game, some other type food is always available."[10] Hadza men spend more time gambling than hunting. Over the year as a whole, the tribe spends less energy obtaining their subsistence than do neighboring sedentary agricultural tribes. A bush woman gathers on one day enough food to feed her family for three days and spends the rest of her time resting in camp, doing embroidery, visiting other camps, and entertaining visitors. It is not unusual for a man to hunt avidly for a week and then do no hunting at all for two or three weeks.[11]

Such recent studies are not conclusive, but they do indicate the simplistic nature of assumptions about the relation of necessity to culture. They tend to support a conclusion reached separately by other disciplines that the roles of nature, environment, and necessity in the elaboration of culture are very far from dominant, but are secondary to social and political processes. Man is free even under conditions of a simple life and a high level of environmental stress to create himself and his own reality arbitrarily from among a virtual infinity of options.

Such writers as Daniel Bell and Charles A. Reich view culture as supreme. Man constructs a reality in his own mind, confirming and dramatizing it by behavioral rituals. Bell states, "Culture has become supreme for two complimentary reasons. First, culture has become the most dynamic component of a civilization, outreaching the dynamism of technology itself. . . . Secondly, there has come about in the last fifty years or so a legitimation of this culture impulse." What is played out in the imagination of the artist, the intellectual, and the technical innovator foreshadows the social reality of tomorrow. In art and in all forms of social behavior, there is an impulse toward the new and the original, a self-conscious search for future forms and sensations; "the idea of change and novelty overshadows the dimensions of actual change." Society accepts the place of imagination actively rather than passively, and provides a market that eagerly gobbles up the new, believing it superior in worth to older forms. Bell concludes, "Thus our culture has an unprecedented mission. It is an official, ceaseless searching for a new sensibility."[12]

Reich sees culture as the true fount of revolutionary change. Today's politics, he writes, deal only with the "trivial and ephemeral, and it is only culture that puts in issue the true political questions that confront us."[13] In *The Greening of America*, he calls for a remaking of the consciousness of men, rather than the useless preaching of solutions to specific problems or proposing of government policies. He considers the latter kind of discussion puerile and factitious, full of meaningless phrases uttered in defense of or in attack on official doctrines that merely preserve the old culture forms by taking them seriously.

Revolutions begin in culture because culture is not only more accessible but also ultimately more potent. Politics, economics, and technology are constrained by existing institutional structures, by existing methods of resource mobilization and commitments, and by the inertia of the existing balance of interest groups with their panoplies of policy powers, vetoes, and initiatives. Culture, in contrast, is free to create new rituals of protest and dramatizes the real parameters of values. Within the realm of culture there is little resistance to expressive symbols and forms. In effect, cultural abstractions provide a low-risk, flexible, and universal forum where any new value or ritual may seek an audience and may promote itself from obscurity to legitimacy.

The cultural revolution has created what critic Harold Rosenburg of *The New Yorker* calls "the tradition of the new," allowing creation of structure and forms outside of existing genres, exploring all modes of new experience, technology, and sensation. Fantasy projects a stimulus-hunger for anything bizarre, cultish, and opprobrious. As Bell observes, "even madness, in the writings of such social theorists as Michel Foucault and R. D. Laing, is now conceived to be a superior form of truth!"[14] Masses of people need not immediately absorb the general onslaught of the new for it to be effective. In the abstract process of social learning, small groups experiment with values competitively. Those values that survive tend to diffuse rapidly, imperceptibly and silently transforming the images and actions of large groups of people. Consider the silent victory of the Beatles' hair style as it moved up the ladder of the generations! Consider the nudie magazines now on sale in family food stores in nice neighborhoods! However, far from being given a blank check, new trends undergoing the process of cultural assimilation must still be subjected to the test of appropriateness, as the fate of some of them attests. Many overnight sensations dissolve in the wave of newer sensations, while others leave a profound residue and blend with tradition.

If we examine revolution as an abstract cultural fact, we see that the recent cultural revolution represents less a radically new process and more a change in the source of inputs. During the preceding thirty years, culture inputs came largely from above. We experienced a highly legitimate centralized government whose purposes appeared self-evident; thus, government, intellectuals conducting government business, business and production entrepreneurs, and executives were the common input sources. Scientists, Think Tanks, operations analysts, electronic priests of IBM, teachers, professors, military experts, planners, engineers . . . all the official innovators carried legitimacy and concerted the sources of culture change. For an entire generation, the whole emphasis of social science and psychology served this perception of legitimate purpose by supplementing public and private activity systems centered on national authority. The loss of credibility of the centralized government and its associated structures opened the way for the restless overload of inputs from every self-appointed insurgent source below.

The collapse was universal. All the minions of old authority and official inputers were themselves in personal and professional disarray, succumbing to the rush of the new and looking for ways to get with it. With uncertainty and paralysis rampant in the upper echelons, legitimacy had to come from below, and it came from the outsider, from "the people," from children, from the old and rejected, from Indians, Blacks, and Hindu mystics, from the talented and the untalented, from the fits, unfits, and misfits, from the proper and from the obscene.

SELF-FULFILLING PROPHECY

Culture constitutes the learned man-made part of the environment; in a civilization as rich in resources and technology as our own, the contrived and the invented constitute virtually all. There is an abundance of solutions to every problem posed by the environment. It is difficult to find a single behavioral form that is clearly determined by biological and physical imperatives.[15]

All organisms, after their fashion, live in a sea of informational stimuli, feedback, sensitivity, and relatedness. The constant flow of information orients the constant flow of behavior. Self-conscious, intentional efforts are made to acquire information from events, with the purpose of using it to deal with those events. Just as every individual requires information, Goffman notes, so every individual must "control and manage" the information that his own behavior conveys, for in this way he influences the response of others to situations in which he has an interest. The role of behavior as information thus becomes highly specialized and extended as an interacting social tool for bargaining, influencing, and controlling. Random reaction in the presence of the unfamiliar (either physical or social) may be spontaneous, but the reaction is immediately assimilated in a secondary mode by the subject and the audience and becomes a culture input. Its specialized informational function becomes a form of ritual—that is, it becomes subject to the conventions of the process of communication in order that it may express and optimize the intentional values of the actor.

Social behavior becomes highly conventionalized in order to draw attention to itself and to specify and clarify its meaning. Its meaning is distinguished from other possible meanings in the same context in all the subtle ways by which nonverbal symbols and language develop both denotative and connotative dimensions. All behavior has a rich infusion of conventional performance. Most of our performances are private and occur in what Goffman calls "a highly bounded region." The impression and understanding fostered by the performance will "tend to saturate the region and time-span so that any individual located in this space-time manifold will be in a position to observe the performance and be guided by the definition of the situation which the performance fosters."[16]

Even unfamiliar and unstructured situations at the frontiers of culture do not elicit purely spontaneous behavior. Search behavior itself becomes stylized and subject to a ritualized process of trial and error in an attempt to apply stereotypes already part of the behavioral repertoire. The failure and frustration of attempts to apply existing stereotypes gives rise to invention and new contrivance whose elements of spontaneity may cause drastic transformations in the catalog of rituals already available in the culture. Search behavior is characterized by both regression and sophistication and leads inexorably away from chaos and randomness toward ritual and meaning.

Functionally, the autistic nature of ritual action, while occasionally inappropriate and harmful to the individual, greatly augments the power of social organization and complexity. Highly articulated patterns of collaboration and competition in societies are made possible only by the capacity and craving for ritual forms. The key ingredient of ritual is a modicum of isolation, which preserves the integrity of behavior from capricious challenge, background noise, and the crippling effects of doubt and passivity where action is required. This isolation enables ritual behavior to maintain an abstract form in spite of the uniqueness of every new engagement, transaction, and situation. The form holds meaning and makes meaningful the divergencies and atypical elements in each new situation. Ritual provides a means of asseverating the significant variables of a situation despite the distracting buzz of events. It enables the organism to conserve, organize, and focus all components of behavior, imposing forms available in the culture upon experiences that could not be dealt with at all in the welter of half-forms, competing structures, or formlessness in which they are encountered.[17]

Actions that are self-fulfilling prophesies make perfect rituals, for they affirm their own legitimacy. Even the private individual alone in his cave tends to fall into elaborate fetishes of behavior, stylized repetitive actions insulated to some degree from instrumental and physical effects, that become a celebration of form, a definition of self, and an assertion of values that are argued to a larger audience that may or may not exist.

Like any other symbol, a ritual stands for something other than itself. Everything is at once itself and a symbol having diverse meaning and is constantly being revised, however stable and insulated it seems, as each new situation and each new enactment enlarge and color its form. No symbol exists in isolation but is part of a structural hierarchy of significance, a gestalt in which everything has meaning and is related to everything else from the simple act of retrieving a fallen stone to the complex performance of a person in a therapy group.

In modern man, belief in the omnipotence of thought (Malinowski's definition of "magic") takes the form of a persistent assumption that behavior flows from one's intellectual world view. Like a Bible-thumping preacher, modern man continues to believe that exhortation and verbal conditioning can capture and control the minds of people and determine their actions. Many psychologists now appreciate the fact that actions and reactions can exist in a sphere almost entirely independent of subjective thought. The inner hierarchy of significance may be largely reactive, *post hoc* coloring that the mind adds to events. For example, a young job applicant reinterprets the behavior of a potential employer in a wholly different way after he discovers that no job is available for him. Inconsistencies between thought and behavior are apparent everywhere—between normative rules and actual behavior, between prescriptions and actions, between actions and alibis.

Verbal formulae are but a part of ritual. Culture is full of subtleties and humor and provides opportunities for fanciful counterpoints between actual behavior and verbal behavior. The meaningful context of behavior is the web of action and reaction between individuals engaged in various interpersonal transactions. This behavior is often governed by an impersonal archetypal logic that contains its own compelling dynamic—almost as if the individual's behavior is controlled by the cues provided by others rather than by the improvised train of thought that trails along behind the motor responses.

Ritual responses are related to the culturally defined requirements of the social situation confronting the individual. Rationalists like John Dewey consider ritual action mere "embroidery" performed for fun; they assume that their own rituals are legitimate and therefore not rituals at all. This fallacy demonstrates the power of culture in the legitimization of myth: in spite of rational pretensions, when a modernist talks about "myth" he is attacking someone else's values, or values that are already dead. When he talks about "reality" he is talking about his own myths, which work for him and which are given reality by the self-fulfilling prophecy of his own ritualized behavior.

People who routinely occupy a common space with others must develop a moral order that includes all those present or they will fall into conflict. In fact, they do both. All societies create a public morality that reflects the interest of minority subcultures and specialized functions, excluding as well as including values in accord with some structural principle.[18] All individuals and groups are in a constant process of maintaining and revising organization, managing competitive demands, values, and shifts in personnel. Constant attention is needed to modulate the interplay of symbols, both verbal and behavioral. Ritual establishes the provisional forms of this interplay and provides the methods for its process whether to facilitate or disrupt the values of dominant groups. The common repertoire of symbolic actions in a culture creates probability and predictability. Ritual is an abstract creation that eliminates the blur of infinite possibility, opening for human use a clearing in the forest of chaos and anxiety.

Myths and symbols of authority express the collective identification of the group, past, present, and future. "Ritual performance is the group's formalized dramatization of an emotional state. And, through the identical repetition of the ceremony, a past event is commemorated as a permanent 'it is.' "[19] Ernst Cassirer states, "Man is a symbolic animal. Symbolic transformation allows man to transcend the immediacy of experience, to convert memory of the past and vision of the future into present possession."[20] The arts present the universal through the particular, thereby mediating between the archetypal forms of behavior of the culture and the social forms of the present. The artist conducts this "bridging function," his imagery and invention permitting otherwise "unlawful discharges" to occur that for the laity are held in check by the grammar of language.[21]

In summary, ritual not only elucidates behavior but transmits it by imitation, strategic interaction (that is, defensive imitation by others who seek to deny its efficacy or to emulate it), competitive collaboration (supportive behavior), authoritative example, and simple imprinting. In all the informal transactions between individuals, physical interactions are inferior to symbolic interactions.

Such physical contacts as may occur (whether simple touching, or pushing, or love-making, or anything else) gain much of their efficacy symbolically through the process of internal fantasy, vastly amplified by ritualized behavior, that endows and augments the meaning of the interchange.

Ritual is an energy-conserving method of social facilitation comparable to the trigger actions of technology (by which a small switch triggers a huge earth mover, or a series of small actions arranges materials as to bring about nuclear chain reactions). Psychogenic factors are the concrete linkage between the fragile tissues of social life and the concrete behavioral interactions of people. Through the discovery and development of social trigger actions, that is, human interventions in physical relationships by which a small action causes a disproportionately large reaction, culture achieves its impressive power. The trigger actions of culture are symbols, small low-energy signals that release organized human energy for large undertakings. They are the energy-saving devices by which conflict can be expressed and facilitated with a minimum waste of resources and energy. Energies that have been allocated to different tasks may be, for the most part, undiminished, and yet be subject to a restructuring as an outcome of symbolic processes, as has been the case in America during the turbulent decade of culture storm.

ACTS AND EVENTS

The means by which the individual expresses information are highly conventionalized but are not limited to intentional transmissions. As Freud discovered, all kinds of physical movements, errors of speech, even accidents, may be primarily communications. Modern psychiatry has discarded the notion that "intentional" is the same as "conscious" or "admitted." The preferred working assumption is that all communications are controlled, intentional, and problem-solving, whether self-conscious and voluntary or not. Signs of all kinds, mostly nonverbal, are produced in the presence of an audience or recipient, whatever the openly avowed purpose of the sender. Symptoms of mental illness may be viewed as communications designed to influence the environment. In order to express information, all such signs must be conventionalized; in other words, they must utilize ritual elements. Every individual is engaged in ritualizing a shared repertoire of communicative acts by means of his reactions to the acts of others. Drug addicts who depend on the doctor for methadone will be reinforced in a pattern of drug dependency as a way of communicating their desire to maintain a supply. In other words, the information that the sender seeks to transmit determines the form of the action. Since it is the ritual definition contained in the culture bank that supplies the information, the ritual definition itself has a strong determining impact on the form of the action. The cycle of reinforcement of abstract ritual forms is thereby maintained; the individual becomes the vessel of culture, his behavior the hard and objective artifact of a corporate abstraction.

Once again, the reality of this abstraction is self-supporting and self-serving. But it is subject to "events," that is, episodes of revision and invention that arise from the unprogramed transactions among individuals and groups as well as the natural events that may change the environmental setting of the culture. All such events, whether the outcome of social exchanges or acts of nature, demand to be assimilated and tamed by ritual. This is the primary means by which the culture adapts itself to conditions external to it. There is a reciprocal relationship between social and natural events in the generation of ritual. The less mastery a civilization has over its physical environment, the more natural events figure in its ritual reenactments. The more mastery a civilization has over its physical environment, the more social events contribute to its ritual forms.

We have already noted that all symbolic systems (mathematical as well as verbal) are tautologies. Conclusions reached by syllogistic reasoning are already presupposed by the definitions or by the assumed relationships between symbols expressed as principles or axioms. However, tautologies are useful; as they wind back to their starting points, they posit symbolic representations that the individual can use to separate, identify, isolate, and control those of his own experiences that are useful in doing, making, or communicating with others. Man breaks out of the tautologies of symbols by acting and communicating, by using them to achieve goals. The act is thus the most meaningful and essential form of meaning, not the subjective knowledge in the mind of man by which he rationalizes and manipulates the operational code, nor the symbols that may arbitrarily fuse one or another set of actions. The *act* changes, commits, or makes, representing the only real meaning. Sequences of acts and events are the only true empiricism whether in the laboratory or on the battlefield.

There is no raw and direct definition of an event as independent of man and culture. It may be defined as any circumstance that is unprogramed and that imposes adaptive revisions upon existing cultural forms. As does Bertrand Russell, we may view culture as we do individual personality, as "a collection of events connected with each other by memory-chain backwards and forwards. We know about one such collection of events—namely, that constituting ourself—more intimately and directly than we may know about anything else in the world."[22]

Events are discontinuous; it is the very purpose of culture to seek to maintain an arbitrary and abstract stability in the face of the flux and infinite perversity of nature. The whole function of culture and ritual is to minimize events. However, the eruption of transforming events is inevitable. The very success of culture creates opportunities for social groups to force events as a means of augmenting their own factional values and leadership against those of prevailing groups. The very success of culture makes it subject to disruptive acts of nature because of its own confident complacency. Culture represents contradictory functions; as a hedge against chaos and background noise, it maintains an arbitrary order, but thereby loses some of its adaptability and becomes vulnerable to shocks inflicted both by dissidents or by environment change.

In the individual, the periods of tranquility between events contain in delicate microform the relics and sacred objects of past events, much as a museum collects representative artifacts of past cultures. The inner reaches of individual personalities are like dimly lit galleries, full of events of a life embalmed in ritualized extensions that buffered and softened shock. Psychiatrists call these artifacts *ego states,* which still exist in microcosm within the prevailing ego state and may be evoked in full form by some new event. In epileptic subjects, electrical stimulation of the temporal cortex of the brain can evoke distinct sets of ego states. "The subject feels again the emotion which the situation originally produced in him, and he is aware of the same interpretation, true or false, which he himself gave to the experience in the first place." Such evocations are discreet and "not fused with other similar experiences." Different ego states can occupy consciousness simultaneously as discreet psychological entities.[23]

Many formal social ceremonies, especially rites of passage that mark changes in status or seasons, reenact traditional ego states of the whole society. Historical events that represent the founding of the group, or the endurance of the group during war and adversity, typically become ceremonial forms expressing values of underlying unity. The ceremony stimulates the temporal cortex of collective fantasy, evoking a past event with full immediacy and palpable reality.

Transactions are social events, most of which are private, bilateral, and of little social importance to the group. Some are of major social scale involving groups and requiring participation by many individuals. Transactions create obligations that are based on a presumption of closure, compliance, and performance and that are fulfilled voluntarily, without reopening the transaction. Changes of status in individual relations, due to generational succession, age-group membership, political reorganization, and adaptation of the group to events are always accompanied by elaborate rituals that alleviate stress, liquidate old obligations, and sanctify new ones. Rites of puberty, marriage, and death, for example, involve change and/or reinforcement of obligations in exactly the same sense as do all of the outcomes of bargaining transactions and exchanges of values of daily social events.

FANTASY AND CULTURE

A symbolic reward or punishment is more effective than a real one. Fantasy has a power of exaggeration and vividness, while the import of real experience may be screened and undermined by memory. In addition, real experience has a tendency to promote counter-strategies and resistance to external coercion so that real punishment may effectively destroy the legitimacy of the punishing authority. Each man's fantasy is his personalized vest pocket edition of the culture, including all the rules of conduct, moral prescriptions, examples from literature, hearsay, legend, and observation, all structured in accordance with the individual's natural history and learned behavior, subject to testing and reevaluation by each new day's grief.

Ritual may be looked on as a paradigm or model, presenting to the individual in a concrete situation an implicit range and inventory of possible socio-political strategies to employ in attempting resolution of a conflict or accumulation of influence. Charles C. Hughes notes, "Every person has numerous latent social identities or statuses of the types sketched in the paradigm, each potentially actualizable, called into play under appropriate constellations of personal circumstances."[24] Acts of violence, even suicide, may be the enactments of a ritual that for persons in extreme situations appears inescapable, reasonable, and legitimate.[25]

Ronald D. Laing argues for the validity of fantasy as "a mode of experience," equal in its effects on personal development and behavior to objective experience. Fantasy colors and embroiders sensory inputs with all of the permutations and combinations of memory and prophecy engendered by the anxiety of existence.[26]

Like ritual, of which it is an intrinsic part, fantasy is the real thought process that links action and response, that intervenes in all sequences of action and reaction, modifying behavior through a learning curve.

Fantasy is more than day-dreaming self-hypnosis. It is rather an individual sample-case borrowed from the storehouse of culture forms that are available in the collective subjectivity of the group. It is the simultaneous presence of all the story lines of all the actions that are relevant to any present circumstance. Relevance is not limited to direct transference of learning, but may be evoked by whimsical analogy, themal inversion, rhyme or consonance of language, and all manner of stray associations that culture and art may combine in the subconscious of the individual.

Fantasy is an automatic prophecy machine grinding out cautionary tales incessantly, grandstanding to our hopes, fears, and regrets. In fantasy, every action is instantly extended into the future in all its permutations and combinations; all possible outcomes are available for consideration as if in a Sears catalog. In fantasy, we are all rapists, murderers, sarcophages, homosexuals; in fact, the range of instantaneous prophecy is bounded only by the limits of energy and time in which the fantasy-generated action is located. Children do not require the model of violence and sex in comic books or on television. They consider killing or maiming their younger siblings three times every day in any case. The explicit pornography of contemporary movies could be rated G; it can hardly compare with the sequences that fantasy screens at will in the private theater of the mind, which enacts every possible response to every situation, allowing us to skim through a thousand scenarios in order to select one for immediate presentation. In this sense, the sequences of our actions are edited versions (pruned and curried to an amazing succinctness and economy) of our fantasy life.

Just as culture symbols are shorthand for actions in certain prescribed situations, so action itself may be viewed as "an edited fantasy." We select a limited number of ritualized components of behavior based on a strategic evaluation of appropriateness. We then implement and perform these, hopefully with conviction and grace.

Even if unconscious, inarticulate, unsophisticated, the fantasy process mobilizes and weighs the options and potentials of response in every human interaction. Every possibility is reviewed for pertinency and efficacy. Thus, in some mysterious way, fantasy colors and determines behavior. All the materials of one's experience, conscious or unconscious (including the secondary inputs of observation, example, and symbolic communication, and the tertiary inputs of artful forecasting dramatized by theater, by plot and story conveyed through the media, as an art form, or through rumor, hearsay, ideology or peer group instruction) are mobilized through fantasy by a process that is not necessarily improved by education; it garners, activates, and selects the appropriate coils of the human memory bank, shapes the perception, and determines the circuit of the body's complex systems of electro-motor responses.

It is through fantasy that ritual behavior is projected and assimilated. That is why symbols can have powerful psychic and bodily effects, acting from a distance without physically touching the individual. What passes for "external reality" for the individual is a compendium of life experiences and organic conditions tested by trial-and-error experiences of the past, as well as those experiences observed or communicated, all of which condition the response to new sensory inputs. Reality, therefore, is a modified fantasy that in its group manifestations becomes ritual and culture.

Fantasy operates by plot and story to project and complete action. It provides a spontaneous total field approach to experience, refusing to be bound by analytical distinctions or artificial methodologies. Moral precept embodied in stories appeals to fantasy because fantasy is a great story-teller. Everything is seen in a causal chain of events. A tennis ball in the gutter suddenly has a life history and a future. The tendency of primitive man to personalize his relation to the machine is shared by moderns; every workman does the same with his tools and his car. This is part of the irrepressible demand for total unity and story line that fantasy imposes.

Fantasy contains a wealth of pictorial hypotheses about the nature of reality; it is alive with concrete images, anecdotes, pictures, parables. This is true even in the educated man whose vocabulary includes many thin-blooded abstractions, and whose discourse is status-conscious and dull. He struggles to put story back into his discourse.[27]

THE REALITY PRINCIPLE

Rituals of action, whether formal group ceremonies or individual and situational excursions, serve to bind time and to objectify memory. Loaded with moral meaning and carrying the subjective freight of past events, social relationships, and expectations, they make the past, present, and future simultaneous and tangible. They accomplish this because they are imbued with moment and necessity, which give them the two aspects of the social reality principle, structured action and milieu significance. The ability of the ritual process to conquer time and condense long tracts of memory into present action endows life with significance and summons for the work of society all of the resources of fantasy that exist in its members, whose energy constitutes the basic resource of the group. Fundamentally, this evocation of fantasy and its mobilization in culture constitutes the basic political stuff of legitimacy, stability, and change, in organized societies.

The particles of action plucked from the stream of fantasy are responsive to a reality principle that is essentially social and cultural and not verifiable in any absolute sense. As fantasy is a pocket edition of the culture, there is a built-in automatic information retrieval system. Every individual is an audience for the edited version of everyone else's fantasy as represented in their actions. Such actions sometimes represent the testing of a wide range of options, the outcomes of which modify the store of culture forms and the fantasy life of the audience. New information is assimilated not only directly and indirectly, but also by ritualization which leads other people to profit from the learning of others without awareness of the specific origins of the behavior form. Everyone is part of the general audience for everyone else, and all are performers for each other in an existential theater.

Daniel J. Boorstin's bitter attack on the ascendancy of pseudo-events in American culture stumbles on the failure to clearly distinguish between real and pseudo.[28] The distinction is difficult to make. Even the most highly ritualized event (a parade or football game) has dimensions in common with unprogramed events. It is difficult to imagine a real nonpseudo event, unless it is the ancient pine that falls unseen and unheard in the depths of an isolated forest. Natural events are quickly assimilated by culture and given man-made qualities. All events are culturally real in some sense, in spite of their pseudo manifestations. The power to make a reportable event is the power to make experience and to shape the direction of culture. Those culture heroes and innovators who capture the culture front may carry it with them as they age; the values and rituals that they develop may be generalized and adopted by the whole society.

A careful reading of Boorstin's powerful harangue reveals that his hatred of the pseudo event is rather directed against those whose purposes and visions of the future are embodied in *certain* pseudo events. His book is the last agony of the old middle-class pretense that nineteenth-century aristocratic culture is the only culture worth preserving, while pop culture is unworthy of serious attention.

Each of us is a living theater for the rest and our actions adorn each others' fantasy as scholia or emendations. This is the process of collective learning and mutual adaptation. All the media of communication, including the informal grapevine, direct observation, and eavesdropping, are part of the network. Each of us portrays himself fragmentarily and unconsciously all of the time, and only occasionally conspicuously and with control. Each of us develops a set of rituals for purposes of identification. Our signature, our style, gestures, accents of speech, are tokens of self-cultivation to maintain a symbolic identity.

Like all symbols, the function of these rituals is to imply a code of behavior that we want others to follow in dealing with us. Our symbolic identity is part of our strategy to influence and control our social environment; it serves as an independent variable in the transactions of social intercourse.[29] In his famous work, *The Presentation of Self,* Goffman analyzes the complex array of "signed vehicles" that the individual uses for self-identification. Each self cultivates a number of ritual roles for different occasions and relationships.[30] Individual behavior is highly ritualized to overcome dramaturgical problems of face-to-face interaction.[31]

The power to create a reportable event is a power to create social reality. Political action is most effective when it is merely symbolic and evocative. The whole success of the Black Panthers in 1969 and 1970 was based on the theatrical staging of confrontations with the police. Yet with the movement's loss of legitimacy in 1971, Eldridge Cleaver, speaking from Algeria by telephone on a television talk show, attacked the very basis that had served the party well in its growth phase: "The trouble with this society is that it is pop culture–oriented. Some people can only dig stage center. They need a martyr to kill every month."[32] Martin Luther King, Jr., marching in Alabama, with the help of white politicians and police provided a theatrical enactment on a small scale that revolutionized values and institutions throughout the country. The clubbing of black pacifists by Sheriff Bull Connor's men did more to unite the blacks and prepare white society for fundamental change than all of the violence of young militants who later sought to ride the wave.

The theatrical quality of ritual action was nowhere better used than by Abbie Hoffman and the Yippies. The Democratic National Convention of 1968 was turned into a clash between puritan and pagan armies. The showdown came in the "great conspiracy" trial, a confrontation in the headlines between giant ritual figures. Cast and directed by Abbie's promotional genius, with the cooperation and support of Mayor Richard J. Daley and the U.S. Attorney General John Mitchell, how could it fail? Yet, an attempt in 1971 by the May Day Tribe (with most of the members of the "great conspiracy" aboard) failed to close down Washington and also failed as ritual drama to point a moral lesson. The result was not a riot, but an extended game of hares and hounds in which the hunters and the hunted remained united in a mutual desire to avoid serious injury and damage. Their rival campaigns of annoyance could not be accommodated within the law, but neither did either side profit by the opportunity of improving its legitimacy at the expense of the other side. Improvement of one's own legitimacy is after all the main function of symbolic political action and is the ultimate arbiter of theatrical success.

An individual identity is defined by the response it elicits from others. This response check is the ultimate reality principle. The ability to judge the audience and to build continuous feedback and interplay between one's own performance and the audience enhances the response check. Without this check, the same gestures and performances become symptoms of madness. The need for a reality check provides the chief distinction between mental health and illness. In the wrong context, the same behavior becomes a neurotic caricature of great achievement. As Theodore Reik observes, "Obsessions are a caricature of religion and accordingly obsessional neurotic ceremonial is an involuntary caricature of religious ceremonial."[33] The performance that ignores the appropriateness of the occasion, or the receptiveness of the audience represents a serious psychological dysfunction.

Man has ritualized a wide variety of signals to express the universal need for a continuous response check. Convention requires the proper response, the nod, the grunt of approval, the smile, even when the significance of the gesture is feigned. Hass notes, "In conversation, the face of the listener often echoes what the other person is saying. If the latter says something serious, the listener grows serious; if he speaks of a surprise, the listener performs a facial movement conveying the same."[34] Ritualization of a response check is so complete that the response can even precede the communication, the laugh may come before the joke, the agreement before the assertion. As a low form of response check, greeting rituals are clear-cut and easily performed. In contrast, the interplay of competitive collaboration that occurs in the body of the encounter is much more threatening and difficult and requires much greater resourcefulness in the use of ritual components. Consequently, many social encounters progress splendidly up until the end of the greeting ritual. Also many schizophrenics enact the greeting ritual endlessly and *in vacuo* as their only form of social intercourse, without an attempt to bring the transaction to closure.

Every ritual option that exists in culture and in fantasy may be looked on as a strategy for encompassing the situation.[35] The whole fabric of personal interactions in a society may be viewed as a transactional network, a dynamic moving welter of continuously changing structure, combining motivations, perception, impulse, affect, mood, sentiment, value, performance, wit, and insight in the unique combinations that characterize each transaction. Hughes states, "It is out of this very cauldron of interpersonal dealing, the shifting field of forces, that a behavioral product emerges; it is in this microcosm that is the personality, that the incoming stimuli, challenges, dilemmas, and opportunities of the environment are confronted, where they are placed in categories, appraised, evaluated as a concomitant of faction."[36] The bargaining continuum of interpersonal relations requires a continuous exchange of cues and signals that highlight the values involved in the interaction and thereby provide a reality check to the parties.

Bargaining relations are essentially ambivalent. The nature of bargaining is uncertainty of outcome and reciprocal thrust and counter-thrust based on the available resources of the parties. The process of action/reaction among individuals and groups is the underlying concrete reality that constitutes learned behavior. Such learning tends to reinforce and stabilize attitudes, habits, and responses, in like, similar, and transfer situations. When new situations prove such behavior to be inappropriate and frustrating, the individual turns to search behavior and the process of trial and error. Improvisation and *ad hoc* reactions are exceptional but always possible. Every such action and reaction becomes immediately available for ritual reinforcement or extinction. Cumulatively, such events modify the culture through strategic interaction and competitive collaboration.

A reality principle lies in the continued legitimacy of any culture form in a given population over a period of time. To constitute a socially significant change, the new must be adopted by sufficient numbers of the members of the population to give it currency, and so integrated into other patterns of the culture as to accomplish values for those who embrace it. As in psychological therapy or religious conversion, significant changes in a culture are accomplished by this unheralded process of interaction and exchange of values among individuals and groups. It is seldom possible to detect and recognize these developments until they are already highly ritualized, formal, and open to challenge. The receiving of legal and/or institutional recognition is a symptom of incipient decline.

Ritual does not guarantee effective action except insofar as the reenactment of the ritual itself provides the essential design for action. The reality principle encompasses the legitimacy of the prescribed behavior and of those persons and offices identified with its authority. As we have seen, legitimacy is a support that attaches to an object through a symbolic exchange between those who give the support and its recipients. It reflects the vitality of the underlying consensus that endows the state and its officers with whatever authority and power they actually possess, not by virtue of legality, but by the respect that citizens pay to the institutions and behavior norms. Legitimacy is earned by the ability of those who wield the power of the state to represent and reflect a broad consensus. Legitimacy cannot be claimed or granted by mere technicality of law; it must be won by the success of institutions in cultivating and meeting expectations, in mediating interests, and in aiding the process by which the values of individuals and groups are allocated.

The components of the informal polity that vest the formal institutional structure with legitimacy are indispensable to the working of the political and social systems. Law enforcement and court and correctional activities are particular aspects of the system of social control, and probably the least important ones. They will not work when the informal systems by which individual behavior is integrated into a social order break down. That which has the greatest legitimacy is taken for granted and is frequently inarticulate. The verbal and intellectual dimension of social values precipitates out as values are defended and attacked in the process of continued change. As we become aware of air only when we gasp for it, we become aware of the artificiality of theatrical conventions, as McLuhan has pointed out, only when new conventions have changed our point of view. Analysis is therefore mostly backward-looking, while future probes that surround us only become palpable after they are incorporated into the culture.[37]

An exchange of values of some kind, however intangible, is essential to a human interaction. It is even essential to relationships with nonhuman subjects. David Premack, in studying the development of language in chimpanzees, could make no progress until a social exchange between subject and trainer was well established. A feeding routine provided the effective transaction that prepared the way for leading the apes into elaborate symbol experiments. The rituals of human relationships facilitate, channelize, and conserve the transaction process. The action/reaction process can be supported or not as the interaction moves toward closure. Collaborative competition does not preclude conflict. The pattern of bargaining may escalate and disrupt the transaction. This danger cannot be erased and is part of the range of available responses that may make possible a constructive closure. The competitive element of collaboration means that there is a constant interplay and search for advantage in the transaction. This in turn means that the rituals themselves will undergo adaptive change in the process.

The fact that there are dangers implicit in every transaction—escalation, withdrawal and rejection, and miserable performance—provides the basic reality principle and response check for determining the appropriateness and truth of culture forms. To quote William James, the "whole feeling of reality, the whole sting and excitement of our voluntary life depends on our sense that things are *really being decided* from one moment to another. . . ."[38] A transaction based on an exchange of positive consensus values does not require tangible benefits or positive feedback to be legitimized and sustained. An outcome based on negative values, coercion of one kind or another by either or both parties, may only be legitimized by the positive benefits bestowed. The latter form of legitimacy is shaky and tends to be of the "what have you done for me lately?" kind. A reality check arises from the fact that the outcomes of interpersonal transactions are sustainable and accountable without further major effort by either party to reopen the transaction. The transaction itself is repeatable and has a heightened probability of being repeated. The available energy committed to fulfilling the obligations of the transaction will not readily be diverted by competing claims.

NOTES

1. "Scarecrow Crusader," *Time*, *November* 9, 1970, p. 41.

2. William James, *Principles of Psychology* (New York: Holt, Rinehart and Winston, 1950), p. 638.

3. Yehudi A. Cohen, ed., *Man in Adaptation: The Cultural Present* (Chicago: Aldine, 1968), p. 1.

4. *Ibid.*, pp. 8–10.

5. Gabriel A. Almond, "Comparative Political Systems," *Journal of Politics*, 1956, p. 396.

6. Lucian W. Pye, "Introduction: Political Culture and Political Development," in Lucian W. Pye and Sidney Verba, eds., *Political Culture and Political Development* (Princeton, N.J.: Princeton University Press, 1965), p. 7.

7. Sidney Verba, "Comparative Political Culture," in *ibid.*, p. 516.

8. For the old view, see Richard E. Dawson and Kenneth Prewitt, *Political Socialization* (Boston: Little, Brown, 1969), p. 29.

9. The study of the Dobe area bushmen shows that they live well on wild plants and meat in spite of the fact that they are confined to the least productive portion of the bushmen range. One anthropologist writes, "It is likely that an even more substantial subsistence base would have been characteristic of these hunters and gatherers in the past, when they had the pick of African habitats to choose from." (Richard B. Lee, "What Hunters Do For a Living, or How to Make Out on Scarce Resources," in Lee and Irven Devore, eds., *Man the Hunter* [Chicago: Aldine, 1968], p. 43.)

10. James Woodburn, "An Introduction to Hadza Ecology," in *ibid.*, p. 53.

11. Donald W. Lathrop, "Ecology and Economics," in *ibid.*, p. 36.

12. Daniel Bell, "The Cultural Contradictions of Capitalism," *The Public Interest*, September 1970, p. 17.

13. Charles A. Reich, "Beyond Consciousness," *The New York Times*, March 8, 1971, p. 311.

14. Bell, 1970, p. 17.

15. Ashley Montagu, ed., "Introduction," *Man and Aggression* (New York: Oxford University Press, 1968), pp. xii–xv.

16. Erving Goffman, *The Presentation of Self in Everyday Life* (Garden City, N.Y.: Doubleday, 1959), p. 106.

17. W. C. Allee, *Cooperation Among Animals* (New York: Henry Schuman, 1938), pp. 12–13.

18. See Gerald D. Suttles, *The Social Order of the Slum: Ethnicity and Territory in the Inner City* (Chicago: University of Chicago Press, 1968), p. 7.

19. Harry Slochower, *Mythopoesis* (Detroit: Wayne State University Press, 1970), p. 334.

20. Quoted in *Ibid.*, p. 29.

21. See Lawrence S. Kubie, "Distortion of the Symbolic Process in Neurosis and Psychosis," *Journal of American Psychoanalytic Association*, 1953, pp. 59–86.

22. Bertrand Russell, *My Philosophical Development* (New York: Simon and Shuster, 1959), pp. 26–27.

23. Eric Berne, *Transactional Analysis in Psychotherapy* (New York: Grove Press, 1961), p. 17.

24. Charles C. Hughes, "Structure, Field, and Process in Siberian Eskimo Political Behavior," in Marc J. Swartz, ed., *Local Level Politics: Social and Cultural Prospectives* (Chicago: Aldine, 1968), p. 171.

25. Charles William Wahl, "Suicide as a Magical Act," in Edwin S. Shneidman and Norman L. Faberow, eds., *Clues to Suicide* (New York: McGraw-Hill, 1957), p. 24.

26. Ronald D. Laing, *The Self and Others: Further Studies in Sanity & Madness* (London: Tavistok Publications, 1961), p. 3.

27. McLuhan notes that disparate film images shown to children could not be recalled except in the form of invented stories that used some of the elements that appeared on the screen. (Marshall McLuhan, *The Gutenberg Galaxy* [Toronto: University of Toronto Press, 1962], pp. 36–37.)

28. Daniel J. Boorstin, *The Image, or What Happened to the American Dream* (New York: Atheneum, 1962), pp. 10–15.

29. Herbert Read, *Icon and Idea: The Function of Art in the Development of Human Consciousness* (New York: Shocken Books, 1965), p. 111.

30. See Goffman, 1959; also Goffman, *Interaction Ritual: Essays on Face-to-Face Behavior* (Garden City, N.Y.: Doubleday, 1967).

31. "The pre-established pattern of action which is unfolded during

a performance and which may be presented or played through on other occasions may be called a part or routine." (Goffman, 1959, p. 16.)

32. *The New York Times,* March 1, 1971, p. 1.

33. Theodor Reik, *Ritual: Psycho-Analytic Studies* (New York: International University Press, 1931), p. 16–17.

34. Hans Hass, *The Human Animal: The Mystery of Man's Behavior* (New York: Putnam's, 1970), p. 118.

35. Kenneth Burke, *Terms for Order,* edited by Stanley Edgar Hyman (Bloomington, Ind.: Indiana University Press, 1964), pp. 124–25.

36. Hughes, 1968, p. 164.

37. See Alvin Boskoff, "Social Change: Major Problems in the Emergence of Theoretical and Research Foci," in Howard Becker and Alvin Boskoff, eds., *Modern Sociological Theory* (New York: Holt, Rinehart and Winston, 1957), pp. 260–302.

38. William James, *Psychology: Briefer Course* (New York: 1892), p. 237.

4 | SACRED & PROFANE

Everyday routines are part and parcel of a familiar world. This is a world which can be managed by ordinary action. Its "reality" can be grasped by the ordinary senses of ordinary men. . . . The strata of significance to which everyday life is ultimately referred, however, are neither concrete nor unproblematic. . . . That "reality" cannot be dealt with habitually; indeed, it is beyond the control of ordinary men. The domain transcending the world of everyday life is experienced as "different" and mysterious. If the characteristic quality of everyday life is its "profaneness," the quality that defines the transcendent domain is its "sacredness." (Thomas Luckman, 1967)[1]

Yali, the spiritual leader of the Fifth Cargo Cult in New Guinea, visited the Brisbane Zoo and the Queensland Museum during an Australian visit. Designed to soften the nationalistic tendencies of the Cargo cults, the visit had quite the opposite effect. He was deeply impressed by the European habit of keeping pets, on which were lavished a degree of care and affection unknown in a New Guinea village. Visiting an agricultural station, he was shown how European animals were housed, and how experiments were conducted to help them adapt to the tropics. Suddenly, the truth dawned on him. "The zoo animals, the pets, the bones in the museums, all were European totems. The form of Christianity taught to his people by the missionaries was false!" White men did not really have one God, a Trinity, or a common descent from Adam and Eve; he saw that, like his own people, Christians had a wide variety of totem cults including the horse, cow, dog, cat, lion, tiger, zebra, and other animals. The respect accorded them were of the same order as the taboos and totem observances that missionaries were stamping out back in the forest. It became clear to Yali that Christianity was not an invitation to his people to join in a sacred state of equality with whites, but a fraudulent attempt to deny his people their traditional truths.

Yali returned to New Guinea pensive and shaken. It was not long after this that the Fifth Cargo Cult became an antiwhite, anti-Christian nationalist sensation throughout the territory.[2] As the scales fell from Yali's eyes, he saw and understood more than the white Christians, whose self-justifying cultural blinders were taken for granted and invisible. Yali observed the actual rituals; he failed to make the artificial distinction between secular and sacred. Instead, he used the common-sense definition of the sacred, not as a convention of language, but as the power of objects to command a wide variety of ritual observances, expenses, and inconveniences. The agriculture station and the zoo constituted culture forms more sacred than the conventions of a dying church with its empty verbalisms and denatured ceremonies. The former were truly sacred, the latter merely sanctimonious.

THE POWER AND THE ECSTASY

Essentially, anything is sacred that has intangible and mysterious powers over our actions and emotions. For example, I consider certain passages of Mozart sacred because in their presence the world is transformed. A sacral light of piety and transcending love adorns my face. I am physically transfixed and immobilized. The banalities of life lose their hold; my spirit glides on the lines of contrapuntal song and is lifted by joy, wonder, selflessness, and serenity. If those passages are not sacred in the truest sense, then nothing is. Yet, I discovered this ecstasy by listening to the scratchy 78-rpm platters of my youth. Today, kids get their kicks from doctored stereo sound blasted at 100-watt levels. The sacred character and the responses are the same, but the technology and the conventions of form are different. Even in the concert hall, an audience accustomed to high-fidelity amplification has difficulty relating to undoctored sound.[3] Scratchy 78's with tinny monophonic speakers are considered quaint and incapable of providing the impulse for an ecstatic sacrament. The variable is not the technology, but the ritual act. One must be open for a sacral experience, sensitized to its values, prepared to react to it as though it has great power to move. Then, unsurprisingly, the magic comes, the piety and transforming love descends. In short, things acquire a sacred character and mysterious powers through the influence of culture. The act of endowing anything with power over oneself tends to make it sacred.

The penis is a sacred symbol of legitimacy in our culture. White male fear of the configuration of the black penis expresses the guilty conscience of a shaken social order. The conventions of nudity and pornography aim at the desanctification of the penis, as is evident from the prevalence of jokes and skits based upon the absurdness of an organ that is frequently unable to perform at all, and at best requires long periods of recuperation between brief and often poorly timed interludes of real work.

Individual readiness and vulnerability to certain forms reflect ritualized values. Identity with a sect or group may lead an individual to endow certain objects or acts with a sacred character. Personal or public events that combine unknown elements and risks heighten anxieties, thereby invoking the same vulnerability, augmenting the intensity and the profoundness of the experience. We are sensitized both by events and by culture (the apotheosis of past events). Our sensitivity is ritualized into a patterned response to the sacred stimulus.

Anything can be sacralized, that is, raised up into a symbol of concentrated power that can evoke and express complex messages and can refresh the incentives of old and familiar ritual forms. The most hardened atheist still thrills at certain invocations of God. The most militant revolutionary never fully erases the tremors of childish adoration for his country's flag whipped by a clear breeze against a deep blue sky. The energy-saving trigger action of culture symbols is achieved by sacralization that augments efficiency and power. All symbols of legitimacy and authority take on a sacred cast. As ritual figures, political leaders with a high degree of legitimacy are crowned with sacred qualities. They assume responsibility not only for government policy but also for the weather, the good or bad fortunes of their followers, and the preservation of their own ritual character.

Christianity was once a battle with death and a conquest leading to resurrection; Billy Graham has truncated this confrontation to the point where the blood and flesh of the lamb become Coca-Cola and Wonder Bread. Under the regimes of recent presidents (Johnson and Nixon), a cult of the Potomac has flourished almost as an official church. "Salvation of the 'soul' is given priority by the cult over the bodily condition of men, women and children—including refugees created by the Nixon Doctrine in Cambodia and America's indigenous refugees in urban ghettos."[4] The cult's philosopher, Bob Hope, and its high priest, Billy Graham, acted as cochairmen of "Honor America Day" in Washington on July 4, 1970. On that occasion, Graham said: "Jesus said, 'Render unto Caesar the things that are Caesar's.' The Apostle Paul proudly boasted that he was a Roman citizen. The Bible says, 'Honor the nation.' "[5]

Every individual, whether truck-driver or classicist, sensitizes himself to the symbols he respects. In this way, he endows them with the power to transfix and transport his emotions. Sacred trust and internalized obedience are aspects of the sacramental habit. It is only cultural chauvinism that convinces the intellectual that his love of opera is in any way sweeter, higher, or more satisfying than is any truck-driver's feeling for "Melancholy Baby." Sacredness as a cultural quality provides a clue to understanding the operation of all kinds of culture symbols. The social meanings that attach to symbols rise from the predisposition to act in certain specified ways in their presence. The profane or the secular represents the common, the specific, the instrumental, which demands and gets but little special attention even though it characterizes a large part of behavior. This kind of behavior, though an important aspect of culture, does not require special significance and subjective integration. It contains automatic rituals, routines, and techniques that pertain, as long as they remain profane, to the steady-state conditions of the culture. In contrast, the profound or the sacralar represents the uncommon (and the familiar that culture decrees as uncommon) and the dangerous, elevated for special attention, requiring ritual safeguards and subjective interpretation.

Classical writers have followed Émile Durkheim in distinguishing social actions into major classes—religious rites, which are sacred, and technical acts, which are profane. With Victor W. Turner and contemporary anthropologists, this sharp polarity is abandoned. In its place is a continuum; *profane* and *sacred* do not denote *types* of action but *aspects* of almost any kind of action. Technique has economic material consequences that are measurable and predictable; ritual, in contrast, is a symbolic statement that "says" something about the individuals involved in the action.

In his study of ritual in Tikopia, Raymond Firth notes the intricate commingling of sacred and profane activities in a complex work/ritual cycle whose manifest intent was "the promotion and sanctification of the economic process."[6] Within the performance, sacerdotal and mundane elements were mixed. The provision of materials for ritual offerings required time and energy; once offered to the gods in ceremony, they were withdrawn and eaten by the celebrants. The atmosphere of the occasion allowed quite rapid oscillations between "recognition of the sacred" (by silence and obeisance) and "recognition of the profane" (by ribaldry, clowning, and good nature). This mixture was essential for sustaining a long and involved ceremony which went on for days, whose intensity and focus demanded variation and release as well as the need to break from ceremonial behavior in order to engage in the profane pursuits of sleep and work.

The relation between the events of everyday life and the rituals of the sacred domain is indirect. Many graduated strata of meaning mediate between trivial profane routines and the ultimate significance of a biography, or a social tradition. The indirectness of this relationship necessarily gives rise to sacred occasions and to events that may be sacralized by future observances. Helplessness in the face of natural events like death is accompanied by anxiety or ecstasy or a mixture of both. Such experiences are apprehended, as a rule, as direct manifestations of the reality of the sacred domain. Thus both the ultimate significance of everyday life and the meaning of extraordinary experiences are located in the sacred domain. The sacred possesses no less reality or legitimacy than does the more palpable domain of the profane. Actually, as we have seen, both are mediated by culture in the same way; any differences in reality are purely subjective and are determined by theoretical paradigms.

While the two domains tend to become polarized, they are necessarily related. This relationship ranges from a relatively high degree of segregation between a profane world and a sacred cosmos in some societies to a high degree of interpenetration in others. Animism, totemism, and eschatology are some of the more typical systematic elaborations of this relationship. The sacred cosmos is socially actualized in performance (rituals), images (sacred icons), and language (divine names). Performances such as eating and planting embody a world view. They have purpose in the context of everyday life, but only indirectly are they integrated into "higher" levels of significance. But acts that embody an element of the sacred cosmos are, strictly speaking, meaningless within the immediate context of everyday life. Their purpose refers *directly* to the sacred cosmos. Sacrifices, rites of passage, and burial rites, represent ultimate significance without the necessity of intermediate levels of translation into the profane context of everyday routine.

Symbols unite "the organic with the socio-moral order, proclaiming their ultimate religious unity over and above conflict between and within these orders." Turner writes that the ritual process divests all the divisive drives of sex and politics "of their anti-social quality" attaching them to the normative order, "energizing the latter with a borrowed vitality, and thus making the *obligatory* desirable. Symbols are both the resultants and the instigators of this process, and encapsulate its properties."[7]

ABSTRACTION AND FEAR

Personal objects and occasions may acquire a sacred character as a way of combining two contradictory motives and forms of behavior, namely, fear and exploration. New objects and events release tremendous anxiety, combining both attraction and avoidance signals, taking on a sacral glow that commands attention and caution. There is a natural tendency for the new and the dangerous to stand out in any situation, and to elicit a standard series of exploratory behavior patterns that aim at incorporating the new thing into existing and familiar uses or expelling or destroying or avoiding it.

This reaction to new things is an individual or social crisis, whether small or large, that must be culturally defined and ritualized. Raw experience and the unknown are dangerous—they draw energy from the necessary on-going processes of life until they can be assimilated into familiar categories. This kind of crisis is the primary motive for abstraction and symbolization, and the biological anxiety of attraction/avoidance provides the archetype of all sacred behavior.

Studies of animal behavior show that a sudden change in stimulation elicits the whole syndrome of behavior toward "a sacred source." Attention is riveted on the new object or event; actions are characterized by a highly-measured and deliberate tension between approach and flight. The two tendencies, Hinde writes, are of course "incompatible and mutually inhibitory. Both monkeys and children, as well as lower forms, when released into a strange area or confronted with a strange object, alternate passive staring with active exploration."[8]

Being visual creatures, men and other animals preface every act with a stare. The eyes become the beacon of the soul, and are therefore used as symbolic threat, direct communication, or dissembling. A stare is a question, a stimulus that represents alertness in the starer. When addressed at another person, it represents an invitation or a threat that immediately heightens the alertness of the target. The stare in response to danger is the basis of abstraction. Any new object or unexpected movement in a field of perception threatens the organism and thereby leads to a sudden change in organization and priorities. The visual stare is the first reaction, the mobilization of the early warning alert system. All of the input from the other senses is suddenly reduced or halted while the organism strains its attention toward the source of change in its environment. This intense concentration is the essential element of abstraction. It frames an event so as to illuminate or outline its form and meaning independently of background noise and context. It is the same concentration of attention that gives objects a sacred quality. The genuflection of adoration or the framing of an object or action in a field of intense concentration, whether of art forms or of experience, constitutes the elemental basis of abstraction. Search behavior is stimulated and oriented by this primeval mode. Social ritual adopts this mode by endowing certain objects and behaviors with the conventions of sacredness.

Occasions that are most dangerous are also, therefore, most ritualized. This is not a contradiction in any sense, but a confirmation of the role and function of ritual. Abstractions of cultural invention (not only in the fine arts but in all culture forms) lie close to the fearful entropic abyss of the human condition, and thereby acquire an operational code that must be classified as lying within the sacred realm.

It may be that events, behavior forms, objects, and persons that cultural usages endow with sacred qualities elicit a dimension of search behavior in spite of the fact that they may have long since been reduced to predictable and familiar forms. Culture forms endowed with tradition and familiarity may still contain, close to the surface, inklings and hints of the fearful unknown that threatens personal and social life. Chaos and death lurk behind the façade of all conventionalized conflicts. The occurrence of a disruptive event that cannot be managed or assimilated by the group without important and difficult social adjustments is never impossible.

The dangerous and the powerful, and especially the unfamiliar, are taken to be sacred and are ritualized in order to preclude their disrupting the social order of the group. Social institutions reverse the process; they endow the familiar with sacredness through ritual in order to give meaning to the governing system of the social order.

By virtue of the same sort of action (anxiety, attraction/avoidance, heightened attention, and so forth), an object, person, or occasion is endowed with sacramental quality. Power and danger become cultural acts maintained by the artifices of ritual in order that they may serve a variety of social and personal functions. The sacred elevates and gives meaning. It consecrates feelings and raises experience to a universal and elemental level. Sacred ritual provides behavioral verification for what is otherwise only a symbolic conceit. What Herbert Read calls "the purity and singleness of an act of vision" gives unchallengeable presence and reality to the inventions of culture, creating a tactual, sensual, and aesthetic apprehension of the world, imbuing with significance and meaning the values and customs of the individual, his time, and his society.[9]

All of the spontaneous acts of search behavior are used to maintain the symbolic artifacts of culture: man freezes into immobility, his attention arrested, all of his senses alert, his mien suspicious. All of the gestures of fright are combined with cautious approach and regard. The heart pounds, the breath comes deeply through the mouth, the reaction to every sound or motion is exaggerated, but controlled. The hand is involuntarily raised as if to protect the face, the head inclined, the eyes wide. All movements become stylized like a ballet. The behavior says of the object, person, or occasion: "This has power to move me. I am vulnerable and responsive to this!"

In a ceremonial ritual, where objects are not intrinsically dangerous or unfamiliar, the behavior itself makes them so and thereby communicates a social attitude to the others present. It also has a bonus effect on the sensibilities of the young. Through imitation and learning, they may indeed regard the ritual as powerful and dangerous, thereby making it so.[10] The secrecy and myth that such cultural conceits (like Santa Claus, sex, and traditional religious symbols) are given by adults for the benefit of children *tend to facilitate and preserve the sacred in the face of inevitable familiarity.* In the same way, political leaders (like Hitler, De Gaulle, or MacArthur) attempt to surround themselves with sacred attributes by maintaining a veil of mystery and distance between themselves and the public. The use of masks, disguises, costumes, and fearful weapons in conventional rituals have the same function.

Search behavior is a pattern acquiring sacred attributes from the existential anxiety and danger that elicit it. The intensity of attention and abstract framing is a condition of inquiry into the unknown. In the same way and for the same reasons, sacred qualities enhance scarce commodities and goods. The law of supply and demand, as the paradigm of all exchanges of value, tends to transfigure and augment the properties of any experience or object whose supply is uncertain and for which a great demand exists. For the low-income photographer, Nikons and Leicas are sacred objects. Merchandizing and marketing have turned this process into an industry. For the unrequited lover, the woman that spurns him is transfigured into more than human. For love to endure, the love-object must continue to be dangerous. The inchoate political group that requires a leader and an unifying symbol (in order to organize its resources) actively recruits ritual figures from among the accidental celebrities of the day, endowing them with godlike grace and wisdom. The hunter on a strange mountain, the swimmer beyond his normal range, the social climber who succeeds in getting a cabinet member to her party, all are in unfamiliar and dangerous situations that elicit from them stylized sacral behavior, including attempts by fantasy to project already available symbols and rituals into the encounter.

It is a curious inversion that the conventions of search behavior are adapted to highly stylized ritual functions that are fully integrated by cultural definitions. Yet the motivation for search behavior is present. All formal sacred rituals release a self-conscious search for personal significance in terms of one's life experience. The highly controlled performance releases the unconscious and reenacts real search episodes of the past and future in a microcosm of sweet anguish. The tensions of normal social engagements within the group fall away; in their place mounts the sense of commonality, protection, understanding, and grace that group life affords. The collective presence becomes real and personal whether symbolized by a deity or another collective symbol. Characteristically, rites of control and inner-searching are usually followed by rites of raucous release through dance, joyous singing, drunkenness, and other permissive acts.

The sacred intensifies and makes authoritative, internalizing the requirements of discipline and order. Authority, writes Hannah Arendt, "is commonly mistaken for some kind of power or violence." In fact, it precludes "the use of external means of coercion; where force is used, authority itself has failed . . . the authoritarian relation between the one who commands and the one who obeys rests neither on common reason nor on the power of the one who commands; what they have in common is the hierarchy itself, whose rightness and legitimacy both recognize and both have their predetermined stable place."[11]

Sacral qualities may inhere in anything that acquires social scale. The first component of sanctity is the ability to command attention. Therefore, anything that has this ability (however inappropriate the cause) may take on sacred overtones and become available as an integrating and coordinating symbol for modal culture forms. Interpersonal relationships of all kinds are elevated by national attention through the media or by the political process, and take on a sacred dimension comparable in every way to the legends of Olympian Gods.

Every new event tends to become a shorthand symbolic embodiment of social learning. The black children of Little Rock, Arkansas, whom Governor Orville Faubus kept out of school, noted, "We spent most of that time getting interviewed. One day you would be sitting down with some reporter from Toronto, another day with some guy from London . . . it was great. We felt like celebrities. Some of the kids who had been selected to go to Central with us had got cold feet and dropped out, but they wanted to come back in when they saw all the publicity we were getting. It's kind of strange for me to say that, knowing the history of lynching and so-forth in the south. . . ."[12] In every such event, individuals play their roles with circumspection and self-consciousness, knowing that public attention has transformed them from simple ordinary folk into ritual images whose every word and deed takes on a magnified archetypal quality, ringing down the marble halls of history for hours, months, or even years. A weak and miserable slob may accidentally fall into a ritual role and be transformed into a paragon of taste, style, and control, just as many individuals may promote themselves into this role through inventive or shocking action, such as suicide or assassination, or through public relations and media exposure. As was noted in Chapter 3, the Black Panthers achieved celebrity by cashing in on the black rebellion by means of stagy public relations stunts.

Who has not discovered the difference in words uttered privately to an indifferent listener and the same words addressed to an attentive crowd? Similarly, there is a sudden relapse into the secular as the performer leaves the theater and takes off his sacred role; he crumples into an unremarkable and lonely private person. A dirty joke told in private has a different character from one told on a late night television talk show by a celebrity. Unsupported charges and aspersions that one communicates harmlessly to one's friends change their character when one is testifying before a Congressional committee. Attention and framing add a sacred element because they create a capability of social coordination and simultaneous reaction, an essential characteristic of formal ritual and of political action. A dialog in the living room, without a tape recorder or the presence of a passive audience, is bounded by the relationships and interactions of the individuals present. Hire a hall or bring in a television camera; the same interplay of personal relationships is suddenly transformed into large social ritual of competing legitimacies. Each person in the room becomes masked in archetype and performs a different dance full of different meanings.

There is a critical number of participants and audience for any given transaction that tends to elevate it from the profane to the sacred realm, all other considerations being equal. In India, *darshan*—the mystical experience of being in very large gatherings —is one of the most important religious practices. Perhaps, a general rule of sacred number might be discovered; but more likely it depends upon the strategic interaction and claims of legitimacy that are part of the process.

Abstractions are not simple symbols but represent behavior. The significances of names are the bodies of practice that they imply. To give something the right name is to know which body of practice is appropriate to it. Symbols of culture, including ritual actions, are like all abstractions; that is, their essential nature is behavioral. The sacred is an apotheosis of an act. A conventionalized ceremony is an apotheosis of an event. Like Plato's Essences, the original event is preritualistic, a variety of search behavior and outcome. Once assimilated by culture, abstracted, and ritualized, the original on which it is based acquires an esoteric status, like a prototype, the dies from which mass-produced items are manufactured. A new or original art form, life style, or solution to a problem, is quickly incorporated into the body of social ritual and performed by all kinds of people for all kinds of purposes, often quite divergent from the original unprogramed enactment. The copy acquires more reality than the original because it is socially defined, has a beginning, middle, and end, and a self-consciousness of permanence and form. It is made to fit into an integrated system and serves to facilitate and orient behavior under a wide range of conditions. "Piety is a system-builder," writes Kenneth Burke. It irrepressibly strives to round things out, to fit experience together into a unified whole. Piety is *the sense of what properly goes with what.* "A kind of symbolic cleanliness goes with altars, a technique of symbolic cleansing goes with cleanliness, a preparation or initiation goes with the technique of cleansing, the need of cleansing was based upon some feeling of taboo—and so on, until pious linkages may have brought all the significant details of the day into coordination, relating them integrally with one another by a complex interpretative network."[13]

There is a strong tendency to sacralize the anomalous, to regard it as holy, to use it as a symbol for the whole system. Village idiots are regarded as living shrines, entitled to food and clothing from everyone; the stone the builders rejected is remade to represent the simple unity of society itself. A thing becomes sacred when it is abstracted from the particular and is thus generalized, symbolically framed, and surrounded with elaborate special observances. By ritual, the symbol becomes modal, an archetype for a whole class of behaviors.

The nature of art is the elevation through abstraction from the profane to the sacred realm. Contemporary artists have found that any object, however common and familiar, can be separated from its context, framed in splendid isolation, and, thereby abstracted, become a symbol of its entire class, or of man himself. A soup can, a toilet seat, or a nail can be transformed into art objects, and the audience can be sensitized to endow these symbols with sacred power. In the same way, a photograph can be elevated from an informational message of everyday events, like the common news picture, into a pristine and powerful symbol of a whole class of events, like the works of art photography.

Individuals may also be endowed with sacred character, as happens to charismatic political leaders, artists, and heroes of pop culture. The groupie phenomenon is not new and is not limited to teenage girls who follow rock bands. Culture heroes are always endowed with a sacred character that justifies holding them in a regard quite above normal personal relationships. Worship of the sacred tends to be voluntaristic and one-sided, flowing from the worshiper without the necessity of response in kind or mutuality from the worshiped object. The groupie phenomenon can be seen in the adoration by middle-aged wives of wrestlers and television personalities. Every subculture has a pantheon of more-than-human figures in regard to whom all kinds of otherwise deviant behavior appears justified. Women want to seduce their doctors, secretaries their admired and dynamic bosses. A popular political candidate on the cocktail circuit needs protection from his admirers. Everyone wants to incorporate into himself a piece of the sacred object, whether it be a Beatles' plaster-of-paris penis, or a touch from the hand of an astronaut. Businessmen offer attractive terms to famous football players and seek to recruit the sons of famous men. In the presence of a sacred personage, the worshiper loses his aplomb and begins to manifest all kinds of strange behaviors.

Modern societies have not dispensed with shamans although modern shamans may be unaffiliated with formal religious institutions. They are found informally, whether in the role of neighborhood clown, family schlemiel, cab driver (whom *Time* defines as the world's most sensitive barometer of opinion), television entertainer, or teacher. The informal shaman is a sacred character outside the status structure and not bound by the conventions of tact and manners. He is required to remind all of unmentionable truths. Far from being devastated or insulted, his audience takes his pronouncements as humor and they laugh. Because he is outside the ordinary tensions of personal interaction, his audience is not required to give him back in kind, to drive him out of their company, or even to take him seriously. He is often the culture antihero. He is the exorciser of public demons and "his art is based on the same mechanism as a neurosis or psychosis. The shaman makes both visible and public the systems of symbolic fantasy that are present in the psyche. . . . They are the lightning conductors of common anxiety. They fight the demons so that others can hunt the prey. . . ."[14]

Social myth, legend, and folklore are not romantic hypotheses but rather "living principles." James Frazer, Bronislau Malinowski, Paul Radin, G. Thompson, Henri Frankfort, and Margaret Mead have pointed to the practicality of myth. The social myth is not, Malinowski writes, "an idle rhapsody, not an aimless outpouring of vain imagining, but a hard working, extremely important cultural force . . . not merely a story told, but a reality read." It is a warrant and charter expressing belief and action, and a precedent that shapes the practical daily life of the group.[15]

What passes as history (even that which calls itself scientific) plays the identical role. It is self-justifying story-telling, a projection of group values and claims into a causative theory of the past as a method of seeking greater authority and credibility for values and claims in the present. For example, Harry Anslinger, former director of the U.S. Bureau of Narcotics, sees the history of the world as one of conflict over drug traffic; Freud sees it as an acting out of his theories; and every budding academic school or discipline offers its own version of how the world got into its present mess, building into the authority of past events their own claims to authority and prophecy. The functions of myth (and history as myth) are ideological. Mythical symbols are seeds of specific ritualized behavior sequences. They are, in Turner's view, "a set of evocative devices for rousing, channeling, and domesticating powerful emotions, such as hate, fear, affection, and grief."[16] They are artifacts of cultural control, of group and individual bargaining, of influence and counter-influence. Rulers are invested with *mana*-power, and existing power-relations are mythicized into sacred institutions. History, immobilized and fixed to the past, becomes a kind of eternal spatial present.[17]

Similarly, ritual is converted to private use as a form of interpersonal influence. Stereophonic rock music that can vibrate the air and shake the walls weaves a magic spell, transforming a room into a sacred locale, suitable for the ritually defined occasion, party, or college dorm seduction. Every kid wants a magic machine to provide a sacred setting for his encounters. Small speakers and low power amplifiers will not do; the conventions of the sacred depend on the latest and most expensive technology.

IS ANYTHING SACRED?

Transitions from sacred to profane are a significant subject matter for the student of social and political change. In general, the use of a highly charged symbol to a saturation point devalues that symbol and removes its luster; overstimulation of the individual eventually raises the threshold and dulls sensitivity. The cycle of ritual responds continuously to this dynamic; whatever becomes too cheaply available obeys the law of marginal value. It is soon devalued and useless as a symbol, its cloud of glory swept away as it fades into the light of common day.

Turner, adopting Van Gennep's concept of rites of passage, discusses the sacred character of "liminality" or "threshold" status transitions. Ceremonials that characterize status change involve a stripping away of the symbols and rituals of one status (preliminal), a temporary and transitional statuslessness (liminal), and finally an induction into a new status with all its attendant obligations and rituals (postliminal). Statuslessness is the most exciting period, and one that, in American culture, he sees growing each decade more protracted and less structured. It is, he writes, becoming a stable subculture of its own which he calls "Communitas."[18]

The sacred need not be holy. The unholy and the befouled bears a similarly sacramental character surrounded with prescriptions and prohibitions. Obscenity and blasphemy can be as sacred as Mozart, Schnabel, and Jesus. Elaborate proscriptions surrounding sex tend to maintain its sacred character. Available and familiar as sex is, its cultural power is dependent on maintaining sensitivity to its symbols. The charms and secrets of sex are fragile; they are readily destroyed by cheap and mindless familiarity like the dust on butterflies' wings. The segregation of boys and girls at puberty in unenlightened times tended to make each sex sacred objects for the other, compounding fear, desire, danger, and power, ritualistically preparing the adolescent for the transitions and obligations of married life and family ahead.

A study of male puberty rites notes the universality in simple cultures of a pattern whereby women of certain classes become available for sexual intercourse to boys. In Papua, after circumcision and a period of seclusion, the youths have access to women who are not their relatives. Among the Zulus, Basutos, and other tribes of Central Africa, there is a belief that youths must have sexual intercourse after initiation or they will die. Thus the boys are encouraged to follow their sexual appetites, even though this runs counter to the avoidance of women inculcated prior to puberty celebrations. Reik notes that by this practice "each sex is practically inoculated against the other. . . ."[19] Prepubescent practices tended to maintain women and sex as sacred with great powers of inhibition and awe over the young male. Unmodified, this sacred regard would stunt the postpubescent patterns of behavior that lead to courtship, marriage, procreation, and head-of-family responsibility. The puberty rite, therefore, secularizes the sex act and womanhood. A sexual relationship thereby becomes psychically available, yet, because of the old sacred status, it is still surrounded with an ambivalence that acts to socialize and orient the conduct of young men toward their future brides. While less formalized, similar rites have prevailed in Western society for generations. The French romantic novel of the nineteenth century, featuring the amorous experiences of young men of the upper classes with low-caste women, is typical.

Today, the segregation of the sexes has become anathema; even the Boy Scouts of America are encouraging coed camp-outs and mixed activity groups. Similarly, four letter words, which gain their power to express and to shock by an elaborate set of rules that maintain their quality as evil and secret, have been deprived of special significance by overexposure and uncritical use. "Hot pants" was part of the sacred language of the male world until it became the season's new name for short shorts and could be used without a blush by any father's daughter. Is nothing sacred any more?

The effect of secularizing verbal obscenities is to make their use less obscene, and to force us to invent or resurrect new uses to take their place. The effect of permissive pornography and explicit sex in the arts and the media may not make us sexier, rather the opposite. The desanctification of sex probably means less sex rather than more. The admission of four-letter words into polite discourse in mixed company probably means the decline in the currency of these words. It is likely that informal defenses may come into play to maintain mystery and interest between the sexes, but new barriers will also arise spontaneously between the sexes to maintain the role of sacred power.

As was stated in Chapter 2 the study of courting and mating patterns in the animal kingdom discloses a tendency for greater ritual elaboration and complexity when there exist awkward, difficult, and dangerous impediments to successful consummation. Typically, the mating rituals combine both defensive and aggressive components, the habit of territorial distance, and the vulnerability of contact, all of which must be moderated and redirected while familiarity socializes the male and female to the mating. The intensity of ambivalence in itself generates elaborate ritualized displays, dances, and strategems of indirections. All the conditions of search behavior exist, and behavior is converted into standardized sacred rituals of high intensity.

Animal studies suggest that circumstantial and physical obstacles to any goal generate tremendous orientation pressure, worked out by elaborate rituals. In human affairs, the hypothesis holds that the more difficult it is to concert and coordinate social activities, for whatever reasons, the richer will be the proliferation of culture forms and the more social energy will be diverted from profane to sacred pursuits, or from instrumental to ceremonial occasions. One might speculate further that the increase in ceremonial occasions and holidays signals the incipient breakdown of social unity and the integrity of group values.[20]

New rituals will always replace old. The process is natural and inevitable, although not necessarily painless. Transitions of legitimacy and social purpose are universal and implacable. Nothing can hold its magic forever, but new magic is available.

Just as search behavior becomes ritual routine, so all culture forms undergo a cycle, passing through alarm, anxiety, interest, exploration, improvisation, ritualization, extinction, and replacement in turn. As culture selects from among the infinite inputs of new forms, what was exciting becomes commonplace and dull. What was sacred, transfixing, capable of holding an intense field of concentration, falls into indifference and passivity. All purposes of a mode of communication or a ritual action may be drained of significance or may assume a new function.

In the early days of radio, each word declaimed by the mellow-voiced announcer was carved in granite. The impact of the new medium created a field of attention and of sensitivity that made it a sacred object, forcing station managers to prohibit ad libs, converting all the stylized theater arts of the time into self-important and stilted program forms. Yet the ubiquity and availability of radio, in time, dissipated the sacred aura. At first, the broadcasters resisted the trend by elaborate public relations campaigns, hard-sell promotions, and an exaggerated, almost satirical, use of the Delphic oracle style. But the sacredness of radio could not last. Soon, someone tried the anti–hard sell commercial, and the informal ad lib, and was an overnight sensation. Radio became desacralized at the very moment that television assumed the sacred role. It, too, in recent times is abandoning the conventions of the sacred, and is now well along toward becoming a profane and more flexible instrument of communication. The same desacralization can be seen in all the media. It would be the height of camp today for a person to pose for his photograph as though the act were the same as being immortalized.

There is a relentless tendency constantly to refresh old culture forms by variation and invention. Each new and successful action is reiterated and becomes a ritual. Once a child finds out how to build a tower of bricks and knock it down, he will repeat the process. Once he has summoned the courage to slide down a chute, he will do it again and again. Every new ability resembles a victory, a pleasurcable accretion of power. Step by step, the child and the culture conquer their environment and bring more and more resources within their sphere of influence. Inevitably, variation creeps in. Partly, it is because of strategic interaction (an element of search behavior persists as conditions change or as other people vary their response to the same stimulus). But even without this competitive process, man craves the sacred. He has a hunger for anxiety and evokes the new and the unfamiliar that chill him, especially when the prevailing culture forms do their jobs most successfully. The exploratory habit causes man to look for trouble, elaborating and embellishing ritual for its own sake as an art form, and also functionally, as a rehearsal for the surprises of future events.

The entropy of the sacred is irresistible, especially in an electric technology that accelerates the rate and number of culture inputs to a syncretistic maelstrom that is insulated by wealth, comfort, and technology from natural events, and that permits an almost infinite overload of invention, tinkering, pluralism, and autism without exploding. In a period that witnesses the emergence of new constituencies into the political process, the most dynamic groups and their leaders tend to be sacralized by the rhetoric of the day, a testament on the part of broad elements of the society to the need to modify the structure of rights and duties among prevailing power groups. In the 1930's, there was an apotheosis of labor and the working class; in the 1960's, a similar sacralization of the blacks. The social capabilities of invention and imagination, though temporarily fatigued and overloaded, are far from dead. "The world is still full of surprises!"[21]

78

NOTES

1. Thomas Luckman, *The Invisible Religion* (New York: Macmillan, 1967), p. 58.

2. See Peter Lawrence, *Road Belong Cargo: A Study of the Cargo Movement in the Southern Madang District of New Guinea* (Manchester, Eng.: Manchester University Press, 1964), p. 175.

3. But the cycle of ritual never ceases to turn. The most recent wave of music-lovers has returned to simple lifelike audio, and live concerts without electronic embellishments.

4. Malcolm Boyd, "The Cult of the Potomac," *The New York Times,* February 17, 1972, p. 37.

5. Quoted in *ibid.*

6. Raymond Firth, *The Work of the Gods in Tikopia,* 2nd ed. (New York: Humanities Press, 1967), p. 11. Leach writes of a Kachin sacrifice that may be regarded as a purely technical and economic act. "It is a procedure for killing livestock and distributing the meat, and I think there can be little doubt that for most Kachins this seems the most important aspect of the matter. A *nat galaw* ('nat making,' a sacrifice) is almost a synonym for a feast. But from the observer's point of view, there is a great deal that goes on at a sacrifice that is quite irrelevant as far as butchery, cooking and meat distribution are concerned. It is these other aspects which have meaning as symbols of social status, and it is these other aspects which I describe as ritual whether or not they involve directly any conceptualisations of the supernatural or the metaphysical." (Edmund R. Leach, *Political Systems of Highland Burma: A Study of Kachin Social Structure* [Cambridge, Mass.: Harvard University Press], 1954), pp. 10–11.

7. Victor W. Turner, *The Ritual Process: Structure and Anti-Structure* (Chicago: Aldine, 1969), pp. 52–53.

8. Robert A. Hinde, *Animal Behavior: A Synthesis of Ethology and Comparative Psychology,* 2nd ed. (New York: McGraw-Hill, 1970), p. 351.

9. Herbert Read, *Icon and Idea: The Function of Art in the Development of Human Consciousness* (New York: Shocken Books, 1965), pp. 88–89.

10. Hans Hass, *The Human Animal: The Mystery of Man's Behavior* (New York: Putnam's, 1970), pp. 114–15.

11. Hannah Arendt, *Between Past and Future* (New York: Viking Press, 1961), pp. 92–93.

12. "The Talk of the Town," *The New Yorker,* May 8, 1971, p. 30.

13. Kenneth Burke, *Terms for Order,* edited by Stanley Edgar Hyman (Bloomington, Ind.: Indiana University Press, 1964), p. 51.

14. Albert Goldman, *Freak Show* (New York: Atheneum, 1971), p. 194.

15. Bronislau Malinowski, *Myth in Primitive Psychology* (New York: Doubleday, 1957), p. 42.

16. Turner, 1969, pp. 42–43.

17. Harry Slochower, *Mythopoesis* (Detroit: Wayne State University Press, 1970), p. 334.

18. Turner, 1969, pp. 62–90.

19. Theodor Reik, *Ritual: Psycho-Analytic Studies* (New York: International University Press, 1931), p. 131.

20. Margaret Bastock, *Courtship: An Ethological Study* (Chicago: Aldine, 1967), p. 95.

21. Elizabeth Mann Borgese, *The Language Barrier: Beasts and Man* (New York: Holt, Rinehart and Winston 1968), p. 151.

5 | POLITICAL THERMODYNAMICS

Individuals, like other objects in the world, affect the surrounding environment in a manner congruent with their own actions and properties. Their mere presence produces signs and marks. (Erving Goffman, 1969)[1]

Nature imposes limits. The laws of impotence determine what is and what is not possible. Arthur Koestler says, "A man can hold his breath for so many seconds and not longer; he can cling with his fingers to a ledge of a precipice so long and not longer."[2] Energy and resources to serve human purposes are limited, while purposes are infinite.

Human behavior is comprised of learned responses within a largely man-made environment; the options for social order are at once infinite and changeable. Any given system is orderly only in relation to values. Slavery may be an orderly state of affairs for the slave owner but at the same time make personal order difficult for the slave. The natural process of growth is one of conflict, that is, relative disorder. The definition of order for any given relationship of social groups tends to reflect the values, interests, and behavior of those who dominate the hierarchical structure of bargaining relationships. The values of dominant groups are modified by shifts in the locus of power brought about by the emergence of new groups. A process of social bargaining forces modification, accommodation, and even revolutionary changes in the hierarchies of power.

In the process of shifting, integrating, and reintegrating the formal and informal hierarchies there is a tendency toward humanizing power and conserving both energy and values. Organized groups are essential to human survival, and hierarchy itself is essential to the practical functioning of group life. But there is no absolute arbiter to determine among the options of changing order that are available to social systems and that are concretely represented by the conflicts of individuals and groups. In the midst of this uncertainty, there must be a process of choice and provisional consensus.

ENERGY AND ENTROPY

We assume that all individuals and groups seek to impose order around them. The boundaries of conflicting systems of order overlap, creating arenas of social entropy (relative disorder) and competition. Within these arenas one set of values may become hierarchically dominant over other values. The formal institutions of state authority reinforce them through socialization, consensus, and ultimately, a monopoly on legal violence. This enables dominant groups to determine the choices available to the lower orders of the hierarchy. They organize and manage social policy, resources, and the environment in such a way as to reflect their own values of order, which limits the choices that remain open to groups with conflicting value systems in ordering their own proximate environments. If the whole multileveled and differentiated hierarchy retains legitimacy (that is, achieves values for at least those groups capable of challenging its authority), the social system will remain stable, its power and negative reinforcement mostly passive, and the processes of collaboration and accommodation relatively successful.[3] Such an integrated social order minimizes disruption, destruction, and potential schism.

One may postulate a thermodynamic law of behavior. Drawing a comparison with the law of conservation of energy, we may assume that organisms seek to conserve energy and values. Keeping in mind the law of entropy (the tendency in nature toward disorder and decay), one may assume that social disorder and decay are constant threats that energy and values must overcome. In any specific bargaining engagement, one party's order becomes another's entropy. All parties at all times seek to maximize the former and to manage and overcome whatever amount of the latter is forced on them by particular bargaining outcomes.

Organized society is a hierarchy of corrective and adaptive activities. While arbitrary and man-made, the structure of the hierarchy becomes authoritative and "natural" for all those for whom it has legitimacy. At each level of the hierarchy, Turner observes,

each more inclusive activity corrects and redresses the deflection or breaches of the activity below it in the hierarchy. . . . The activities that make up a society are patterned by custom, and pattern only emerges in corrective and adjustive situations. Society is a process, a process of adaptation that can never be completely consummated since it involves as many specialized adaptations as there are specialized influences in the environment to be met.[4]

Ritual prescriptions of culture constitute mechanisms for conserving energy while maintaining structure, form, and meaning in social life against hostile entropic processes. The myths of culture hold chaos and disorder at bay, providing meaning for sickness and horror, rationalizing suffering, making death bearable. The rituals that give concreteness to myth release the tensions of disruptive and painful experience by providing orderly routines of action. Ritual in culture works against the decay of order and provides the means for integrating social relationships disrupted or threatened by the inevitable competitive process.[5] Ritual makes the social structure explicit, symbolizing and dramatizing the socially approved systems of relationships between individuals and groups. Turner notes that Ndembu people use the same word for ceremonial ritual that is used for *landmark* or *blaze*. This usage is profound, implying that tribal rituals are connections between known and unknown territory, like axe marks on the trail that lead the hunter back from the unfamiliar bush to his village. "It conveys the notion of the structured and ordered, as against the unstructured and chaotic. . . . It makes intelligible what is mysterious and also dangerous."[6]

All symbolic behavior may be viewed as aspects of a thermodynamic "cost economy," like the cash nexus in economic relations. Man searches his environment for vital signs that provide the cues for his behavior. He cannot afford to relearn the meaning of these signals on each occasion. The allocation of attention and energy to search behavior at all times in all things is a biological impossibility. The laws of impotence impose a requirement for mythologized acts of faith and ritual repetitions. Every action is at once an exploration, a reenactment of past actions, an example for future actions, a communication, and an instrumental manipulation; but the priorities of each of these functions must be allocated on the basis of values.

Through the conventions of culture, we are capable of responding to danger signals abstractly, while the danger is still only potential or theoretical. Indeterminate external stimuli are assimilated into psychogenic patterns that are determinate and limited in their energy demands. Ritual indicators possess greater saliency as sensitive and specific control mechanisms, able to use the information of poor quality that is generally available to the senses. Without the editing provided by culture and fantasy, all information is a blur of vagueness, ambiguity, and overload. A single datum cannot be extracted from the environment except arbitrarily. Only the conventions of culture relieve the arbitrary element and impose a paradigm in terms of which poor information can be useful.

As Turner points out, what is made sensibly perceptible in the form of a symbol is thereby "made accessible to the purposes and action of society."[7] Social ceremonies embody the intangible and the invisible and make them probable, concrete, and real. In this sense, ritual creates reality by permitting the reinforcement of group action. The magician or hypnotist who can make subjects behave as though in the presence of a golden pig has in fact created a golden pig. The bereaved widow, acting out the old patterns of her married life, creates the presence of her husband. Hysteria is the acting out of old, once-meaningful patterns in inappropriate conditions. What may appear as dysfunctional behavior (by the values of the observer) may be problem-solving behavior for the actor who thereby preserves the integrity of deeply felt, learned values against the disruptions of personal tragedy.

Ritual makes tangible and concrete, in a time and place, changes of status that otherwise would be acted out under conditions of unmanageable conflict and self-defeating, costly learning. Rites of mutilation and pain (like initiation or circumcision), rites of sacrifice and punishment (like the isolation of pubescent boys or menstruating women), give greater reality to symbolic action. Pubescents in many primitive tribes are terrorized by shadowy ceremonies in which they are tortured and harassed by masked demons, thereby dramatizing indelibly their change in status. They are better prepared to learn new forms of behavior and obligations while putting aside childish habits. Frazer points out that

the candidate is supposed to die or be killed and come to life again or to be born again; and the pretense of a new birth is not uncommonly kept up by the novices feigning to have forgotten all the most common actions of life, and having accordingly to learn them all over again like newborn babes.[8]

Through ritual, the intangible can be experienced directly and assimilated into behavior. Many cultures achieve this object by such intensification acts as sacrifice of the hair in reconciliation ceremonies, tattoo or marking of the body by scars, cutting and punctures, fasting, dietary requirements, sexual abstinence, special clothing and concealment of parts of the body, periods of solitary confinement or enforced isolation from the home, and so on.

Rites that may seem cruel and barbaric are in fact evocations of cultural reality that maintain systems of behavior between generations and act as safeguards against their dissipation through time. In Western cultures, having abolished most of the means for dramatizing status change, parents and children must discover their new obligations by the trial and error of search behavior, with the accompanying heartbreaks, alienations, and long-term psychic costliness. School, or work away from home, or military service may serve as separation rituals for the passage from childhood to adulthood; but the implications of the change of status are nowhere dramatized. Eventually the change of status must be acted out with all of its terrible consequence of escalated and negative bargaining tactics, as parents seek to maintain the rituals of the past whose legitimacy the young adult must resist.

As cost economy, ritual relieves the inevitable stress of transitions by making sensible the senseless, familiar the unfamiliar, and providing the substitute experience that will legitimize and rehearse the behavioral requirements of a new status. Changes of status are a hazardous attack on the flow of individual energy and the structures of the social group. Rites of passage attempt to structure changes so as to conserve energy and facilitate adjustments.

As expressive action, ritual enables a small investment of energy to achieve a large result. The actual form of the ritual responds to a thermodynamic rule. In a noisy place, people are accustomed to yell at each other at the top of their lungs. The energy invested in the form of ritual action varies directly with the noise level and inversely with the responsiveness of the object or audience. Every behavior pattern is influenced by a tendency to minimize energy and risk, and to maximize learning and communication. Ritual display in conflict or mating enables expressive actions requiring only low-level energy to substitute for physical combat or coercive exertions. The bargaining continuum of interpersonal relationships is transformed into an artful, competitive collaboration, using all kinds of behavioral symbols as a substitute for the behavior itself.

A test of nerve, will, and endurance can be enacted in psychogenic paradigms, leading to real adjustments, reconciliation, and the sweet closure of anxiety without major cost and risk to the organisms involved.

All of the system problems of social groups (including the regulation of entering and leaving, capacity for collective action, division of labor, leadership, socialization, and so forth) can be resolved symbolically and indirectly, thereby preserving the group's available energy for positive values, overcoming the danger that these preliminary and essential requirements of group life will soak up all of the available energy.[9] McLuhan notes that a Japanese wife never speaks irritably to her husband. Instead, she rearranges the flowers. This has the effect of preserving the structure of priorities in the relationship while still effectively punishing the husband. Symbolic action conserves legitimacy partly because of its cost-saving function. Anything that costs too much puts a strain on the structure of priorities.

Culture uses all kinds of notational devices to express and encode values, sanctions, threats, and predictions of future behavior. Gestures, colloquial language, conventions of dress and style embody group norms, goals, standards, and relationships, marking the boundaries of loyalty and group membership. In Hitler's Germany, Physicist Werner Heisenberg reports, the government required professors to start every lecture with the Nazi salute. Thus, the small signal became the basis of both a rite of mortification and a test of loyalty.[10] There are many forms of symbolic threat intended to influence behavior at minimum risk, like the dead kitten on a neighbor's doorstep, the telephone call in which no threat is uttered, only heavy breathing, the package of dung delivered in the mail. The celebrated Mafia symbolism, the system of graded warnings from the cutting down of a vine and the maiming of a mule, to the deposit at a man's doorstep of a dog or sheep with his throat cut—all such threats are found all over the world. Similar contrivances, such as ceremonies of sacrifice, initiation, blood-drinking, and artifacts of death connected with mystical rites frequently are incorporated into group rituals as a kind of implicit threat against member disloyalty or as a means of intimidating outsiders.

Black leather jackets and dark glasses are rich in symbolism. The jacket goes back to the Gestapo (Stokely Carmichael said Hitler is the white person he most admires). Picked up by the British Rockers, and the American Hell's Angels, it expressed a threat of merciless violence. The dark glasses worn by the Black Panthers are derived from detectives and jazz musicians. The style has threat value also. The wearer can stare at another person surreptitiously. The object is unable to read the intentions of the person whose eyes are shielded. The role of the Black Panthers as the "muscle" of the latter stages of the civil rights movement provides the black community with an element for which sociologists have been searching in vain—that is, para-police enforcement that provides a base not only for organized criminal activities, but also for organized political influence. Earlier waves of immigrants who took up residence at the bottom of the pecking order in American cities eventually formed criminal syndicates and gangs that aided the fight of the group into the social, economic, and political systems, into the suburbs, and into a loss of group identity and an end to the need for para-police muscle.

All effective political action is symbolic display. Fidel Castro in the Oriente Mountains concentrated on the survival of his small revolutionary band. He avoided tests of arms with Batista forces. Guerilla warfare is always a political campaign, revolution as theater, designed to inspire resistance by example by making the regime appear inept and ridiculous. Every serious writer on revolution cautions against indiscriminate terrorism. Its effective use depends on selecting appropriate targets that dramatize the legitimacy of its users. Terrorism must be used sparingly in order to preserve its dramaturgical value. As such "it promises returns far out of proportion to the amount of time, energy, and materials the insurgents invest in it."[11] Aggressive threats are a form of economy. Challenges escalate from the less to the more costly, from symbolic display to the symbolic act of violence, toward action on a larger and more unmanageable scale that inevitably will be more costly and self-defeating. The possibility of escalation tends to limit aggressiveness and to enforce the display ritual, but it also gives efficacy to threats based on this possibility. The energy economics of conflict accomplish the purposes both of limiting violence and of causing some major violence to appear meaningless (that is, too costly) in retrospect. You cannot have one without the other.

Like other kinds of extreme behavior, violent acts may be regarded as society's early warning system, revealing deep-rooted political conflicts that are gathering strength beneath the surface of social relations. In a real sense, the unbalanced individual is a sensitive telltale. He suffers from the social cleavages that run through his very life. Distraught and disturbed persons act and react without waiting for a new consensus. In this manner, they are both the victims and the heralds of social change.

Political extremism, whether for or against the status quo, is an indication that pressure is building against the chain of social relationships. The weakest links are the first to break and may precipitate larger crises. The assassination of Chicago car dealers (the Foreman brothers) by a black (who had bought a car he could not afford) foreshadowed the smashing of loan offices and automobile dealerships that erupted soon thereafter in Chicago and other cities. Many individuals in crisis signal a society in crisis. Whether violent action is deliberately contrived by those who wish to create a crisis situation or haplessly enacted by distressed individuals, the result is the same. It is a commonplace that war and revolution are great catalysts of social change, but other forms of extreme behavior may have similar causes and effects.

Major social crises and dislocations by definition have major social causes. They are not the result of isolated conspiracies and plots, and they cannot be alleviated by efforts to stamp out all present and future conspiracies and plots. Social fits and seizures can be viewed as a form of search behavior, a pragmatic trial-and-error method leading toward new political and social norms that better satisfy the requirements of organized groups for security, predictability, and low-risk methods of conflict resolution. Thus it is not enough to explain extremism by pointing to conditions that justify it. Rather, one must study patterns of behavior and the process by which they evolve from testing to selection and reinforcement.

Symbols of aggression are system-maintaining, linking social learning, low-risk experimentation, and reporting for the benefit of the whole group. Lorenz identifies "displacement" as a key process by which behavior that may be dangerous to the individual or the species is redirected by "evolution's most ingenious expedient for guiding aggression into harmless channels."[12] Displacement permits a substitute action to resolve the tension of a situation that is threatening. Its function is not merely surrogate, but also creative in making available new directions and substitute goals by which individuals and social groups may recover from reversals and from the exactions of impotence, turning the energy release to good account in other areas. Societies use individual deviant behavior as paradigm-learning, either to maintain prevailing norms or to revise them with minimum risk for the nondeviant majority. Lewis A. Coser notes, "Deviance is taken as a warning that there is something foul in the state of Denmark. . . ."[13] In a study of mental hospitals it is observed that deviant patients serve as "fire-alarms for the ward." By disrupting social equilibrium, such patients highlight and compel adjustments by the hospital staff.[14]

The social role of symbolic behavior is perfectly illustrated by the most highly developed symbolism of exchange money. Like other symbols, money is a concentrated measure of value. It is a pure claim by its possessor to impress his own values on the resources of the environment and the energy available in the social group. Cash was the original credit card, invented as a convenient, concentrated, durable, and portable representation of the vast array of values and resources of the exchange process. Money is an abstraction, just as a computerized plastic credit card system is an even more highly abstracted metasymbol for money. Money is the concrete embodiment of diverse social institutions surrounding the giving and taking activities of cooperating people. It is a distillation of legitimate obligation and performance. It is a record of interpersonal promises, a miraculous and sacred talisman. Like spellbound savages in the presence of the holy, we watch the solemn proceedings of the stock exchange, "feeling in a vague, somewhat fearful way, that our lives and the happiness of our children are at the mercy of mysterious forces beyond our control."[15] Money is a specialized form of legitimacy. It is more negotiable, liquid, and impersonal than political power. Society requires that certain kinds of exchanges be at least partly isolated from political bargaining. In the exchange of commodities and technical services, a measure of interchangeability needs to be segregated from the general milieu of interpersonal bargaining. Other symbols of value outside this segregated market, such as gold, are more fundamental and underlie the economic realm itself.[16]

CULTURE HEROES, SCAPEGOATS, AND SHAMANS

In the more general range of social values, heroes and scapegoats that receive public attention constitute a form of cost economy. They provide cheap and convenient cultural paradigms. A study of witchcraft in Rhodesia reveals the witch as a culture antihero, the personification of disruptive forces. "For that reason, the reactions to a person accused of witchcraft have a ritual aspect—the community as a whole participates in the divination and also participates in the action against a witch." The concepts of witchcraft are catalogs of cultural no-no's.

Cannibalism is the most detested of all crimes, therefore she is a cannibal; family ties are the most sacred of all ties, therefore she destroys members of her family; medicine and magic are the forces with which one can control the environment in the interests of one's society, therefore they become perverted in the hands of the witch; animals such as snakes are dangerous because they can kill, owls are feared because they fly when other birds sleep, therefore the witch has these creatures as her familiars.[17]

The opposite of the witch is the culture hero or champion. In classical myth, the hero's quest became an expression or critique of existing social norms and pointed to a social order "which is envisaged as integrating the valuable residues of the past and present."[18] In modern culture, gossip and legends of superheroes play this immemorial cost-saving role. In the words of Daniel J. Boorstin, ancient heroes were known by "the great simple virtues of their character," while celebrities are differentiated mainly "by trivia of personality:"

Entertainers are best qualified to become celebrities because they are skilled in the marginal differentiation of their personalities. . . . We identify Jimmy Durante by his nose, Bob Hope by his fixed smile, Jack Benny by his stinginess, Jack Paar by his rudeness, Jackie Gleason by his waddle, Imogene Coca by her bangs.[19]

Celebrities become well-known primarily "for their well-knownness," which infinitely annoys Boorstin. Certainly, even in pre-media days, well-knownness, that is, the ability to command an audience, has always been the primary attribute that makes a person available as a symbol, able to perform all the legitimate functions that symbols serve. Andy Warhol, John Lennon and Yoko Ono, Richard Burton and Elizabeth Taylor, Leonard Bernstein, Jackie Onassis, Abbie Hoffman, Eldridge Cleaver, Timothy Leary, Daniel Berrigan, all are available as symbols mainly because they are known and can attract attention. Whether their contribution to manners and morals, and to high or pop culture is heroic or not depends on the values of the critic. But the cost-accounting of social behavior requires agents and agencies of learning and assimilation.

Celebrities cannot, in spite of Boorstin's outrage, be made to order. Culture symbols compete for attention and those that become archetypes are the product of forces beyond their control, the deeply rooted currents of culture change, the problems and fantasies of the season, the success or failure of behavioral inventions in that mysterious melange of swarming culture inputs. Ritual sacrifice, the sudden blackening of a culture hero and his role reversal, the ceremonial regicide of political leaders in the public esteem, the canonization of saints, the elevation of dead martyrs, scapegoats, and heroes, all are learning paradigms that follow careers not of the individual's own making and never fully understood or controlled.

The cultural hero (or antihero) plays a ritual role like that of the shaman or high priest. The high priest, in the words of Claude Levi-Strauss, is "a professional abreactor," that is, in psychoanalytic terms, he relieves the disturbing situation and overcomes it.[20] As a professional and a specialist, he resolves crisis indirectly at second hand, without yielding his generalized prestige to a single occasion. His life-style aims at resolving the problems of others rather than his own. He belongs to a third category between culture hero and scapegoat, that of outsider, disinterested peacemaker, untainted innocent, remote and detached wisdom. The clown, the jester, the dwarf, the Jew, the Holy Beggar, the Third Son, the Little Tailor, the Mysterious Stranger, all acquire symbolic roles as observers and mediators, rather than as actors. They are lightning rods rather than champions, commentators rather than protagonists, passive rather than active symbols.[21]

In all kinds of species, including man, certain individuals may assume a role essentially outside the dominance hierarchy. Wandering in and out among high ranking members, they avoid all challenges and surrender to all threats, disregarding the proprieties of rank entirely. In a study of monkeys, John H. Kaufmann noted that one of the lowest ranking peripheral males "boldly stayed around the feeder. Submissive and appeasing to all he met, he was tolerated, and fed easily, with no need to be furtive."[22] Many animals make a good living by drifting among the rigidities of rank as special characters.

This has been called the schlemiel syndrome, the ritual role of an individual who by nonaggressively and persistently ignoring rank assumes a kind of sacred character of clown or idiot, regarded with tolerant amusement by his betters, and permitted to make a good living. As a farmer, I have noted the same phenomenon among chickens, dogs, and horses. Obviously, it is not limited to human society; indeed it appears to be a common attribute of structured social groups. Whatever the life history of the individual so selected, he becomes an outsider in his own group. He may be teased and befriended even by the lowest ranking scapegoat. He becomes like the stone of the arch that did not fit but became a symbol of the whole, a unifying factor that maintains a behavioral link cutting across caste, class, and rank lines, providing an informational input that the group makes available by violating the conventions of the social structure.

Pantheons of champions, scapegoats, and shamans permit major social conflicts to be acted out in microcosm, bringing far-reaching results with only minor inconvenience to the on-going activities of life. Political trials are a leading example of this process, joining the conflicting claimant groups in a morality spectacle. Black Communist Angela Davis, with the help of *Life* magazine and the FBI, became an instrument of culture change. Because of the controversies over her lectureship at the University of California and the deadly shoot-out in a San Raphael courtroom, her exquisite features have become familiar to millions. The first beautiful black female radical, her plight and elevation to the FBI's Most Wanted list made her a kind of Jackie Onassis of the militant left, glamour queen of the revolution, hot copy for every newsmagazine that could get her picture. She knocked Kathleen Cleaver off the cover of *True Confessions* into the obscurity of an Algerian exile.

The Chicago conspiracy trial of 1969 became the box office smash of the season, sucking into its shrill ripostes the fantasies of every group on all sides of every issue of the turbulent 1960's: the confrontations at Berkeley, at Columbia, at the Pentagon, hippie culture, the antiwar movement, and so forth.[23] The Berrigan brothers' case had the same appeal. Following the destruction of draft records in Catonsville, the Berrigans became self-conscious role players representing a vast collection of issues. The audacity and imaginative detail of their act inspired a whole series of road shows, enabling them to hold the stage of public consciousness for months. Indictment by the Justice Department for an alleged conspiracy to kidnap Henry Kissinger fulfilled their wildest ambitions and maintained their roles against the vulgarizing impact of success and imitation. As the letters of Philip Berrigan reveal, he and his accomplices discussed the kidnapping scheme as a method of preventing the vulgarization of a tactic pioneered in Latin America. They wanted a responsible kidnapping without violence, with a trial of the victim in an open dialog with leading dissenters, filmed and recorded to be made available to the television networks after Kissinger's release unharmed.[24]

This process of acting out through political trials is like the use of hired champions as a form of judicial settlement in the Middle Ages, in which an inarticulate or ungifted defendant could have a professional warrior take his place in a wager of battle.[25] Little has changed in modern society. In large social questions, prosecutors and defendants are champions for the common man in a symbolic wager of battle, out of which (regardless of judicial forms and technical decisions of juries) will come the more fundamental decisions about social values, group adjustments, and the introduction and reinforcement of new behavior norms. Champions are used symbolically when Black Panthers, Hell's Angels, and student revolutionaries are invoked to support all kinds of threats and claims, by all kinds of spokesmen, as though their potential for violence gave them special authority as the muscle for every kind of special interest.

RITUAL IN POLITICAL INSTITUTIONS

Ritual behavior is a form of cost economy in two other respects as well. First, symbolic action and ceremony represent passive or latent political behavior and organization held in reserve for occasions that may demand its use. The reception line at a wedding, offering personal contact and identification between the friends and the families of the bride and groom, opens up possibilities of future interactions that did not exist before. The rituals of a religious holiday organize the group and create obligations and loyalties that help to maintain group interests against outsiders as well as facilitating all kinds of new transactional opportunities among members. The military parade and the drill-field create the latent capability for organizing the activities of a vast number of men as may be required for the purposes of national diplomacy and warfare. A school fire drill is a form of ritual whose function as training for emergencies is obvious. However, the ritual of the fire drill has other effects. It manifests the unified whole of the school, it confirms the power of the principal, and it provides the students with an opportunity of mass assembly. Most important, of course, it teaches behavior that can be invoked in the event of a real fire. The inability of most of the students to distinguish between the real and the ritual is one of the most important functions that the drill performs, making evacuation of the building possible without panic and even with considerable gaiety. The requirements of group life impose many difficult actions on individuals. Individuals suffer and die in order that group purposes may be achieved. Rituals like marching or holiday ceremony teach group unity and facilitate leadership control over the behavior of its members. Most primitive societies have warfare rituals celebrated as great occasions especially in peacetime, making it easier to mobilize the group's war-making resources and manpower when policy requires.

Second, agonistic behavior is also a form of cost economy. Through playful games and symbolic conflict, social hierarchies emerge. The agonistic phase of conflict facilitates the common interest by creating unified activity systems, by creating structures of relationships of subordination and superordination. Conflict and competition remain subordinate to the emergence of structure, and the agonistic phase establishes hierarchy, trains all of the participants to their roles, and reinforces the legitimacy of the result. By remaining primarily symbolic, such competition softens the inevitable defeats and disappointments that are necessary to hierarchical structure. Agonistics conserve energy and sweep back entropy through ritualized games whose ritualized outcomes may be termed political institutions.

Many of these structures become formalized by constitutions, laws, policies, agencies of government, customary practices, and so on. These formal elements tend, insofar as they retain legitimacy, merely to regulate the informal bargaining relationships. In the course of political change, the matter rises to the level of legislative debate and consideration when the existing code no longer provides an adequate basis for private bargaining claims or for third party adjudication. That is, it is no longer acceptable to those who have the power to challenge it. Proposals of new laws, repeals of old laws, amendments, appropriations for enforcement, and the appointment of judges *formalize the process of social consensus building symbolically.* Lawmaking summons to the public forum all the interested social groups, bringing into a ritual display the values and resources of power and influence of the whole community.

Such tests of strength, and the accommodations that emerge from them, are more durable and significant than the elections of congressmen and presidents. The alignments and coalitions of slate-making, balanced tickets, endorsement, and election do not in themselves create substantive norms of social behavior. Representation is significant but rarely determining. Most of the elected legislators assess and respond to a given bill in terms of the new legal norm's consequences for the social bargaining situation it will modify. The reason for this independence of judgment is simply that such considerations reflect the social consequences and costs that private groups can impose.

In legislative debate, alignments and coalitions emerge as interest groups trade off marginal values in order to enhance their strength in regard to values that are more central and significant and command broader support. Every individual and group with an interest, active or passive, in the regulation of a particular kind of behavior is likely to be drawn into some level of pressure activity. The process of changing a word or inserting a comma becomes a form of symbolic maneuver that aims at consolidating forces, mediating demands, assessing bargaining terms and positions. The problems of language are not only a technical matter. More important, they are symbolic surrogates for the larger, more sensitive, and more divisive issues, and they present a test of strength for all the parties in the society who play a role not only in spelling out the new law but also in spelling out the changed equation of social relations and the new norms of individual and group behavior, many of them informal, which are much broader and more far-reaching than the legal fictions. What must emerge is not merely a law but changes of attitude and an accommodation of conflicting interests which will give the law and the lawmaker legitimacy, and the new behavior practical support and efficacy.

Legislators and politicians become brokers and mediators for constituencies far wider than those that nominated and elected them. Their dedication tends to move toward the new consensus, toward the emerging social system whose norms of behavior have, in effect, been created by the ritual charade of making a law. Through this process is performed the indispensable services of keeping the authority of law intact, of enabling the nation to retain a workable legitimacy, of supplying new norms of political sociali- zation, however provisional, when they are needed, and of inducing a general efficacy of social control that operates through the formal and informal, private and public, individual and group bargaining processes, and that will win the general support of the community in the few instances where it must be policed and enforced by the state.

Political leadership has a responsibility and a motive to assess the informal power behind the conflicting demands of social groups and to find the most economical basis of accommodation in terms of cost and risk. In doing this, political leaders must adjust their followers' values to make the accommodation feasible, or face the dangers of direct action and escalated violence and counter- violence. When a community drifts toward alienation and violence, leaders of the establishment cannot evade the responsibility of adjusting majority values in order to moderate minority needs. In such a situation, a popular referendum may widen the cleavages and intensify the danger. Lawmaking shifts the confrontation to a manageable dialog that changes the norms and attitudes of the whole society. The law may be viewed as the scar tissue of the body politic. Those laws are most tough and resilient whose mak- ing involved the most representative bargaining process and whose prescribed behavior norms and structural relationships permit con- tinued flexibility, bargaining, and generally fair and acceptable accommodations between social groups. Among the great functions of the formal order are the methods it provides for terminating disputes, replacing the informal methods of reprisal and retaliation (with all their counter-productive potential) with a method of im- personal conflict reduction and closure, improving the chances of a sustainable outcome.

Social catharsis helps to maintain the continuity and stability of the society in the face of the inevitable and frequently insoluble tensions that exist at all times in all human groups. Not all problems can be solved, and conflict is omnipresent. The more people have in common, the more intensely they argue about less important things. The more closely men collaborate, the more things they find to differ about. Tension is as universal and inescapable as the search for tranquility and order. The means of transmuting and releasing tension, of converting persistent and chronic elements of conflict into constructive forms, are not without value in controlling potential disruptions and maintaining general continuity. This process is an important factor in insulating the legitimacy of the system. In the face of inevitable corruption, miscarriages of justice, bad policies and bad laws, personal and group antagonisms, personal failures, aging, sickness, and accidents, in the face of all this there is a human need to avoid too much reality. A great deal of real accommodation of conflict occurs under a slight blur of ambiguity that permits graceful retreats, tacit threats and promises, and an emphasis on common interests, however marginal, rather than on divisive facts, however massive.

The legal process may be viewed as a set of unifying myths and institutions that serve a wide range of uses, including that of a theater-in-the-round, a circumambient divertimento that dramatizes and gives meaning to our lives, even if it lies a little. In the legislative theater, the actors more or less consciously recognize their roles and cultivate contrivance, artfulness, dramatization, plot, and story. They act as if their function, far from being limited to lawmaking, includes the venting of the collective subconscious of the nation. Most of the issues thrown at government are not capable of being solved there and may be insoluble altogether; until these problems can be solved, the healing balm of time must be purchased by artful delays and dodges. The doctor's bedside manner constitutes more than half of his healing art and has little to do with medical knowledge. The "tale told by an idiot" may be an important tale that serves to ease our deeper recognition that new conflict will replace old and many old conflicts will remain; that it may be more important to find ways to live with unresolved conflict than to seek to force a consensual solution for every issue.

IDEOLOGY AS RITUAL

The rituals of political faith reflect the political structure itself. The hierarchical nature of the structure of leadership and influence is reflected in the way political reality is perceived at various levels. This may be described as the principle of inverse verisimilitude.

Verisimilitude refers to the correspondence of mental images and concepts to concrete and specific experiences, the plausibility and immediacy of works of art. At leadership levels, the relationships within and without the group are seen concretely and specifically in terms of interpersonal bargaining relationships, struggles for power, personal idiosyncracies, and conflicts of personality. As one moves down the ladder away from the leadership level, the realities of the group are more and more generalized, theoretical, and abstract. Grandiose and ideological reasons are found to support policy decisions and actions of leadership, conflicts within the group, and conflicts between the group and other groups. Communications from the leadership to the membership tend to be generalized to support and maintain the ideological commitments of the group. Actions and policies forced by compromise, alliances of convenience, conflicts of interest, ignorance or powerlessness, are rationalized for the membership in terms of general values and ideological myths. Strategy and tactics, means and ends, reinforcement of simplistic assumptions about the political universe that the group inhabits—these are the rationalizations of group members who are far from real responsibility and initiative. The further a member is from power, the more general and ideological is his perception of group policies, values, and motivations. On the top of the political structure the reverse is true. Descriptions of interpersonal bargaining are very concrete and specific but may not inspire support from members. They may, in fact, be considered trivial, selfish, and unprincipled, if frankly presented to the membership in place of the ideological myths.

Political belief, therefore, tends to become more and more generalized as individuals depart more and more from real responsibility. Political rhetoric satisfies the requirements of verisimilitude at each level, creating reality, maintaining structure, orienting and conserving energy. In the words of Kenneth Burke, political rhetoric is "secular prayer," whose function is "to sharpen up the pointless and to blunt the too-sharply pointed."[26] Political leaders have the task of providing men "with good and acceptable reasons to dress up the choice which is more effectively determined by underlying social affiliations."[27]

The function of ideology is to provide a vehicle for symbols with a built-in automatic authority, in the name of which the requirements of political maneuver by the responsible leadership can be continuously rationalized, in order to maintain the unity of the group, the commitments of its members, and the continued effectiveness of the leaders. Ideology provides a framework and a vocabulary that enables its interpreters to establish the authority of utterances made in its name. For the same purpose, the conventions of certain systems hold that the gods or the dead speak through the lips of the leader, or through mediums and priests. The social function of spirit-possession, like that of ideology, is a claim of authority.[28]

RITUAL AS COUNTERVAILING POWER

Ritual can provide means of countervailing power, a balancing in behalf of the weak and against the strong. Those who are denied the opportunity for decision-making and control over resources in the world of trade, production, and public politics, rectify the situation by asserting ritual roles in which they play leading parts and are served in turn by the great and powerful of the mundane world. Ritual encompasses a variety of checks and balances. The presence of a disinterested mediator and peacemaker forces the political leader to share legitimacy, and maintains a means of accountability. In any given organization, the chaplain is outside the chain of command. He embodies the principle of mercy as opposed to the formal principles of justice. The ultimate legitimacy of the organization rests on some mixture between mercy and justice, and the balance is preserved by the ritual power of the chaplain to chastize the politically powerful and to intervene against them, forcing conciliation and mending as a higher value than *post hoc* punishment.

Ritual status is an elementary form of political office.[29] Its function may be interpreted in exactly the same way as formal separation of powers in a constitutional system. In the ancient Greek state, the center of legitimacy was the Oracle. Since secular leaders had to seek oracular support and guidance, the High Priests of Delphi became, in a sense, the Supreme Court of the State.[30]

Witchcraft may provide another source of countervailing power. Anyone who has wealth and power and who abuses them may be singled out and accused of witchcraft. The conventions of witchcraft thereby constrain powerful individuals from exploiting their advantages selfishly or from flaunting their power too conspicuously.[31] Conversely, the conventions of witchcraft moderate the treatment of the poor and powerless, by inducing fear that the latter in their desperation may turn to witchcraft in retaliation.[32]

The effects of witchcraft on political power may be seen in all kinds of diverse social groups, both primitive and modern. Monica Wilson describes African tribes in which the ritual power between chiefs and commoners is balanced. The divine kings have an "innate creative power" while commoners have "pythons in their bellies with which to destroy their enemies." The destructive power of the commoners can be used morally, to maintain the established order, as well as irresponsibly by witches. Chiefs maintain their position by feasting their men on beef, and this, Nyakusa think, prevents the witches from attacking; sated with meat their pythons lie quiet.[33] Women in Rhodesia openly confess to witchcraft in spite of the onus and risks. One native informant thought such confession was aimed at enhancing the status of the self-proclaimed witch: "To be feared has, after all, many advantages."[34] The tendency for witches to be women, rather than men, is an expression of women's need for ritual power to offset their generally inferior status. Similarly, the ritual role of motherhood expresses a feminine claim for sovereignty in the nest against her dependence on the breadwinner's excursions into the outside world. Witchcraft provides a way in which the old and rejected, and the young and powerless of either sex can play roles of importance.

In modern countries, rituals associated with religious institutions, recreational interest groups, politics, voluntary service activities, and sports create rank and office independently of the structure of authority vested in formal political office, property-holding, and work skills. The ceremonial offices act as countervailing power that formal power holders cannot ignore without jeopardizing their own legitimacy and effectiveness.[35] This reflects the importance of the psychogenic components of culture that give meaning to action. Successful businessmen would rather be popular members of the volunteer fire department, a ritual group of instant legitimacy, than to outwit competitors in a business deal.

Turner conceives there to be "a human need to participate in both modalities. Persons starved in one of their functional day-to-day activities seek it in ritual liminality. The structurally inferior aspire to symbolic structural superiority in ritual; the structurally superior aspire to symbolic communitas and undergo penitence to achieve it."[36] The mesh of ritual collaboration and the rites themselves insure that office holders and those endowed with formal power in the political structure are accountable to ancestors, to confreres, and to all kinds of other ritual figures in the community. Shamans and priests have authority over holiday celebrations, invocations, religious services, and funerals in an elaborate ritual cycle. The property owner or politician looks to them to reconfirm him in office and remind him that office is a sacred trust.[37]

The powerful must share power. In ritual blessings and ceremonial acts, legitimacy is shared and responsibility for the enterprise is not borne entirely by the authority figure. He has a strong incentive to cultivate the protection of ritual figures as a form of self-protection and social control.[38] For example, the new baby or the new car must be blessed. Recently in Jakarta, Indonesia, the founding of a racetrack was marked by the slaughtering of a water buffalo whose head was buried on the site to appease local devils. In subsequent ceremonies, a local ghost was befriended by offerings of food on bronze platters while a large ensemble of priests and worshipers engaged in rites to chase away other unfriendly ghosts. The carrier of legitimacy without authority, the ritual figure shares power with those who exercise authority but whose legitimacy is not self-contained. The relationship is not unlike the practice of administrative clearance, or the requirements of budgetary support by legislative bodies.

In simple societies, A. R. Radcliffe-Brown notes, the effective force that controls or limits conflict, or that compels the wrongdoer to give satisfaction to the person injured, is "public sentiment." There is often some conventionally recognized procedure that an injured person may use to get public sentiment on his side. "The kinds of belief which underlie ritual or supernatural sanctions may provide a basis for what may be called indirect penal sanctions." The person who has committed an offense will be cursed by his victim, and the latter may seek by some ritual act to make the curse effective. The audience for this procedure will be the acquaintances of both parties who, acting like a jury of peers, will judge the matter. As a form of self-fulfilling prophecy, they may ostracize the wrongdoer, and thus make the curse succeed. The wrongdoer himself may be convinced of his danger, even if he is wrongly accused, and may seek to propitiate and resolve the situation by some conventionalized means of reparation. He may even fall sick and die a psychogenic death as a kind of ritual act. Through the cultural pattern of ignominy, he may become depressed and cease to function in his normal role, weakening himself by lack of nourishment and by accident-proneness. He becomes vulnerable to the entropy of a suicidal urge, taught by his cultural milieu and internalized as a powerful behavioral trait.[39]

The magician is the opposite number of the headman and acts as an ombudsman for the group.[40] In this way, a rudimentary separation of powers is embodied in the ritual order. Even in a highly articulated and modern political system, the existence of a ritual order survives and retains great salience. The formal political structure may only be a court of last resort, the basis of desperate claims when the conflict-resolving and mutual-adjustment machinery of the ritual order proves inadequate to the task. By and large, *most of the disputes of the informal polity are resolved on the basis of the ritual rather than the legal order.*

But the ritual structure also becomes a way of formalizing political organization when governmental institutions have no real legitimacy for certain groups or lose their legitimacy because of a crisis of credibility, the failure to achieve minimal objectives for the nation, defeat in war, the inability to maintain internal order, and so on.[41] Secular sanctions alone cannot maintain by coercion or threats the body of moral and legal norms that are necessary for the maintenance of social systems. Under European rule, African kings retained their ritual functions long after they lost any secular authority. Similarly, since independence, the formal and constitutional authorities in African capitals discover that all the king's horses and all the king's men cannot give real power or legitimacy, which still rests with the ritual order of the tribes. The formal government can only strive to bring some of the ritual authority to their side, to incorporate some of it in government, or to conduct matters as they have been from time immemorial, disregarding the façade of constitution, law, and courts.

What may appear to Europeans as corruption, nepotism, personalism, and superstition may be in fact the timeless ritual order that constitutes the real basis of authority, legitimacy, social organization, and social power. The Cargo Cults of the East Indies and medicine men and witchcraft practices in Africa and Australia represent the mystical form of the body politic. Segmented, tribalized, social organizations are held together by a ritual order. Sacred personages mediate between the segments and myths, and ceremonies and dogmas allocate powers and responsibilities among the segment.[42]

Inchoate groups, minorities whose values are not represented in the formal institutions of society, maintain identity and a political order through ritual bonds, such as those that characterize Gypsies, Jews, overseas Chinese, and other groups. Such groups formalize their bonds and create national institutions based purely on legitimacy. The great authority of their leaders and their values is maintained voluntarily as a means of survival and defense in hostile majority cultures, although it lacks all of the formal panoplies of national authority.

In late 1970, Gypsies of the Evans clan suddenly began rolling their trailers, pickup trucks, and campers into Tempo, Texas, where an obscure carnival barker, Yogi Evans, was on his death bed. License plates showed them to be from points as distant as New York and San Francisco. They filled the parking lot and crowded the hospital lobby awaiting the results of a lung cancer

102

operation on their king. Shingle salesmen, roofing contractors, carnival barkers, itinerant jobbers of palmistry and hustling, how did the word pass among them that Yogi might die in Tempo, Texas? Crises of succession, funerals, weddings, and certain calendar holidays marked the occasions that maintained unity and communication among a landless windblown tribe that fiercely resists assimilation and a sedentary life.[43]

NOTES

1. Erving Goffman, *Strategic Interaction* (Philadelphia: University of Pennsylvania Press, 1969), pp. 4–5.

2. Arthur Koestler, *Reflections on Hanging* (New York: Macmillan, 1957), p. 94.

3. R. M. MacIver, *The Web of Government* (New York: McGraw-Hill, 1947), p. 77.

4. Victor W. Turner, "Mukanda: The Politics of a Non-Political Ritual," in Marc J. Swartz, ed., *Local Level Politics: Social and Cultural Prospectives* (Chicago: Aldine, 1968), pp. 135–50.

5. In the words of Anthropologist A. F. C. Wallace, both religion and science are processes of "maximizing the quantity of organization in the matrix of perceived human experience." (*Science,* November 20, 1964, p. 1018.)

6. Victor W. Turner, *The Ritual Process: Structure and Anti-Structure* (Chicago: Aldine, 1969), p. 15.

7. *Ibid.,* p. 25.

8. Quoted in Theodor Reik, *Ritual: Psycho-Analytic Studies* (New York: International University Press, 1931), p. 95.

9. Julian Morgenstern, *Rites of Birth, Marriage, Death and Kindred Occasions Among the Semites* (Chicago: Quadrangle Books, 1966), pp. 84–100.

10. Werner Heisenberg, *Physics and Beyond: Encounters and Conversations* (New York: Harper & Row, 1971), p. 42.

11. Thomas Perry Thorton, "Terror as a Weapon," in Harry Eckstein, ed., *Internal War: Problems and Approaches* (New York: Free Press, 1964), p. 88; see also Carl Leiden and Karl M. Schmitt, eds., *The Politics of Violence: Revolution in the Modern World* (Englewood Cliffs, N.J.: Prentice-Hall, 1968), pp. 30–33.

12. Konrad Lorenz, *On Aggression* (New York: Grosset & Dunlap, 1967), p. 54.

13. Lewis A. Coser, *Continuities in the Study of Social Conflict* (New York: Free Press, 1967), p. 117.

14. Stuart A. and Helen Swick Perry, "Deviant Behavior, Function and Dysfunction in the Psychiatric War," cited in *ibid.,* p. 117.

15. William Herbert Desmonde, *Magic, Myth, and Money: The Origin of Money in Religious Ritual* (New York: Free Press, 1962), p. 4.

16. See James S. Coleman, "Political Money," *American Political Science Review*, December 1970, pp. 1074–87.

17. J. R. Crawford, *Witchcraft and Society in Rhodesia* (London: Oxford University Press, 1967), p. 71.

18. Harry Slochower, *Mythopoesis* (Detroit: Wayne State University Press, 1970), p. 34.

19. Daniel J. Boorstin, *The Image or What Happened to the American Dream* (New York: Atheneum, 1962), p. 65.

20. Claude Levi-Strauss, "The Sorcerer and His Magic," in John Middleton, ed., *Magic Withcraft, and Curing* (Garden City, N.Y.: Natural History, 1967), p. 37.

21. See Paul Bohannan, ed., *Law and Warfare: Studies in the Anthropology of Conflict* (Garden City. N.Y. Natural History Press, 1967), p. 249.

22. John H. Kaufmann "Social Relations of Adult Males," in Stuart A. Altman, ed., *Social Communication Among Primates* (Chicago: University of Chicago Press, 1697), p. 82.

23. Tom Hayden, *Trial* (New York: Holt, Rinehart and Winston, 1970), p. 24.

24. "Letters from the Berrigan Case," *The New York Times*, May 1, p. 1971, p. 12.

25. Henry Charles Lea, "The Use of Champions," in Bohannan, 1967, p. 249.

26. Kenneth Burke, *A Grammar of Motives* (New York: 1945), p. 393.

27. Paul F. Lazarsfeld, Bernard Berelson, and Hazel Gaudet, *The Peoples' Choice* (New York: Columbia University Press, 1944), p. 83.

28. See M. J. Field, "Spirit Possession in Ghana," in John Beattie and John Middleton, eds., *Spirit Membership and Society in Africa* (New York: Africana Publishing, 1969), p. 12.

29. Meyer Fortes, "Ritual and Office in Tribal Society," in Max Gluckman, ed., *Essays on the Ritual of Social Relations* (Manchester, Eng.: Manchester University Press, 1962), p. 61.

30. See Mario Attilio Levi, *Political Power in the Ancient World* (New York: New American Library, 1968), p. 99.

31. A. L. Epstein, "Power, Politics and Leadership," in Swartz, 1968, p. 66.

33. Monica Wilson, *Communal Rituals of the Nyakyusa* (New York: Oxford University Press, 1959), p. 155.

34. Crawford, 1967, p. 60.

35. Ronald Frankenberg, *Village on the Border: A Social Study of Religion, Politics and Football in a North Wales Community* (London: Cohen & West, 1957), p. 154.

36. Turner, 1969, p. 203.

37. See Fortes, 1962, p. 78.

38. The ritual role of medical doctors is interesting because of the sacred quality of their office. They must maintain social distance and a bag of secret practises. The preference for Jewish doctors in the nineteenth century or in twentieth-century America and the great prestige of doctors with European accents helped to enhance the sacred status. Monica Wilson notes the universality of this trait, which she found among the Nyakyusa: "The doctors with the greatest reputation are those at a distance, and a high proportion of the practitioners in the country are of foreign lineages, their fathers, or grandfathers, or great-grandfathers having come in, bringing medicines with them, and begun to practice." (1959, p. 151.)

39. See A. R. Radcliffe-Brown, "Preface" in Meyer Fortes and E. E. Evans-Pritchard, eds., *African Political Systems* (New York: Oxford University Press, 1940), pp. xvi–xviii.

40. Bronislau Malinowski, *Magic, Science, and Religion and Other Essays* (New York: Doubleday, 1954), p. 46.

41. Peter Lawrence, *Road Belong Cargo: A Study of the Cargo Movement in the Southern Madang District of New Guinea* (Manchester, Eng.: Manchester University Press, 1964), p. 206.

42. Fortes and Evans-Pritchard, 1940, pp. 21–22.

43. See *The New York Times,* November 15, 1970, p. 28.

6 | THE RITUAL CYCLE

What of the young kids who became Bikers only yesterday, adapting the conventions already pioneered over a decade to the point where they have become campy clichés? Adopting Nazi symbols, Kaiser helmets, hirsutz and flattulence, can they play the role without self-conscious satire? Wearing steel chains for belts, they invade a tavern. Challenged by another gang, they leap to the attack, tearing the chains free from their waists and swinging them in deadly arc, while their pants fall down . . . .

Acting styles go in fads. It is like girls at a dance. One night a fellow walks in wearing a motorcycle jacket and blue jeans and he takes the first girl that he sees and embraces her and crushes her rib cage. What a man! all the girls say, and pretty soon all the boys are coming to the dances in motorcycle jackets and blue jeans and taking direct action. Then one night in comes a fellow in a blue suit carrying a bouquet of flowers. Now the girls say, what a charmer! and they are off on another cycle. (Cary Grant, 1965)[1]

Making the cover of *Time* magazine has long been known as the "kiss of death" for any politician or celebrity. This is not merely a conceit, but may actually reflect the natural cycle of celebrity. "By the time you make *Time,* you've had it!"

The very qualities that brought fame and attention in time become sufficiently familiar so as to inspire incipient boredom. The attention span is stretched to its breaking point. Other competing sensations are clamoring for attention and now receive more than their due because of an inclination to challenge success. Even more important, a host of imitators will have entered the field, adapting by more or less imaginative variation the same values and forms embodied in that which has succeeded. Now, vulgarized by repetition and imitation, dulled by familiarity, success itself elicits a motive of challenge and contempt. It comes to represent the antithesis of its original meaning. It is abandoned and despised by the next wave of innovators. Modern technology liberates ritual more and more from functionality; it makes it more arbitrary and creative and also diffuses it more quickly, guaranteeing both its spread and its demise.

All values follow the natural cycle although some have greater impact and may endure longer than others. Ritual arises from repetition of action. A successful outcome will reinforce a random search behavior, thereby fix and orient it, and make it available for cultural diffusion. Repetition arises from an attempt by the organism to recapture and augment the gains of the original experience. Eric Berne proposes "script analysis" as a means of psychiatric therapy for the patient who has a "repetition compulsion" and tends to reenact ritualistically, regardless of outcomes. The object of "script analysis" is to close the show and put a better one on the road, to free the patient from "the compulsion to relive the situation" and to start him on some other path.[2]

GAME ANALYSIS

All actions may be viewed as *transactions,* that is, as part of a sequence of value exchanges between and among individuals and groups. The archetype of transactions in a closed system of values is the game. In this terminology, behavior may be described as game-playing, a strategic interaction among actors, each seeking to maximize certain values. Berne writes that "the individual will strive to engage in transactions which are related to his favorite game; he will strive to play games which are related to his script; and he will strive to obtain the greatest primary gain from each engagement."[3]

Game analysis is an inadequate metaphor for social behavior. The terminology suggests a kind of automatic drive toward oneupsmanship that takes place in a value and has no real impact on behavior change. Berne's whole analysis is saturated with opprobrium and disapproval, implying that games are pathological and unworthy of the well-balanced personality. Berne defines the term with a sneer: "A game is an ongoing series of complementary ulterior transactions progressing to a well-defined, predictable outcome." It is a recurring set, "superficially plausible, with a concealed motivation" or a series of moves "with a snare or 'gimmick.'" He differentiates games from "procedures, rituals, and pastimes" which he says are "candid." "They may involve contest, but not conflict, and the ending may be sensational, but it is not dramatic." Every game, he says, "is basically dishonest." The pattern of behavior that aims at influence in the transaction, he calls "an operation," which he defines as *"maneuvers;* not honest requests, but moves in the game."[4]

With this limited definition, he is forced to invent a meaningless function for the game that, he says, lends it efficacy as a means of exploitation, deceit, and ego-aggrandizement. The legitimizing function of games is "to structure time," to provide surrogate activity as a substitute for "real legitimacy" and as a prop to maintain the psychic stability of mentally ill people. "These people's psychic stability is so precarious, and their positions are so tenuously maintained, that to deprive them of their games may plunge them into irreversible despair and even psychosis." He postulates a utopia of human relations that can be gained through psychiatric game analysis in which patients achieve "the rewards of game-free intimacy, which is or should be the most perfect form of human living," rewards so great that "even precariously balanced personalities can safely and joyfully relinquish their games. . . ."[5]

Such an approach to transactional analysis and ritual behavior is self-serving and limited. As a basis for strategic analysis, game theory places emphasis on ploys and decisions in the abstract, ascribing to them an indifference and cynicism rarely characteristic of live social transactions. In real transactions, the chief ingredient is mutuality of interest and influence. The very uncertainty of outcome and the variability of values, both controlled by all the parties involved, creates a reciprocity that effectively limits and defines the options available in real time. The bargaining parties are not free, but are deeply involved and committed. No transaction can be separated from the web of multilateral transactions and actions of the total social milieu. Each transaction and its outcome has a powerful impact on subsequent transactions both positively and negatively for all participants.

Status is an important vantage point of bargaining. Behind every transaction lies a fundamental authority issue. Though frequently unrelated to the specific quarrel, it overrides and often becomes the main issue. The question of status or authority affects the viability of bargaining positions in future issues and quarrels, either among the same parties or with other parties. This is what teenage gang members refer to as "saving my rep," and what nations regard as "prestige." Every transaction provides a model for settling other issues and predisposes outcomes that replicate the model without other costly tests of strength.

Once a quarrel is escalated to a fundamental test of authority and status, the high costs of such a test tend to enforce its outcome without another major challenge for a long time. It is not uncommon for individuals to force a test of strength on relatively unimportant or silly issues. This tends to limit and control the danger implicit in the dispute by focusing on less sensitive and provocative questions. For example, people often remember major arguments with loved ones without recalling what the argument was about. As diplomats prepare the way for negotiations to end wars, every symbolic element of procedure becomes a matter of intense bargaining.

That is why status values (reflecting the rank of individuals and groups in the hierarchy of authority) constitute one of the most fundamental aspects of human aspirations. It is literally a matter of life and death in the sense that the higher the individual or group status, the greater the power to bargain and to organize life boundaries in accord with a principle of order, thereby reducing relative entropy and optimizing the ability to manipulate and control the requirements of life and growth. In this sense, status values are not unlike the requirements of living space and territoriality for other members of the animal and vegetable kingdoms. The loss of the ability to eliminate entropy and bring order to one's personal boundaries is the greatest source of personal despair, desperation, and death. Recent studies have found the rate of heart attacks and other physical disorders to be clearly related to the achievement or nonachievement of status values. Drastic status reversals are closely related to accident-proneness, suicide, and aggression.

Sequences of transactions and outcomes, or actions/reactions are a form of learning and mutual adjustment. The process is not a game in any cynical and invidious sense, unless one chooses to attack the specific values embodied in any given transaction. One cannot hope to escape by any process of psychiatric analysis from transactions, uncertainties, the strategic use of one's resources, and the rituals of bargaining. Whether for good or ill, social behavior has consequences. Otherwise it is without meaning. The game-free relationship exists only in the mind of the euphoric honeymooner who wishes to minimize the components of tension that characterize a given transaction before closure. The honeymoon period that comes with closure cannot be indefinitely prolonged but will soon be disrupted once again as the restless elements of the next exchange of values begin to collect and assert themselves.

In the words of Eric Fromm, "two persons fall in love when they feel they have found the best object available upon the market considering the limitations of their own exchange values."[6] The moment of closure of this particular transaction is an exhilarating miracle that lasts a little while. "The two persons become well acquainted, their intimacy loses more and more its miraculous character, until their antagonism, their disappointments, their mutual boredom kill whatever is left of the initial excitement."

More recent trends in psychiatry reject the formalistic detachment of game analysis, along with the whole notion of mental health and the "well-balanced" personality. Dysfunctional behavior symptoms, instead, are seen as patterns of value exchange arising from a corrupt transaction. In his recent work *The Politics of Therapy,* Halleck writes, "Symptoms are behaviors that arise from the need to influence what is often an oppressive environment; they are also efforts to change that environment." If a husband acts in a manner that indicates sadness, depression, or anxiety, it is because he is trying to tell his wife to take better care of him, to treat him like a child, or to feel guilty for having made him miserable. He may be punishing her as part of some old and unresolved transaction, or "trying to alter the distribution of power within the marital relationship." Symptomatic behavior has an obvious influence-seeking purpose. "Symptoms can exert a powerful influence upon the patient's environment: the husband of a frigid wife must deal with his partner's unresponsiveness; the community must respond to the aggressive child delinquent. Symptoms are usually indirect or symbolic attempts to communicate."[7]

Psychiatrist Ronald D. Laing contends that the role of the therapist subjects the patient to "a ritual of mortification and humiliation" that confirms the values that the psychiatrist represents and strengthens the self-hatred of the patient. As such, psychiatric treatment is already completed by the self-abasement of the act of seeking help, which represents a surrender of the patient's rebellious values. The ritual of psychiatric counseling and analysis that follows is merely a face-saving sop; the patient is repaid for his self-abasement by the satisfaction of receiving protracted and serious attention from a ritual figure, who represents approved community values.

Contests of influence elicit the marshaling of resources and support among all the participants. The outcomes of past transactions create webs of obligations that may be looked on as capital to be expended judiciously in new exchanges. Grounds of past decisions are used as claims and promises that can be traded on when new decisions will be made. Values, jural rules (that is, enforceable understandings concerning rights and obligations), goods, people, and the relations between people (whether based on ties of kinship, emotional or material attachments, or some other bond) are among the main resources that the contestants convert into support for their own ambitions. Exchange is not free of moral or jural considerations. Swartz writes, "even if the actor who tries the mobilization should be without either moral scruples or fears of sanctions, others on his side . . . will not be and at least part of the success of the maneuver will depend upon their accepting it and its results." The only way actors can determine whether these new supports and their means of attainment are acceptable is by trying to use them. If they are effective, "they will probably be used repeatedly, and eventually the rules for their mobilization will take their place with other accepted regulations."[8]

Games are real, inescapable, and of consequence. The stakes are important for all of the actors. Pretended indifference or detachment will not wash. The outcomes can be fraught with great psychic danger for all of the participants and this threat may be manipulated symbolically. The awareness that the transaction may be disrupted, or that the parties may invoke real danger, facilitates compromise and adjustment. The ever-present threat of volatile and unmanageable escalation works to reduce the probability of such a development. Symbols, display, demonstrations, and abstractions are enough to change behavior and to hold significance for action. But even highly ritualized action has real costs and effects, even though the ritual tends to reduce and conserve such costs.

COLLABORATIVE COMPETITION

Action/reaction is the continuum of behavior. Ritual repetitions tend to stabilize the pattern, but rituals are not immune to variation, embellishment, strategic adjustment, and development. A student of political extremism should not be forced to recommend frontlash as preferable to backlash; rather, he should see two positions as intrinsically related in a contest that, one hopes, can be moderated, at a lower level of risk, with symbolic confrontation and tactics of display rather than tactics of destruction. At the same time, one can recognize that only the real potential of sudden escalation imposes restraints and limits demands. Such a potential is, indeed, the only means of enforcing mutual constraints, which in turn enable peaceable conciliation and adjustment to operate by means of ritualized symbolic processes in political institutions like parties, legislatures, courts, and executive bureaucracies.

Sequences of action/reaction, stabilized but subject to change, are ritualized in all aspects of cultural learning. All situations struggle to wrench themselves into a ritual definition in order to trigger the appropriate springs of the individual's behavioral repertoire. A great deal of innovated behavior involves the transfer of signals into new situations that broaden the range of behavioral options, or, conversely, lead to inappropriate and counter-productive responses.

The element of surprise may give great efficacy to a new behavior largely because the audience is initially disoriented by the behavior, failing to respond at all, or overreacting so as to augment the attention-seizing quality of the behavior. Every behavior is an appeal to legitimacy, and must express, among other things, a demand for attention. But there is a built-in corrective that denies repeated success to this demand. What begins as regenerative oscilation must be eventually dampened. Goffman describes the process: when the participants in an undertaking "fail to prevent the occurrence of an event which is expressively incompatible with the judgments of social worth that are being maintained," then the participants are likely "to give it accredited status as an incident—to ratify it as a threat that deserves direct official attention—and to proceed to try to correct for its effects." The participants find themselves "in an established state of ritual disequilibrium or disgrace, and an attempt must be made to re-establish a satisfactory ritual state."[9]

Conflict rituals tend to become durable when they maintain values for all of the participants through a process that may be called collaborative competition. The conflict between J. Edgar Hoover and the Communist party was a perfect example of this process, as is that between Vice-President Spiro T. Agnew and the television medium. Rivals locked in a ritual of collaborative competition tend to become more and more alike. Spies and counter-spies need each other and must specialize in legitimatizing each other's function. Excesses in one direction always beget answering extravagance. The American obsession with cleanliness, the worship of Mr. Clean, the elaborate germ warfare on the home front in the form of detergents, deodorants, mouthwashes, antiseptic sprays, specialized forms of paper for the toilet and a thousand other wipes, soaps, and shots—the whole armor against filth—is responsible for the regressions of the counter-culture into funky, raunchy, Ur-slime, sonic and visual slop, scatalogical references, four letter words, litter, dirt, and ritual squalor. The popularity of these anti-clean styles may be viewed as a protest against the cult of the new, the seamless, the plastically undefiled in a pattern of collaborative competition.

Another example of the functionality of collaborative competition is the practice of leaders to accept invitations to address hostile rallies, or to arrange through drummers and advance men to have hecklers represented at every public appearance. Robert Welch, founder of the John Birch society, and George Lincoln Rockwell, leader of the American Nazi party (which provided so many paradigms of political behavior to the student radical movement), were both favorite campus speakers. Alabama's Governor George Wallace built student hecklers into his audience as part of his act.

When behavior is paying off, it tends to remain in the repertoires of the participants in a relatively unchanged form. As the black revolution gathered steam in the mid-1960's, and as white power groups sought to accommodate it, polls indicated that blacks perceived themselves to be worse off and more riot-prone than ever. Why should they be less disaffected when disaffection was paying off so well? But at the very point of maximum success, the behavior begins to die. Those whose interest it does not serve learn to discount it in advance. They adopt counter-strategies. The element of novelty is fragile; the drive of strategic interaction is merciless. Imitation, vulgarization, and overuse aid the cause of those who wish to resist the success of the ploy. Eventually, the behavior is dropped from the repertoire.

It often happens that formal spokesmen and government officials recognize a problem and begin to make speeches about it at this point, when the problem has already changed its form and possibly disappeared. The U.S. Attorney General became very exercised over the threat of the Black Panthers some months after the Panthers had lost their dynamism and legitimacy and were quarreling among themselves over petty and dishonoring issues. The Government launched strenuous programs to combat drug addiction among white youth at about the same time that drugs were becoming passé and an internal dynamic was well-advanced for reducing their use. In each of these instances, the entry of busybodies and government on the scene had the effect of reviving the behavior for a time, as a form of collaborated competition, the opposite of the effect sought.

Official persecution and harassment of informal movements, especially those characterized by mystical and religious ritual, guarantee their endurance and survival. Official persecution validates the claim for attention and importance that is an implicit and rudimentary value sought by every new behavior form. In Australian New Guinea, government attempts to stamp out the New Guinea Cargo cults had exactly the effect of strengthening them. The same could be said for the efforts to repress the Millenarian cults of medieval Europe, the Chinese Peiping Rebellion, the Mahdiya in the Sudan, the American Indian ghost dance, the Navaho peyote sect, a wide variety of witchcraft cults in Africa, Southeast Asia, and Polynesia, and the UFO cults of modern industrialized America.

The attacks of the Nixon administration on the press act to validate the legitimacy of all the dissenting groups that have received press attention in the last decade. The press is responsive to the activities of search behavior from which spring culture change. But as messengers who are punished for carrying a message, the press is being radicalized by the harassment of government. More and more, it has been forced back into its traditional role as a challenging institution largely as a result of the inept actions of a regime of second-rate lawyers and summons servers.

Sooner or later every behavior form turns into its opposite and becomes satire or camp. First, the Beautiful People make the scene. The word is soon out, since the Beautiful People celebrate everything before a national audience. But then they are forced to move on to new fields in order that they be not overtaken by the sweaty public who follow them, trying to act like Beautiful People. Their new behavior having lost legitimacy, they engage in it only as a self-conscious satire of outsider groups who still take it seriously, as an assertion of cultural chauvinism which expresses the infinite superiority of this month's thing as opposed to last month's. Successful improvisation leads inevitably to contagion, mimicry, exaggeration, inversion, counterpoint, and all of the infinite modes of permutation and combination. The variations do not require new and original inputs and tend to run their course rather quickly. The more new styles are ritualized and transmitted to outsiders by this route, the more pressing is the search for variation. Berne refers to the ritual process as "social programming." Within any given social aggregation, as people interact, "more and more *individual programming* creeps in, so that 'incidents' begin to occur." These incidents, he writes, "superficially appear to be adventitious . . . but careful scrutiny reveals that they tend to follow definite patterns which are amenable to sorting and classification, and that the sequence is circumscribed by unspoken rules and regulations."[10]

Another example of behavior reversal can be seen in the police confrontations of recent decades. The success of the black revolution made revolutionaries out of everyone. Freedom Riders and nonviolent marches in the South in the early 1960's trapped police into acting like pigs. Teenage street gangs and juvenile delinquents, and their mimics (white college youth), began to call the police pigs even after the police learned (through the losses of legitimacy brought about by peaceful marchers) how to conserve their image. When police acted with restraint and forebearance, the militants acted like pigs. The ritual roles reversed themselves.

The transference of a ritual to new situations can lead to inappropriate and self-destructive behavior. William Buckley, the conservative columnist, recalls walking through London's Hyde Park and listening with lazy inattention to soapbox orators denouncing the nation. It was, he writes, rather like "the child's dreams of walking in a jungle surrounded by wild beasts who, however, are powerless to hurt you because you are surrounded by a bubble of glass that is proof against their aggressions."[11] But in a similar situation, the rhetoric of provocation and violence led to confrontations with the police, and resulted in tear gas, split heads, and arrests. The youngsters experienced a sense of having been betrayed. People were not supposed to take them seriously; they were not supposed to respond in kind. The ritual was supposed to be performed as a kind of metaphor and symbolic warning. There was, they charged, something unfair in the tendency of the police to take them at their word and respond accordingly.

The word *revolution* soon became the pat formula for the new culture. Anyone who used the rhetoric effectively was flooded with invitations to appear on television and radio talk shows and lecture platforms at universities, and to accept jobs and money from the Office of Economic Opportunity and reparations from conscious-stricken white churches. The most outrageous demands in the name of revolution carried automatic authority and legitimacy. By the end of 1968, Tom Wolfe points out, there were no more fighting gangs in the slums. "Everybody was into Black Power, Brown Power and Yellow Power, and the poverty program in one way or another." Crime did not decrease, but the hoods and the hustlers became "fighters for the people, ghetto warriors." Poverty program confrontations ("the mau-mauing") brought overnight celebrity.

You turn on the TV and there would be some dude you had just seen hanging out on the corner with the porkpie hat scrunched down over his eyes and the toothpick nodding on his lips—and there he was now on the screen, a leader, a spokesman, with whites holding microphones up to his mouth and waiting for the Word to fall from his lips.[12]

Huey Newton and Rap Brown made the front pages with "power comes from the barrel of the gun" at the very moment when the fortunes of war in Vietnam were proving exactly the opposite. Minister of Defense Huey P. Newton: "Army 45 Will Stop All Jive/ Buckshots Will Down the Cops/P-38 Will Open Prison Gate/Carbine Will Stop War Machine/357 Will Win Us Heaven/If You Don't Believe in Lead, You Are Already Dead."

White campus rebellions roared across the land in mimicry of the slum explosions, and when blacks in Panther garb brought rifles to a sit-in at the Cornell administration building, public attention for such sit-ins, divided and fatigued by saturation, suddenly shot to the front pages once again. The white student radicals bought the line that guns were the answer. As one SDS leader, to enormous applause, told an audience at Kent State, one year before some National Guardsmen killed four students there, "They used guns at Cornell and got what they wanted. It will come to that here!"[13] What was it that they wanted? Was it admissions for ghetto blacks, more black instructors and an expanded black studies program? The few blacks at Cornell already had or were in the process of getting all of these things. No one with guns was threatening to deny them these. What they wanted and what they got by using guns at Cornell was national press! They recovered image-making initiative and provided the next variation in the revolutionary model.

In the same way, having temporarily lost attention in favor of black teenagers, Roy Innes, Director of CORE, recovered his personal stage by disrupting services at Norman Vincent Peale's Riverside Church, after alerting the press, and posting a demand for half-a-billion dollars in reparations from white churches. After some initial success, this strategy went the same route of corruption and absurdity. All kinds of self-appointed leaders demanded reparations from all kinds of groups and individuals, selected not necessarily for the likelihood of compliance as for the prominence of the stage-setting of the demand. Most recently, four women psychologists disrupted the annual convention of the American Psychological Association, charging that modern psychotherapy perpetuates male supremacy and contributes to mental illness among women, and demanded a billion dollars in immediate reparations. Such an event indicates that the extinction of this behavior form is near![14]

Revolution quickly became such a commercial success that the word even began appearing in advertising, not only in counter-culture media, but in the citadels of the establishment (for example, "the Dodge Rebellion"). Trying to salvage the image, the *Village Voice* announced in 1971 it would no longer accept ads that played on the revolutionary idiom. But alas, it was too late. Even President Nixon declared "power to the people" in defending his government reorganization plan. The revolutionary rhetoric was already shallow, as discredited as that of Spiro Agnew and deodorant commercials. The makers of the white middle-class mimic revolution began to split, their rhetoric ripped-off by the relentless cycles of culture.

Roy Mungo, successful organizer of the national underground press syndicate, sold his interest and retired to a farm commune.

We dreamed of a new age born of violent insurrection. We danced on the graves of war dead in Vietnam, every corpse was ammunition for our side; we set up a counter-government down there in Washington; had marches, rallies, and meetings, we tried to fight fire with fire. Then Johnson resigned, yes, and the universities began to fall, the best and oldest ones first, and by God, every thirteen-year-old in the suburbs was smoking dope, and our numbers multiplying into the millions.

Then in the spring of 1968, he woke up. "This is not what I had in mind." He found "the movement had become my enemy; the movement was not flowers and doves and spontaneity, but another vicious system, the seed of a heartless bureaucracy, a minority party vying for power rather than peace."[15]

A radical columnist for the *Village Voice* wrote in late 1970 that "Love kills. Love has become the justification for everything from killing a cop to castrating a husband. It is love thy neighbor, unless thy neighbor happens to be a pig, a straight, a hardhat, or a stinking middle class liberal."[16] A student leader at Kent State, a year after the shootings, said, "We have learned that the incessant shouting of 'pig' is dehumanizing. As bad for the shrieker as the shrieked-at."[17]

Bernadine Dorne, exiled to Algeria after the trashing expedition by the SDS women's contingent on the streets of Chicago, called for a fall offensive in 1970, to bring the war home by bombings, sabotage, and violent confrontations. But the mood failed. Fatigue and ennui with empty rhetorical calls for violence, the collapse of SDS as a legitimate cadre in the nation's colleges, brought an autumnal lull and a resurgence of beer drinking and football fiestas. There was hardly a whimper of revolution in the land. By the following spring, Bernadine was renouncing violence and calling for a renewed period of peaceful struggle, citing the explosion in a Greenwich Village town-house bomb factory (not the failure of the fall offensive) as the basis for the strategic change.

Huey Newton, within a year of his emergence, free and no longer sainted, ensconced in his $600-a-month penthouse ("for security"), with the Black Panthers cut off from the ghetto and allied to the dead constituency of white radical youth, fell to attacking the Eastern and Algerian branch of his own organization. The Apostle of the Gun called for a return to peaceful effort through, of all things, "the black churches," which he called a grass roots force in the black community.

Originally, a new behavior form strikes everyone with astonishment and awe. It inspires a false omnipotence in its inventors, which tempts them into actions that end by destroying the linkage with the reality check of their audience. For example, when Arthur G. Barkeley hijacked an airplane he found all of the world's electronic media hooked up to the pilot's microphone. Giddy with his success, overwhelmed by the godlike platform that his action unexpectedly created, the demented hijacker began solving all the problems of the world. He even had a special message for President Nixon: "Resign, you are unfit to rule!"

The syndrome of public attention elevates a man into a god, makes him sacred, and leads him to act like an ass! Fresh from their success in Catonsville (burning draft records and thus setting off a flurry of draft record burnings throughout the country), the Berrigan brothers considered ways to hold the initiative for their efforts against the war. The Tupamaroes had just killed Dan Mitrione in Uruguay. Johnathan Jackson had just been shot outside the San Rafael courthouse in California, the Weathermen seemed at the height of their influence, and the bombings of banks and computers seemed to be increasing on all sides. Daniel was finally arrested after six months of dodging the law on Block Island. In this context, a group of intellectuals who had attached themselves to the Berrigans considered it their responsibility to use the new tactics "responsibly" before someone else left a trail of corpses.

THE GENERATIONAL EVENT

Judged by the history of acid rock, Woodstock, and the youth revolution, an era in behavior styles now lasts two to five years. However, some forms of behavior may endure much longer because of the time-fixing element of events.

The unprogrammed crisis, the unstructured experience, the unpredictable, ineluctable combination of circumstance has a presence that cannot be managed by old forms and that demands a general revision of values. Events that cannot be encompassed by minor revisions in the ritual repertoire require a reorganization and restructuring of the whole. This includes events such as major and worthy wars, the collapse of economic activity in depression, and main struggles for power between important emerging constituencies. Great transformations of the ritual order arise from great events, just as small revisions arise from the commonality of small events. As Sigmund Neumann observes, "Contemporaries are not merely people born in the same year. . . . What identifies them as people of one generation is their common experiences, the same decisive influence, similar historical problems."

Cultural-political generations are far more significant than biological ones. A generation consists of persons in a common age group who in their formative years "have known the same historical experiences, shared the same hopes and disappointments, and experienced a common disillusionment with respect to the elder age groups. . . ."[18] This may be called the generational event, the unifying event that marks an age and tends to be embodied in its rhetoric and rituals for generations to come. To the Chinese Communist students of the 1930's, it was the Long March. The American 1930's brought depression and the new values represented in the writings of T. S. Eliot, Ernest Hemingway, and John Steinbeck. The 1940's brought the Second World War, and also Albert Camus, Jean Paul Sartre, Norman Mailer, and Graham Greene.

Social generations follow on each other more rapidly in critical times than in quiet times. The wars of the first half of this century resulted in a rapid succession of generations that became more differentiated from each other than class systems. Repeated historical crisis in a short period of time multiplies political generations to the point where they may be separated by just a few years of real time.

The First World War differentiated generations in this manner: "First was the pre-war generation, comprised of people born before 1890," whose education, Neumann says, was complete and whose careers had been formed before the war started. For them, the war was an interruption. Next was the war-participant generation, "to them the war meant the great formative experience. Admirable or brutal, it was in their blood. It could never leave them. This was the younger generation called upon to make post-war history." The war, as a massive traumatic event, amplified the wave of the normal generational conflict. Any world event that imposes a diversity of experience on the generations, especially localizing the trauma on one generation and not others, "tends to divide society, to intensify conflict, and upset the generational equilibrium." It was in this sense, Neumann pointed out, that fascism was "the revolution of the war-generation par excellence."[19]

Just as the ritual order acts as a countervailing power against secular authority, so insurgent political movements seek to appropriate for themselves the ritual roles. Ethical ideas become an instrument of struggle and the means by which the challengers seek to demoralize and discredit the incumbents. This process has nothing to do with generations, but rather with a structure of values that runs vertically and horizontally through the generations in spite of the impact of generational events on age group differentiation. Events give specific form and content to the ritualized behavior of an era, some of which may be stabilized by competitive collaboration to endure for a generation or more. But because of this striving for authority the cycle will eventually begin moving again, whether rapidly or slowly, as the search for values and social relationships continues a timeless process of adaptation, reinforcement, and extinction, caught in the relentless tension between stability and change.

NOTES

1. Cary Grant, quoted in Tom Wolfe, *The Kandy-Kolored Tangerine-Flake Streamline Baby* (New York: Simon and Schuster, 1966), p. 150.

2. Eric Berne, *Transactional Analysis in Psychotherapy* (New York: Grove Press, 1961), p. 118.

3. *Ibid.*, p. 125.

4. Eric Berne, *Games People Play* (New York: Grove Press, 1964), p. 48.

5. *Ibid.*, p. 62.

6. Eric Fromm, *The Art of Loving* (New York: Harper & Row, 1956), p. 3.

7. Seymour C. Halleck, *The Politics of Therapy* (New York: Science House, 1971), pp. 68–69.

8. Marc J. Swartz, ed., *Local Level Politics: Social and Cultural Prospectives* (Chicago: Aldine, 1968), pp. 27–28.

9. Erving Goffman, *Interaction Ritual: Essays on Face-to-Face Behavior* (Garden City, N.Y.: Doubleday, 1967), p. 19.

10. Berne, 1964, p. 17.

11. Quoted in Goffman, 1967, p. 54.

12. Tom Wolfe, *Radical Chic and Mau-mauing the Flak Catchers* (New York: Farrar, Strauss & Giroux, 1970), p. 142.

13. Joyce Cecora, quoted in *Kent Stater,* May 7, 1968, p. 1.

14. See *The New York Times,* September 6, 1970, p. 28.

15. Raymund Mungo, *Total Loss Farm: A Year in the Life* (New York: Dutton, 1970), pp. 16–17.

16. Joe Flaherty, *Village Voice,* September 24, 1970, p. 16.

17. Philip Hamburger, quoted in "Aftermath," *The New Yorker,* May 11, 1971, p. 119.

18. Lewis S. Feuer, *The Conflict of Generations* (New York: Basic Books, 1969), p. 25.

19. Sigmund Neumann, "The Conflict of Generations in Contemporary Europe," *Vital Speeches of the Day,* 1939, pp. 623–28, cited in *ibid.*, p. 26.

7 | REBELLIONS

*It's five thirty in the morning—The Woodstock Hour—and Jagger
is jigging on the ruins of Western civilization. He is into his
final medley, with a dozen powerful amps screaming, "I can't get
no satisfaction." Suddenly, the Stones turn the corner into
"Street Fighting Man," and the whole audience levitates. Every
. . . love child mounts his chair, raises his right hand over his head
and makes his biggest, blackest, hardest fist! What pure
Nuremburg! (Albert Goldman, 1971)[1]*

*Under questioning by defense attorneys, Susan Atkins said: "Should
I feel remorse or sorry for doing what was right for me? What I
did was coming from love. Anything that comes from love is good.
I felt no hatred, no malice. I didn't even know these people. But
they were part of the system that jailed my brother for something
I did and I was going back on the system. I told Sharon [Tate],
I didn't have any mercy for her. What feels right, feels good. Touch
a flower, look at the sun, get my brother out of jail." (1971)[2]*

Greek tragedy arose, not out of the apollonian myths of
law and structure, but out of the dionysian cults that celebrated
disorder and unrestraint. Apollo was associated with light, knowledge, and the patriarchal aristocracy of the gods, while Dionysus,
the god of fertility, wine, and drama, represented the underworld,
the principle of growth, change, and rapture.[3] Like Hamlet and
Christ, Dionysus represented both a challenge to prevailing authority (the death of kings and heroes), and renewal (the cycle of
the seasons and the rebirth of heroes).

Orgiastic and unrestrained rapture is the middle act of a purification rite that is found in a variety of forms in all cultures. In addition, small rebellions are ritualized widely in social relations and
private behavior. Festivals, drunkenness, seizures and manias, and
crowd actions may be seen as rituals of rebellion. Comedy and
satire, criticism and political name-calling, even a certain syndrome
of suicide, heart attacks, and obesity can be understood as behavioral options that gain their efficacy as rituals of rebellion.

CATHARSIS AND RENEWAL

The archetype of such rites has been analyzed by anthropologist Max Gluckman. In studies of the Bantus, Gluckman discards "Frazer's intellectual analysis" based on the assumption that ritual acts out religious belief; he asserts instead the structural and functional features of the ritual itself. Assuming that behavior expresses values, he is struck by the large variety of rituals that "openly express" social tensions. "Women have to assert license and dominance as against their formal subordination to men, princes have to behave to the king as if they covet the throne, subjects openly state their resentment of authority."[4] He argues that this universal pattern proceeds within an established system, in which "there is dispute about particular distributions of power, but not about the structure of the system itself." In a complex way, rituals of rebellion renew the unity of the system!

Gluckman notes that among the Bantu, quarrels tend to increase, not during a period of hard work and hunger, but "because of the sudden access of energy from the new food . . . after harvest."[5] Tribes that have no great periodicity of hunger and harvest, he observes, have no great ceremonies. He points out that in a Zulu ritual, the normally docile women become lewd viragoes, and unmarried maidens assume the behavior of men. Superficially, the observer might think that the ritual expressed a protest against social subordination of the women and the practice of exogamy whereby the women were transferred by marriage to stranger groups as a form of chattel. In fact, the suffragette ritual should be interpreted as maintaining, rather than altering, the existing social and political order—the women afterward continue to be good wives and mothers. The mechanism is clearly evident. Forced to tolerate this extravagant transformation in their women, the men are reminded of the fragile nature of the social system that endows them not only with authority but with responsibility to maintain legitimacy—the ritual warns the males of the danger involved if they abuse their social role. It expresses the requirements of social unity to which both men and women must subordinate their private fantasies. Were the males to punish and retaliate against the festival, they would create the basis for a real political suffragette movement.

Turner notes that Ndembu ritual is "obsessed by the hilarious contradiction that the more the sexes stretch their differences in mutual aggression, the more do they desire sexual congress." This mutual aggression is incorporated as a form of therapy for the ill; the sexual incitement makes the audience, the medicines, and the patient stronger against the powers of death and darkness. "They sing ribald and Rabelaisian songs during the collection of medicines in the bush, and toward the end of the public dance, while the patient is being sprinkled with these medicines . . . dithyrambs in praise of sexual union frequently specified as adulterous."[6] To legitimize obscenity and pornography, the Ndembu chant a special formula: "Here another thing is done!" This has the effect of opening the door to the mention of matters that otherwise they consider "a secret thing of shame or modesty." This formula licenses disrespect and immodesty. The songs are in serial order. Members of each sex belittle the sexual organ and prowess of the opposite, and extol their own. The women jeeringly assert that they have secret lovers, and the men retort that all they ever get from women are venereal diseases. Having exhausted this vein of discourse, both sexes join in praising the pleasures of intercourse in lyrical terms. Turner writes, "The whole atmosphere is buoyant and aggressively jovial, as men and women strive to shout one another down."[7]

Nothing expresses group solidarity so much as the massing face-to-face of large numbers of people in some kind of unified activity system, whether a mass meeting, a political demonstration, a march, a sit-in, a picnic, a New Year's Eve celebration in Times Square, a graduation ceremony, a political rally, or a theatrical presentation. Such occasions express the existence of unifying values of great power and legitimacy for participants in the activity. Official occasions, highly stylized and surrounded with formal definitions, or those that contain many spontaneous elements, express the coalescence of group loyalty, the most basic product of the culture process. The structure of festival and carnival occasions, therefore, provides a striking clue to the subtle, inchoate currents of the political process. The mass meetings, speeches, and public debate that make up a major political campaign have a greater effect on culture values and social outcomes than the somewhat artificial counting of ballots and selection of formal leadership. Whoever is selected is destined to seek to encompass the elements of legitimacy established by the ritual interaction of the campaign itself.

The mass activity system of a festival has a variety of functions. It acts as a rite of passage to mark important seasonal, temporal, physical, and political transitions. It acts as a means of displacing energy from other mundane activity systems, thereby making it available for group purposes and for eventual redeployment in new or old patterns. It is an excellent example of a device for maintaining symbolically otherwise latent capabilities, such as the group's potential for warfare or for changing economic priorities. Whatever their functions, the structure of all festivals is that of a rebellion ritual. The normal constraints and specialized activity systems are submerged in the mass occasion. The same process that expresses underlying unity and ultimate adaptability permits the violation of conventional norms and a variety of spontaneous open-region behaviors. The release of energy not only has cathartic value but resolves the tension of the contradictory strains toward stability and change.

The ability of the group to revise its energy allocations depends upon this mechanism of self-attack and rebellion. All rituals of rebellion create a sense of community by virtue of an underlying theme of external hostility. All of the underlying modes of conflict in the society are suspended in a love-fest of good feelings and fellowship. The presence of a common enemy is universally displayed. Human or supernatural forces must be overcome or intimidated by the collective power and determination of the celebrants. The rebellion form always implies a battle with unfriendly demons. These demons may be personalized as the tribe's or nation's enemies, whether within or without, or merely as unsympathetic, indifferent, or hostile outsiders; or they may represent past conflicts of the group and private dangers and temptations that continuously threaten group norms. Whatever the cultural rationalization, the festival legitimizes every excess of behavior as a kind of "military necessity" imposed upon the group by its enemies. The purgation of pity and fear is accomplished not only by the resulting property damage, physical injury, and general fatigue, but also by the transcendance of private values and energies in a mystical union of the whole group in the face of chaos and evil.

Thus what appears to be a love-fest is really a battle with symbolic enemies. In this, it is like the rituals of rebellion that lead to real conflict in a physical form, as in a confrontation of rival gangs, riots against property, or organized warfare. Because the dynamics of both a battle and a festival are the same, both assume the same characteristics. That is why riots are frequently marked by the same gaiety and excitement as a Mardi Gras. That is why even a natural disaster creates a sense of happy abandonment and contagious good-will. That is why more people are killed as a result of New Year's Eve brawls, and euphoric drunkenness than in political rebellions. The small, repetitive, private festivals that we may call Saturday night rebellions account for more murders, rapes, and accidents than those associated with great world wars.

In all such occasions, the purpose of rebellion is not to overcome existing values and activities, but to assist underlying legitimacy and to test the existing order. The test itself is part of the system and necessary to ensure its adaptability and survival. Values and activity systems of everyday life are renewed and supported by the rebellions.

Alfred Adler describes neurosis as a counter-compulsion, a problem-solving attempt in the face of the social compulsions imposed by society. "The realization of this basic fact in the psychic life of the neurotic so lightens the task of obtaining an insight into the psychic interconnections that it is bound to become the most useful working hypothesis in the investigation and curing of neurotic diseases. . . ."[8] Mental illness may be compared with a formal ritual of rebellion. Peter C. Rosenbaum cites from a case history:

Patient: (roaring at full volume with veins bulging, face red, standing six inches away from the therapist.) I am Christ. No goddamn, punk-shit psychiatrist is going to send me to a locked ward. The images of regard have been revealed to me and I have to protect those images. I am God. Do you understand that? I suck off Cougars.[9]

The pattern of logic is a claim for legitimacy, represented by "God." Jesus was legitimate and persecuted. I am persecuted. Therefore, I am legitimate. The God-claim is an aggressive cover for a fear of intimidation, but it is also, as is the case in all rituals of rebellion, a claim for legitimacy.[10]

Whether a rebellion remains merely expressive or becomes revolutionary (in the process of escalating violent confrontation) depends upon the strategic interaction of interested groups, what new opportunities are created by the demonstration of collective power, and the resources of legitimacy available to the parties involved. Attempts to retaliate, punish, or prevent ritual rebellion always backfire, authenticating and intensifying rebellious behavior, and precipitating a counter-productive process in which symbolic conflict is replaced by physical violence. By validating rebellious behavior, the retaliating authority jeopardizes its own legitimacy. This may indeed be unavoidable and necessary—a showdown may be perceived as preferable to the coexistence of groups and values in irreconcilable conflict. However, historically, the expense of violent ordeals brings symbolic conflict back into play at an early stage, and few conflicts are carried to the point of utter and complete extirpation and annihilation of the vanquished.

Animal ritual may involve mass ceremonies related to the cycles of reproduction or the seasons that are remarkably similar to the festivals of human cultures. A herd of horses celebrate a harvest festival in the fall on the night of the first day in which they are switched from pasture grazing to hay feeding. In the weeks immediately past, as the autumn set in, the pasture had become bleak, dry, tasteless and thin. Each day an increasing amount of energy had to be spent grazing in order to secure a bare minimum of nourishment. Suddenly, with the first feeding of hay, there is abundance again. The whole pattern of intensive grazing of recent weeks is broken. They easily satiate their hunger in a few hours, and the energy flow is now available for redirection. The horses have a festival. As the sun goes down, they sing and race around, playing games like young foals, nibbling and biting each other, chasing, hiding, racing back and forth. They may even break through the fences like juveniles after a football game. The very anxiety and fear elicited by someone else's territory that normally keeps them in their own pasture, even when the electric fence is shut off or down, is converted by their excitement into a method to intensify the significance and immediacy of the celebration. Like demon gods, they are rendered invulnerable and sacred by the occasion and cast aside all of the inhibitions of safety that normally control their behavior.

I have observed this phenomenon among horses on five separate occasions under identical conditions. Similar events have been observed in other species, but without enough data to provide a real understanding of the ceremonial significance. William G. Van der Kloot notes the carnival of the chimpanzees as "the most remarkable and the least understood social occasion." In the depths of the forest, some chimps begin to drum rhythmically on tree trunks and to hoot and scream. Others travel through the forest to join the group, increasing the sound and the party atmosphere. Chimps who hear it become apprehensive and timid, as the carnival gathers steam and becomes more aggressive. In the wild, no human has been able to observe the festivities, but captive chimps engage in similar activity, forming circles to dance around a tree, wagging their heads and beating their feet on the ground while individuals perform solo variations.[11]

Many wild grazing animals like deer or gazelles, who normally appear in small family troops or as isolated individuals, reveal the existence of large scale social organizations during the rutting season when they gather in huge coterminous herds for the rituals of mating. Festival-like behavior becomes richly intermingled with the agonistics of mate selection and dominance.

Widely reported in the winter of 1971 was a Malaysian frog war/love-in. On a rubber estate near Kuala Lampur, thousands of frogs gathered for a singing, dancing, biting, fighting, bloody fray that raged for days, leaving a swampy battlefield littered with torn bodies. The Malaysians regard these frog wars as portents of disaster. The Japanese invasion came soon after a particularly vicious frog festival in the early 1940's. The twelve-year struggle against internal terrorism began after a frog festival in 1948. A huge 1969 frog celebration was followed two weeks later by violent race riots. Following the 1971 celebration, monsoon rains brought one of the worst floods in the nation's history, killing at least sixty people and threatening hundreds of thousands with starvation. The prime minister declared a national disaster.[12] Zoologists from the University of Malaya studied the site and concluded that "almost certainly the war was a breeding frenzy typical of frogs who had long lain buried to survive a drought and then had been liberated by heavy rain."[13]

The migrations of mountain lemmings have all the earmarks of mass ritual and are surrounded by superstitions and portents like frog wars. About every four years, millions of the tiny creatures gather and march together like a flood down from the heights into the lowlands. One of the largest migrations ever seen, ominously reminiscent of those of 1918 and 1939, occurred in the spring of 1970. Ignoring their normal migration path in the valleys (toward the northeast Baltic coast), the lemmings swerved instead toward the inland north. Thousands were crushed in ravines crossing the cliffs, trampling each other and drowning in mountain streams. Many were killed by cars crossing the roads. Foxes, buzzards, and owls preyed on them, orchestrating secondary mass festivals of predatory species following the lemmings. Yet the survivors marched on, hundreds of miles from their starting point, driven by the mass of the wave behind them on across the beaches and into the ocean where most of them drowned. Zoologist explain this phenomenon as the result of a periodic population increase that follows on a few good years of nourishment in the mountains. Multiplying into millions, the lemmings overwhelm their natural habitat and eventually one day stampede aimlessly into the valleys.[14]

All members of a social group acknowledge that the maintenance of legitimacy is an overriding requirement of group survival, whatever the transitions and challenges of the physical and social order. This requirement enforces patterns of permissive rebellion whose effect is not merely cathartic and system-maintaining, but also a form of real rebellion and social renewal. Monica Wilson notes that sacrifices among the Nyakyusa of any sort are occasions for "speaking out," for confessing anger that if left to fester will erupt in witchcraft. Unconfessed "anger in the heart" is what the Nyakyusa fear most. Confession and criticism are explicit rituals of rebellion. The acting out of conflict facilitates its resolution as well as its catharsis of tension. Just after the break of the rains, ashes are swept from the hearth and thrown out and the Nyakyusa villagers perform a ritual in which they dance and spear one another. They say, "Let us dance, let us fight, that the homesteads may be peaceful." Ritual is the integrating force "with the widest range in the traditional society."[15]

Goffman, referring to satirical theater pieces by inmates at a mental hospital, said, "to act out one's rebellion before the authorities at a time when this is legitimate, is to exchange conspiracies for expression."[16] Those who exercise legitimate authority in the dominance hierarchy are responsive to criticism when it is couched in a conventionalized form that supports rather than attacks their authority. Rituals of rebellion tend to facilitate conciliations, to purge conflict that is otherwise repressed and dangerous and to emphasize underlying legitimacy, all the while facilitating real adjustments and reforms through voluntaristic processes. There is an element of rebellion in all novelty, but the ultimate maintenance of legitimacy must accommodate novel and experimental values. The ambivalence of these requirements means that every social group must preserve a precise and delicate balance between authority and rebellion. Rituals of rebellion are, therefore, fundamental aspects of energy conservation, countervailing power, and group unification provided by culture forms.

In prisons and mental hospitals, the rituals of theatrical presentations, flower shows, sporting events, and dances occur with well-spaced periodicity and give rise to considerable social excitement, Goffman reports. All the groupings in the establishment join in, regardless of rank or position. Whether "through a sly article, a satirical sketch, or overfamiliarity during a dance, the subordinate in some way profanes the superordinate." This is a sign of the strength, not the weakness, of the establishment state.[17] At the mental hospital, the annual party mixes staff of all ranks and inmates in party games and refreshments. At such times, the participants "will have license to take liberties across the caste line, and social reachings may be expressed through sexual ones." The conventional office party represents a similar process. The most sacred ritual occasion, Christmas, is taken to justify the most flagrant permissiveness in broaching caste lines and disregarding social distance.

The process is seen in private rituals of behavior such as acts of personal inattention, gossip and criticism, work-a-day resistance to authority by real or feigned malaise, tardiness, slips of the tongue, small gestures of profanation, failure to laugh at superior's jokes on cue, and so on. All such little personal rebellions represent low-risk challenges or relationship probes. They are not merely cathartic and expressive, but also represent punishment, threat, and bargaining signals that seek and obtain some sort of response. Like their opposites (attention, civility, positive indications of all kinds), they tend to confirm the fundamentals of the relationship. The general flow of interaction between individuals is punctuated by instances of license, repartee, playful insults, and the like, as an unending and reciprocal symbolic exchange by which the participants constantly judge each other's merit, trust, and power.

A whole variety of private behaviors attests to the self-determination, autonomy, and dignity of the individual. They are symbols of presence, weight, and importance that others may wish to confirm or challenge. The rituals of antagonism, affection, or unconcern, are the daily content of behavior. Goffman notes the systematic violation of these rituals by prisons and mental hospitals. Mortification rites of all kinds are imposed on the inmates to deny their autonomy. The rigidity of these coercive rules leads to a "looping syndrome" that contains the secret of ritualized rebellion: symbolic mortification rites serve to confirm the self-hatred of the inmate, lending legitimacy to the institutional requirements that serve the convenience of society and the staff. Disruption of mortification behavior (essentially a healthy reaction) is interpreted as a symptom of illness, which is punished, in turn, by appropriate treatment ranging from shocks or tranquilizers, to skull-sessions with a psychologist or prolonged confinement. The rebellion thus tends to reinforce the legitimacy of the system.

Coercion by imprisonment and physical constraint achieves legitimacy by dehumanizing the inmates of prisons and mental hospitals. In the world outside, such methods destroy legitimacy and can only be used for limited periods of war, disaster, and crisis. Private rituals of rebellion in the mental hospital and prison are squelched cheaply and quickly by the looping system. Outside, under ordinary conditions, looping occurs as well; that is, people may rationalize causes as symptoms. However, coercion cannot be totally unaccompanied by consideration of and concessions to the underlying cause of the challenge. Thereby, looping becomes merely a diversionary and facing-saving cover beneath which behavioral adjustment may be mutually made.[18] Modern and enlightened psychiatric establishments are more like ordinary society in that a permissive atmosphere encourages the inmate to project or act out his problems, so that the looping process becomes essentially a form of didactic feedback and therapy.[19] In private behavior, under conditions where the capability of coercion is reciprocal (and therefore cannot be evoked by either side for advantage), rebellion expresses renewal and underlying legitimacy; its opposite is an irrevocable dissolution of the relationship by withdrawal or indifference on the part of one or more of the parties.

Many of the most innocent holidays of Western society are rich in rebellion and status reversals. Halloween, for example, in which preadolescent children wear costumes and masks that represent earth-demonic powers—witches who blast fertility, corpses or skeletons from underground, indigenous peoples such as Indians, troglodites, dwarves, gnomes, and hoboes, antiauthoritarian figures such as pirates, cowboys, and gunmen. "These tiny powers, if not propitiated by treats or dainties, will work fantastic and capricious tricks on the authority-holding generation of householders—tricks similar to those once believed to be the work of earth spirits, such as hob-goblins, elves, fairies, and trolls." As with other rituals of reversal, anonymity is preserved for purposes of aggression. "The child's mask is like the highwayman's mask—and indeed children at Halloween often wear the masks of burglars or executioners."[20]

In many primitive tribes, elaborate festivals of succession occur during a changeover of leadership. After the death of a king, tradition provides for some form of interregnum measure to keep the office warm or fill it immediately. The office and the stability of the social order must be protected against not only the possibility of civil war over the succession, but also perhaps more importantly, the sudden suspension of legitimacy that may precipitate a period of ritualized rebellion and anarchy. Public suspense and lawlessness accompany major successions and may in fact tend to encourage rival claimants to office. Political succession becomes a public threshold condition that requires elaborate rites of passage to safeguard the integrity of the polity. Symbolic release from authority suddenly reveals the fragility of the group. A lack of confidence on the part of the heir apparent may lead him to misinterpret the eruptions and thereby encourage the unrest, bringing on the collapse of the regime which may or may not have been symbolically prefigured by social outbreaks.[2]

Rites of status elevation, like those of puberty or the installation of officials, provide a formal release of the tensions of competitive conflict over status. Leadership changes always jeopardize the authority structure itself. Therefore, it must be provided with a means of legitimate succession in order to avoid the inherent dangers. Such ceremonies are designed to emphasize common values and unity through what Turner calls communitas, that is, a state of statuslessness and a period of unstructured relationships from which neophytes in the African circumcision lodge, Benedictine monks, or members of a millenarian movement return when their initiation is completed to assume well-defined and structured roles. Communitas is a state of marginality, and is held to be holy. For most members of the group, it is temporary; however, prophets and artists may dwell in such a state permanently, and are for that reason sanctified by the tribe. Art, poetry, and prophecy are thus incorporated into the body politic as forms of continuous rebellion, much like a process of deliberate infection that vaccinates the body against disease.

CEREMONIAL PROFANATIONS

Many of the disagreeable tactics of political extremists are in the nature of ceremonial profanations, such as the use of four-letter words, public fornication, incivility, and the disruption of dialog. Ceremonial profanation is an accessible means of attack against another group's unity and self-confidence. The breaking up of public meetings and religious services, pioneered in the last decade by the American Nazi party, has proved efficacious as an attention-getting device for small groups in the same way that all acts of surprise and coercion create an otherwise unobtainable forum. Such tactics are designed to shock and disorient. In the search for new ceremonies to profane, antiwar protesters broke up speeches by Senator William Fulbright, and the November Action Coalition, a so-called left faction of the left faction of SDS, launched attacks against Moratorium marches and the New Mobilization.

Profanation is a form of counter-ritual that implies the sacredness of the thing profaned. It is impossible to profane the secular. Such an act bothers no one. But a sacred occasion provides a made-to-order stage where attention, well-defined form, and strictures of propriety exist and are recognized by worshipers and profaners alike. The ceremonial structure implies opportunities for profanation and provides a well-defined set of counter-rituals. Like the urge to explode in laughter during a serious public occasion, the profane urge has its origin in the very discipline of the affair. Common access to the ceremony makes it vulnerable when the motives for cheap rebellion are present.

Small ceremonial transgressions in personal behavior are always possible, and are considered to be attacks on the legitimacy of the occasion and its personnel. Lorenz observes that good manners are by definition "those characteristic of one's own group" to which we conform constantly. "We do not as a rule realize their function either of inhibiting aggression or that of forming a bond."[22] Manners function to produce an effect of mutual conciliation among group members. Nonobservance of these rituals has the same effect and meaning as does overt aggressive behavior; "indeed, such intentional suppression of the normal appeasing rituals is equivalent to overt aggressive behavior." Such acts immediately disrupt or suspend the situation unless the intruder can be chastened, removed, or ignored. Such profanations are ordinarily taken as symptoms of mental disorder when they occur in private situations. As a political tactic on public occasions, they often are subject to the same interpretations. As is true of all rituals of rebellion, this fact does not eliminate their efficacy in changing the values of others.

Many of the highly imaginative profanations of the cultural revolution of the 1960's were invented by Ken Kesey and his Merry Pranksters. The notion of a "hippie wagon," a brightly-colored bus outraging the conventions of traffic, touring the highways like a great itinerant carnival, and his joining together of motorcycle gangs and flower children (an ill-fated action destined to destroy original hippie values) were original acts of profanation, bringing violent misfits into the company of intellectuals, as if to exhibit them as individuals with some simple and primitive contact with reality. Similarly, the celebration of violence and vandalism by self-styled white revolutionary street fighters was by implication a profanation of the deep pacifism of their middle-class values.

Rennie Davis's call for a "marijuana smoke-in" at a July Fourth "Honor America Day" observance in Washington, D.C. illustrates the vulnerability of ceremonies to profanation. Heads and freaks flooded a Billy Graham revival meeting in New York, waiting until the "Come to Jesus," when by the hundreds they took over the aisles and the stage in mimic mockery of Jesus enthusiasm and stopped the meeting. Stokely Carmichael, the former chairman of the Student Nonviolent Coordinating Committee, appeared on the David Frost television program after fourteen months of listless anonymity in Africa and reached for notoriety by profaning the sacred myth of Hitler's pure evil. The same dynamic has caused the revival of all of the paraphernalia and symbols of Nazism, including old uniforms, helmets, flags, and war medals bearing the swastika.

As a result of the prevalence of ceremonial profanation as a culture form in its own right, today nothing is immune. The more highly regarded the event, the more likely it is to be a target of profanation. The chief requirement is that it not have been already overprofaned, so that the act will be original and will not be discounted in advance by its intended audience. Be it a football game, graduation ceremony, ship-launching, the Kentucky Derby, or the Indianapolis 500, somebody will someday deign to profane the event and capture the audience for their own personal fantasy of self-exhibition, social revolution, or simple madness.

The behavior of vandals has been ritualized into a highly conventionalized performance comparable in motive and effect to that of food throwers, kickers, spillers, and stealers found in nursery schools and families. Being a form of direct action, it can hardly be ignored, and by threat of escalation it neutralizes control action based on superior or even overwhelming force. However, violation of the situational proprieties and deliberate assaults on Emily Post have piquancy only so long as there is an element of surprise. When such behavior is generalized as a new norm, it loses its charm. Some contemporary extremists think they are signaling the beginning of a prison revolt when actually they are only throwing a nursery school tantrum.

As a variety of ritual desecration, vandalism is a rite of rebellion run amuck. In New York City, the deliberate destruction of comfort stations has become a spreading form of urban guerilla warfare. Burning and breaking warns respectable people to shun the area, while the destroyers—addicts or others to whom a burnt-out building is valuable—take over.[23] Vandalism is a mirror of the times; the damaged legitimacy of most institutions makes looting and vandalism a heroic action. Day and night, the schools of America suffer befoulment, overturned furniture, splashed paint in classrooms, and broken doors and toilet seats in the johns. British sociologist Stanley Cohen notes the ritual significance of what appears to be meaningless property destruction: "It is a political judgement." Every act of vandalism carries a heavy freight of motivation and logic.[24]

Shoplifting may be looked on as the youth version of Master Charge and Bankamericard. "Ripping-off" has acquired new respectability among affluent whites. Rationalized as a political act, it serves, among other things, the purpose of facilitating a protracted period of economic dependence and adolescence. It is part of a subculture of exploitation that lives off the work of parents and straights by begging, pan-handling, scavenging food from garbage cans, and furniture from public dumps and from Salvation Army stores. "The big stores rip off the people with their profits, so why shouldn't we rip them off," argues the Washington underground newspaper *Quick Silver Times*. "Anything that screws up the system and gets people to flip out is good;" for many people stealing is at once a political act of revolution, a means of survival, and a form of ecological recycling.[25]

The rationale of retaliation does not accord with the actual selection of targets. The occurrence of vandalism and theft seems rather to be related to vulnerability, with communes and free stores, Mom and Pop grocery stores, the old, the high, the helpless, cherry blossoms, trash containers, pay phones, and vending machines being the most common victims. Public schools, universities, museums, and parks are also popular targets because they are universally accessible and usually undefended. The Woodstock Nation has not become a tribe of kleptomaniacs, but, like all culture forms, its values have been used to rationalize patterns of behavior that are neither new, nor restricted to radical youth.

THE WOODSTOCK NATION

The street party, the carnival, the Mardi Gras, and ritual vandalism all have much in common with political demonstrations of recent years. The be-in, and the 1969 Woodstock festival and its countless imitations were recognized street occasions in which roofless and open space, usually in mild weather, became by definition stages for socially defined behavior unlike that which is appropriate in a private setting. The very fact of group encounter, strangeness, anonymity, the reinforcement of numbers, inverts the normal sense of danger and the reflexes of self-protection, liberating people from their private roles. Street theater is an "open region" where instant social accessibility is recognized and facilitated, where extravagant and fleeting claims on life may be projected by every repressed ego. Even Wall Street bankers had a famous be-in during the summer of 1969, celebrating a young girl with an enormous bust much in the same way as the young rebels on the campus seize as excuse the obvious sins and faults of society.

People who are forced together, or come together voluntarily, on such occasions radiate assumptions of trust and good-will. This value system is built into such open regions. It is the only way a crowd protects itself from the implicit dangers of sudden social fusion. The same system of values manifests itself during a natural disaster when individuals suddenly find themselves locked together in a predicament. Tragedy has struck and may strike again, and all are suddenly aware of their mutual dependence for information and help. All of the ordinary constraints on communication among strangers are put aside. The anxiety and tension that exist in all relationships are liberated as a kind of free-floating energy.

Many have remarked on the curious paradox that natural disaster creates a sense of gaiety and excitement whose contagion overrides even the tragedies of the moment. A disaster creates a ceremonial occasion with many of the same dynamics as those seen in convivial carnivals and costumed street demonstrations. The Woodstock festival is cited as an instance of half-a-million people creating a new culture that enabled them to live for three days under disastrous conditions with bountiful toleration, mutual help, and an intense sense of the moment. In this case, the aftertaste was good, the disappointments, inconvenience, and disorientation of the event temporary. For many of the participants, it was the first great ceremonial occasion of their lives, a mass postpuberty rite in a world that offers the young few meaningful ceremonies. Thus, it provided the impetus for a mystique and a cult. It was an ordeal and a ritual such as earlier generations achieved at summer camp in the mountains or during a Boy Scout Jamboree.

The *Village Voice* said it was a "hip version of Jones Beach transported to a war zone in Vietnam during the Monsoon." At one point, local officials asked Governor Rockefeller to declare Sullivan County a disaster area. Camaraderie and bonds of mutuality are commanded by the priorities of circumstance. The same thing existed a month later on the Gulf coast of Mississippi when (as *The New York Times* reported August 23, 1969) "banded together by hurricane calamity, black and white Mississippians were eating together and living together in the biggest exercise of integrated living in the state's history." There is nothing like flood, wind, war, and revolution to join a crowd into a structured and disciplined social order, fused by legitimacy and love.

The mammoth celebration at Woodstock created a three-day utopia. As Stanley Kaufman wrote, this was somewhat easier to achieve than a permanent state: "It proved very little about possibilities for future life, and that may be one reason it had small continuing effect." Woodstock was a ritual of rebellion, a rejection of politics, rather than its assertion. "Everyone was anti-war, but that's like being pro-sex, much more biological than political." The very gentleness that made the weekend a success was rooted in political apathy. The three-and-a-half-hour film of the event reveals "not a culture of opposition," but what young Germans call "a culture of 'ohne mich,' (without me)."[26] In the middle of a performance by Peter Townsend and *The Who,* Abbie Hoffman unaccountably invaded the stage and grabbed a mike, calling on the assembled horde of half-a-million to rise up from the farmsite, overflow the boundaries, and march on surrounding establishment targets. Hoffman was booed off the stage. He retired in ignominy, arguing and laughing like a harmless madman as he retreated into the marijuana haze.[27] If Woodstock represented the turning point from the activist form of rebellion ritual to an inward, passive, and expressive communal celebration, the Hoffman incident was a key event that signaled the conversion. Similarly, the murder at Altamont marked the close of the Woodstock phase and the beginning of a regression from community to solipsism, from group ritual to self-exploration.

It is the sad fate of events to be travestied by repetition. At Altamont, and later in numerous other rock festivals, motorcycle gangs assumed control, and ecstasy turned to revulsion. The epitome of antiyouth, the Hell's Angels are bearded and beefy, affecting the image of warriors past their prime, satiated with food and drink like conquering Romans, hedonists of brutality and sadism. These sated patriarchs, scowling, gurgling, farting, and spitting, became the guardsmen of mass rock rituals, pushing, slapping, punching, and stomping like bordello flatulists. Goldman says, "The most unyielding generation in American history is demanding—and receiving—punishment by big father figures with ogre faces, beer bellies, and the humorless pompishness of dragons rising to the provocation of young twirpy hippies."[28]

At Altamont, these symbols of coercion and intimidation were hired to keep order and they continued to do so through the Louisiana Festival of Life of July 1971. The selection of the Hell's Angels was inevitable, in spite of the recurrent waves of terrorism against youth enacted by motorcycles gangs throughout the land. They were. identified with the counter-culture. They were (at least by courtesy) youth. The effete collegiate drop-outs thought to identify with their dynamism and muscle as a means of avoiding their hostility and also to frighten conventional society with the existence of a praetorian guard. Further, the police functions of the festival had to be performed by someone. Official authorities could not be trusted to respect the values of the gathering, the dope, sex, and nudism that had become indispensible parts of the scene. Finally, and most important, if the Hell's Angels were excluded, they would come anyway in a state of mobilized force to subdue and conquer, if not destroy, the festival. At Altamont, they were the custodians of law and order, high on drugs and drink, with no counterforce to oppose them. With none of the restraints of responsibility or loyalty to the official code of the occasion, they were free to act out their basic infantilism and sadism. Armed with billiard cues, tire chains, and all manner of hidden weapons, they occupied the area around the stage with increasing irritation and viciousness, like tormented Godzillas, practicing self-indulgent aggression at the least provocation. When their authority was impugned by verbal backlash or physical resistance, they combined to stomp the hapless victim. The hopped-up black who drew a gun was quickly surrounded by Angels and stabbed to death. Mick

Jaggar, His Satanic Majesty of Rock, flopped about the stage like a futile puppet. Then, the Stones in a panic crowded into a helicopter and flew out of the lonely crowd, leaving behind the corpse of the Woodstock nation.

The forces that erupted at Altamont lurk close to the surface at every rock concert. The concert becomes a reportable event and a benchmark of culture only by outdoing. The transition from fence-breaking and cop-baiting to an orgy of madness and bad trips is easily accomplished. The power of the rock performer as a sacred ritual figure may have induced Jagger to overestimate his magical powers. Goldman suggests that Mick assumed that

if things got out of hand, he could do his Moses dividing the Red Sea bit and roll back the crowds. . . . One of the film's [*Gimme Shelter*] few valid ironies is the image of a sadly deflated Jagger, standing on stage like a little boy in a Superman suit, vainly pleading with people who have lost interest in his music because they are fighting for their lives.[29]

In subsequent years, rock festivals throughout the country became tangles of unsuccess. Organizers attempted to offset possible gate crashers by recording and filming the proceeds for separate release in the form of films and records, trying to top the commercial success of the original Woodstock. However, once the full range of possibility had been exploited as popular culture, the genre was no longer available as an art form. A thousand would-be Woodstocks throughout the world turned from magic into a tedium of chronic failure without redeeming qualities. Each of the major gargantuan rock festival sequels showed a heavy toll of bad trips and deaths due to drowning, sleeping in the path of traffic, and overdoses by increasingly younger celebrants zonked out of their hulking gourds by every variety of chemical bubbling in their veins.

NOTES

1. Albert Goldman, *Freak Show* (New York: Atheneum, 1971), p. 149.

2. *Binghamton Press*, February 1, 1971, p. B-8.

3. See Harry Slochower, *Mythopoesis* (Detroit: Wayne State University Press, 1970), p. 72.

4. Max Gluckman, *Rituals of Rebellion in Southeast Africa* (Manchester, Eng.: Manchester University Press, 1954), p. 3.

5. *Ibid.*, p. 26.

6. Victor W. Turner, *The Ritual Process: Structure and Anti-Structure* (Chicago: Aldine, 1969), p. 78.

7. *Ibid.*, pp. 78–79.

9. Alfred Adler, "The Practice and Theory of Individual Psychology," in Thorne Shipley, ed., *Classics in Psychology* (New York: Philosophical Library, 1961), p. 690.

9. Peter C. Rosenbaum, *The Meaning of Madness* (New York: Science House, 1970), p. 57.

10. *Ibid.*, pp. 86–87.

11. William G. Van der Kloot, *Behavior* (New York: Holt, Rinehart and Winston, 1968), p. 148.

12. *Time*, January 18, 1971, p. 22.

13. *The New York Times*, June 9, 1971, p. 16.

14. *Ibid.*, July 19, 1970, p. 6.

15. Monica Wilson, *Communal Rituals of the Nyakyusa* (New York: Oxford University Press, 1959), p. 216.

16. Erving Goffman, *Asylums: Essays on the Social Situation of Mental Patients and Other Inmates* (Garden City, N.Y.: Doubleday, 1961), p. 110.

17. *Ibid.*, pp. 97, 109.

18. *Ibid.*, pp. 36–38.

19. Rosenbaum, 1970, pp. 38–39.

20. Turner, 1969, p. 172.

21. Max Gluckman, "Ritual and Office in Tribal Society," in Gluckman, ed., *Essays on the Ritual of Social Relations* (Manchester, Eng.: Manchester University Press, 1962), pp. 70–71.

22. Konrad Lorenz, *On Aggression* (New York: Grosset & Dunlap, 1967), p. 75.

23. Statement of August Heckscher, Park Administrator, *The New York Times*, March 19, 1971, p. 35.

24. Quoted in *Time*, January 19, 1970, p. 45.

25. *Binghamton Press*, September 27, 1970, p. 4.

26. *The New Republic*, May 2, 1970, p. 20.

27. Jim Marshall, Baron Wolman, Jerry Hopkins, *Festival: The Book of American Music Celebrations* (New York: Macmillan, 1970), p. 168.

28. Albert Goldman, review of *Gimme Shelter*, *The New York Times*, January 3, 1971, p. D-9.

29. *Ibid.*

8 | MANIAS & SEIZURES

This isn't a riot. It's a goddam orgy. (a Pittsburgh policeman, 1971)

DOWNTOWN PITTSBURGH TORN INTO SHAMBLES
A massive World Series victory celebration exploded Sunday night into a rampage of destruction, looting and sex-in-the streets.
Newsmen reported two apparent assaults—some of them in full view of hundreds who cheered the assailants—displays of public lovemaking, nudity and drinking.
At the height of the melee a police desk sergeant said he had calls reporting about a dozen rapes . . . .
The disturbance left the downtown area in shambles.
More than 100 persons were injured and nearly 100 others . . . .
(Associated Press, October 18, 1971)

Most private encounters are motivated by the various needs, designs, and incentives of the participants. In typical situations, the usual forms of polite social intercourse provide methods by which a gradual exchange of values or a nonprovocative withdrawal may occur. Social distance and manners tend to protect, buffer, and test the development of mutuality of interest. The ceremonial occasion of a carnival or a disaster, however, guarantees that encounters are not and should not be the basis for lasting relationships and exchanges of value. Consequently, many of the safeguards for negotiating long-term relationships are relaxed. It becomes possible to appropriate a new value here or there with the hope of not paying for it, in a psychological sense. Individuals may fornicate amid the shrubs and cows in much the same way as black teenagers loot liquor and department stores during a ghetto riot.

In such a situation, new values are born every minute as persons ratify each other's acts by imitation, signs of approval, and mutual participation. It is this process that makes it possible for crowds to become mobs, capable of the most unlikely and despicable actions. A desperate youth stands on the ledge of a high building while, amid laughter and obscenities, the crowd yells "Jump, man, jump!" Although it falls short of mob action, a ceremonial crowd also encourages behavior that is improvised rapidly from the materials at hand, whose imitation by others becomes a test of loyalty to the occasion's code. The ritual of spontaneous ratification of innovative acts leads to crowd actions that may have political consequences and characterizations. It may also lead to uncontrollable situations in which violent attacks, counter-attacks, and preemptive attacks may occur. Mass hysteria may arise from this process, as a form of inappropriate and harmful ritual, although most rituals of rebellion are appropriate and useful to the cultures in which they occur.[1]

SPIRIT POSSESSION

Instances of spirit possession, a form of ritual rebellion, are widespread in tribal cultures. Dancing is widely associated with the achievement of a possessed state and is used also by medicine men as a means of therapy for an individual thought to be pathologically possessed. Among the Tonga of Zambia, studied by Elizabeth Colson, a malady known as mad dance was widespread and the subject of considerable social ambivalence. Some authorities sought to punish and prevent it, while for many of the people it had real legitimacy as a form of defense and attack against external authority and injustice. An epidemic of mad dance broke out in a girl's boarding school in 1962, with girl after girl falling into the pattern for days, then demanding soapy water to drink. Under official repression, mad dance began to occur among adolescent girls throughout the country. Colson noted that the statistics demonstrated also that

women under stress seem likely to be possessed. We noted a number of instances of barren wives or wives whose children had died who were treated for possession shortly after the successful delivery of a co-wife. A dance might also follow a period of quarrelling between spouses. Several outstanding dancers possessed by many different spirits are regarded by kin and neighbors as easily excited by trifles, forever running to diviners when others are prepared to wait on further events.[2]

John Beattie and John Middleton note that spirit possession allows an individual to throw off restraints and act in ways not sanctioned by his ordinary social role. Whatever be the physical and psychological difficulties of the "possession syndrome," they note that "some personal benefits may at times accrue. Redress or en-

hancement of status is one such compensation . . . some readjustment in the relative status of the sexes may be promoted. . . ."[3]

Beattie and Middleton conceive of the trance state (locking the
hands together and tensing the muscles, rhythmic swinging of the
head, shuffling the feet in time with the monotony of a drum beat)
as a cultural phenomenon: "Even apart from occasions of collective
ecstasy, as in the charismatic phases of pentecostal sectarian gatherings, the sheer expectations of an audience often help to provide
the situations congenial to the development of trance behavior in
persons in the appropriate social position."[4] The trance state is a
form of medical practice as well as social ritual. Well-known mediums charge heavily for their services throughout tribal Africa.
Rituals of cult initiation are usually carried out under the direction of professional mediums who have mastered highly dramatic
qualities of performance. The professional appears in striking and
colorful attire and a special spirit language and vocabulary are used
that are frequently incomprehensible to the audience. The possession
is drama as well as dance and involves considerable dramaturgical
structure, implying suspense, development, conflict, climax, and
resolution in the same manner as in ancient Greek religious theater. The performances provide not only a means of catharsis, but
a lively form of entertainment.

The problem of analysis of spirit mediumship is not concerned
with "spiritual versus human phenomenon," but of "unconscious
versus conscious production of symptoms." In cases where a medium is thought to "fake it," the social question becomes the issue
of legitimacy. Was the performance poorly done, ill-timed, inappropriate for the circumstances? Were the purposes of the performer suspect, competitively discounted, rejected by other legitimate authorities who themselves represent a social consensus? Did
the social values represented by the performance fail to inspire support for whatever reasons? The medium's own cynicism about the
trance state provides no basis for a decision, for it may reflect merely
the persistent lack of positive reinforcement in the response.

In Australia, the itinerant hunting culture of the bushman contains large amounts of energy devoted to ritual dancing. The primary activities of the men when they are not hunting are visiting,
entertaining, and dancing. The trance dance is the focus of social
life: "At some camps, trance dances occur as frequently as two or
three times a week and those who have inner trances the night before rarely go out hunting the following day."[5]

Pierre Verger describes the role of rhythmic drumming in the
conventions of trance in Nago-Yoruba: "The role played by the
drums in the incitement of possession is a vital one; but it is not

the mere mechanical action of an overwhelming rhythm, thousands of times repeated that causes the trance." Each phase and act of the ritual drama is marked by a separate movement and change of rhythm. "It is only the hearing of his particular rhythm at the stage of the feast when the God is called that incites the trance of his medium." The drums enjoy respect as "the voice of the gods themselves; through them, the gods are called and answer at the same time. The sound of the drums is vital in building-up the atmosphere of the ceremony, and is particularly impressive in a civilization based on spoken words and not on written ones." The drums are a magical form of speech which by their rhythm lock themselves together with the rhythm of movement, of heartbeat, of breathing, of measured development within a framework of regularity, transcending biology and individuality, giving validity and outward form to the moral dimensions of life.[6]

A comparable scene could be observed in one of the famed discothèques of the middle 1960's, L'Oursin, which was typical of the genre, combining a flashing light show with the throb of rock. Goldman writes,

Those dancers out on the floor: what do they look like? It's the tribe readying itself for an orgy. What is an orgy? It is an alignment with force like iron particles patterned by magnetic fields. Combine enough excitement with enough narcosis, and you slip out of yourself and perform acts of public sex with no embarrassment or guilt. Is it a holy act? Yes, because it celebrates some force bigger than the individual's consciousness and outside his consciousness.[7]

The pattern of possession and mediumship is not limited to black tribes. Under whatever name or religious interpretation, whether known as ecstasy, pythonism, devil-dancing, shamanism, spiritism, spiritualism, or rock music festivals, similar rituals occur in all cultures and have generated a vast literature extending over at least two thousand years. In the classical Greek period, accounts of dionysiac cults refer to god possession in which the worshipers see visions and perform feats of an extraordinary kind. Throughout most of its history, Christianity has sanctified possession and mediumship. Anti-Christian spirits representing primitive witchcraft, devils, and paganism were denied legitimacy, but otherwise possession by the Holy Spirit was treated as a divine and sacred condition to which not only saints but all could aspire. Raymond Firth notes that spiritualism has flourished in modern nations, especially after the First World War when "bereaved families wished to get in touch with their loved sons who had died."[8] The continued popularity of ESP, psychokinetics, Christian Science, faith healing, and so on testify to the continued power of rituals of this kind.

Spirit cults provide a way of coping with potentially inimical forces in order to come to terms with them.

Almost always traditional mediumistic cults are essentially conservative . . . yet we have noted that mediumship plays an important role in situations of radical and disturbing social change. The paradox is resolved if we accept that in most traditional societies, change is regarded as something unwanted, even as dangerous and evil. . . . The forces of radical change may be spiritualized in order that they may be accommodated and thus in some way controlled.[9]

The role of spirit possession reported among the Tonga, the Alur, the Zulu, the Banyoro, and the peoples of Southern Ghana provide a means by which are comprehended the agents of change, which are thereby incorporated into a mythological system. Further, spirit possession provides a basis for the legitimization of new patterns of power and authority. In the postwar period, the revival of tribal values and nationalism have become associated with renewed respectability and legitimacy for rituals of spirit possession.

In studies of religious societies of a century ago, Charles Nordhoff notes how spirit possession was a means by which leaders maintained the status of a sacred personage. While in a trance state, this personage could relieve the tensions of the community by talking freely of things otherwise banned, and could obtain divine sanction for policy pronouncements, putting them beyond discussion. A policy decision so delivered could be revised only in a future religious trance.[10] In the Amana community, the "inspired person," possessed by a godlike spirit, plays an important role in the annual inquisition of the community, an examination of its spiritual condition. Nordhoff writes, "This is done by classes or orders, beginning with the elders themselves; and I judge from the relations of this ceremony in their printed books that it lasts long, and is intended to be very thorough. Each member is expected to make confession of his sins, faults, short-comings; and if anything is hidden, they believe it will be brought to light by the inspired person, who assumes on this occasion an important part, admonishing individuals very freely, and denouncing the sins and evils that exist in the congregation.[11]

Nordhoff also reports on the Kentucky revival of the 1820's, in which thousands of people were drawn into a mass seizure known as the jerks. To dance was the only cure, and men danced until they dropped to the ground. "It was of no use to try to resist the jerks. Young men sometimes came determined to make fun of the proceedings and were seized before they knew of it." A young fellow, famous for drinking, cursing, and violence, was leaning against a tree when he was jerked to the ground slam-bang. He swore he would not dance until it was a wonder he was not killed. At last he had to dance. Throughout the hills of Kentucky, the settlers came together to jerk and to dance and to worship God, returning to their farms and to their private lives with a sense of a vast community of which they were a part, "a manifestation of the power of God."[12]

Such instances of mass hysteria occur all the time. In 1955, London's Royal Free Hospital reported a deluge of three hundred patients who had identical symptoms and no verifiable disease. Contagious hysteria has been well-documented in many kinds of situations, such as the witch-hunting in New Salem or the dancing manias of Germany in the Middle Ages. Events of recent years give us insight into the process. Possibly the study of such historical incidents would indicate that they were not isolated outbreaks but were related to conflict groups and social change in much the same way as was the mass hysteria of militant students in 1970 who burned and ravaged Isla Vista and Harvard Square.

Lewis S. Feuer writes of the famous Wartburg festival of October 9, 1817, when the first major conclave of students in the modern world came together. A universal German Student Union was formed during an exalting, rebellious, festival occasion. All Europe took notice of the festival and it evoked a controversial literature, "raising this outburst of student revelry to the level of a European event."[13] The waves of U.S. campus riots in 1969 and 1970 similarly contained a strong festive element.

On many campuses, the storm troopers of Consciousness III reacted to the murders at Kent State and the U.S. Cambodian invasion by occupying student union buildings and staging a week-long binge of togetherness sustained by drugs and wine, sex and vandalism. The exaltation was unmistakable. Virtually everyone experienced a sense of outrage, complicity, and guilt that confirmed the celebrators in their self-righteousness. The new outrages of the Nixon administration seemed to prove all of the charges and were greeted as symptoms of the inevitable collapse of the system. Giddy with this prospect, strikers all over the country rose up to give orders to presidents, congressmen, senators, and commissioners.

Bruno Bettelheim counseled many activists at the University of Chicago, including one of the leaders. The latter "took part in every demonstration he could," Bettelheim declared, because "while they lasted they gave him a temporary feeling of closeness to others.

For the same reason, he pressed for as many and as drawn-out demonstrations as he could." Then one day, on a protest march, the instruction was given that each should hold someone else's hand. "It so happened that he found himself without anyone holding his . . . . Much later recalling the incident in therapy, he still remembered it with tears." Another student activist said the political explosions relieved the tedium and provided meaning and identity: "I could now picket, distribute leaflets, run off to Washington, work and talk to people all over the country as if I had a connection to other people." She confessed that during a confrontation with a university president, "I was aware that . . . if we were granted what we said we wanted, we could no longer protest, we would be useless, we would be nothing, we would have to face ourselves."[14] During the Columbia rebellion, the climate inside the occupied buildings involved "an intense communal life . . . in which the students at last enjoyed a shared commitment and purpose. . . . This enjoyment became one of the chief purposes of the uprising, something that could not easily be bargained nor negotiated away."

Eric Hoffer noted how the clinics of the university are full every day except during a riot. "Come the riots the clinics are empty. Nobody is sick the moment you get a riot."[15] A reporter who sat with occupying students at the University of Chicago administration building reported the scene as follows. During the long two-week seige (which was given official protection by the president) the students found it hard to sustain togetherness. The same rock music was played over and over again. The supply of marijuana had to be replenished from private sources, as the university only sent in food. The guerilla theater group, calling themselves Chicken-Shitters, came in continuously with their orange armbands, water pistols, and toy rocket guns from their roving tours of the campus, where they had been staging guerilla theater skits in classes, trying to stimulate some repressive reaction from the administration. "But no luck. The students were very friendly and happy to talk," but nobody got excited. "There was a good deal of forced hilarity, but it failed to conceal the prevailing sense of boredom and frustration. Some of the people looked suspiciously young, and confessed they were actually pupils from nearby high schools. . . . They wished the police would come, they said, they wished something would happen."[16]

In 1969 and 1970, the phenomenon of "the rebellion festival bum" became common as young people (both students and nonstudents) began drifting from one college conflagration, political confrontation, rock music festival, to another, from Hashbury to the Isle of Wight, going in search of the easy rider, the shimmering legend of Woodstock, drama and love. "I don't know, man. It sure is a groovy way to spend a summer. So maybe the summer was like a party—a goodbye party and a hello party all wrapped up in one. There we were, all of us, outside, all grooving. Sure, some people would take reds and get up tight and cops went on power trips. But most of it was groovy. Like a celebration. Do you dig?"[17]

Tom Wolfe's Pump House Gang set the pattern with their well-publicized "conventions." In the early 1960's, as hippiedom was aborning, the underground press spread the word, and any kid could come. "One was in the Sorrento Valley in the gulches and arroyos, and the fuzz came . . . the last one was at Manhattan Beach, inside somebodies poor hulking house. Everybody was stoned out of their hulking gourds and it got to be about 3:30 A.M. and everybody decided to go see the riots. Watts was a blast. . . ."[18] In Watts, the Pump House Gang found the same atmosphere—a party! Approaching a gang of black teenagers going into a furniture store, the kids were invited, "Come on in. It's a party and it's free." The looting and rioting blacks were happy and friendly to all, even to white hippies, until a group of helmeted cops came roaring up, "Get the hell out of here, you kids," the cops yelled, "we cannot provide protection."

The festivals of radical militancy became *de rigueur* in the late 1960's and developed a pantheon of ritual figures and slogans. Blood-tingling verbs like *smash* and *rip off* and phrases like "Up against the wall, Mother Fucker!" were combined with ceremonial profanations of all kinds, including the strongest obscenities available. Anyone who found such language lacking in taste, if not content, was automatically a power elite manipulator, an imperialist, or an establishment pig. It became imperative to sound like the member of a depressed minority, especially if you were not one. The safest saints were Malcolm X, Che Guevara, Frantz Fanon, Mao Tse-tung, and Herbert Marcuse. (Although in his *New Left Reader,* Carl Oglesby warns against Marcuse: "He is not the kind of writer whose books explode one out of the study."[19] The cardinal sin of the New Left writer is to keep his readers off the street.) At its height of vitality, the New Left was a remarkable combination of evangelism, German sociology, and Madison Avenue, containing the shrillest of placard slogans and jeers to do the work of Jeremiahs. The solution to every problem was essentially "a street party!"

The waves of student rebellion in this period bore an unmistakeable resemblance to the mania for the early Beatles on their first American tour, the hula hoop craze, fraternity raids, and the spring madness of beach riots—rituals that college students in their campus ghettos invent as a way of demonstrating their insulation and insularity. However, such ritual occasions by their very nature cannot be sustained indefinitely. Behavior that seemed so appropriate, original, exciting, amusing, and intelligent in the ceremonial setting is soon found to be quite otherwise when the occasion ends, as it must. But the memory of the emotional binge creates a great incentive to look for socially legitimate occasions, at least from the point of view of the intended audience, for calling the tribes together again for a reenactment. It is never the same. Disillusionment and reservation must set in.

This syndrome helps to explain the imitative rash of so-called political encounters that swept through the nation in 1969 and 1970. The most liberal and free universities were the first targets. In their guilt and uncertainty, the authorities sought to renew their legitimacy by capitulations to demands, however shallow. They were startled and dismayed that such capitulation seemed to precipitate an escalation of demands and a renewal of the ceremonial forms of mass protests. Studies of campus rebellions show that such actions tend to run a natural course, ending after about two weeks as fatigue, boredom, and the call of private values and life situations reassert themselves and soak up the vast reservoir of free-floating fantasy that had been directed into the rebellion. The natural demise of the ceremonial has often had the effect of isolating the activists and forcing them into attempts to reenergize and radicalize their comrades by more extreme and provocative actions. Such tactics are designed to draw the authorities into mistakes and overreactions that may renew the unity of the participants. Tear gas, tanks, and machine guns resurrect the image of the demonstrators as put-upon and manipulated innocents who must stand together to face the official terror of the authorities.

The original people's park rebellion in Berkeley was a great success. It was widely covered by the press and created a new model for festival confrontations and provocation of the police. Ronald Reagan, already a symbol of reaction and repression, was forced to bring in helicopters and tear gas, collaborating with the instigators of the event in making it a public relations success. Reagan desired to stop all future provocations by enforcing the letter of the law, even at the expense of legitimatizing and publicizing the tactic; he thus guaranteed reenactment of the model throughout the country and annually at the original shrine. Charles Palmer, the Berkeley student who led the original park rebellion, was elected president of the National Student Association on the strength of the event's success. Throughout the country, city parks became gathering places for the young, who deliberately taunted the police, hoping to evoke the "people's park syndrome," the re-enactment of the symbolic clash with evil, personified by governors and police. The destroying of shrubbery, urination on monuments and parking meters, beating the bongo drums, and window smashing and looting in nearby business streets spread throughout the country.

As police and administrators learned to avoid the use of terror tactics as a response to low levels of provocation, the provocation level of the activists had risen as if to force an hysterical reenactment of the old situation. After employing hit-and-run guerilla tactics at the University of Wisconsin, combined with window smashing, overturning cars, and throwing fire-bombs, the young people walked hand-in-hand down State Street singing "We Shall Overcome," imbued with a sense of injured righteousness. Ritualistically, they were the tormented blacks of Alabama led by Martin Luther King, Jr., walking with truth and God at their side, heads held high, right in the face of Sheriff Bull Connor and his redneck storm troopers.

Reagan's mistake was not repeated too often. At Holyoke Center, the street fighters and revolutionaries of Harvard and Boston's hippie community gathered together, hoping to fight for the right to expose their sexual organs and smoke pot. But police had learned from past mistakes. "We are not going to start a war to enforce any curfew," an official said. The initial insurgency dissolved in boredom, bad vibrations, and fatigue after two or three days, at which time the police stepped in and enforced the law. Elsewhere, it took more active provocation to force the hand of police and thereby revive the spirit of injured innocence on the part of the celebrants.

The practices of trashing and direct provocation represented the fag end of the revolutionary festivals. Tom Hayden said,

Who were these white kids anyway, planning to run wild in the streets? Did they need to learn something new about the brutality of the Chicago police? Who was going to be mobilized by these actions? Violence should be used in defense—self-defense—when the police attacked programs which the community supported.[20]

Rituals based on the overreaction of the police were legitimate. When the police no longer overreacted, they could be forced to do so by the overkill of the demonstrators. The martyrs would feel justified in using violence first; in fact, they felt put upon, thinking the police more evil and deserving of punishment because of their deeper strategy. The ritual elements of an event destroy the critical faculty. The very tendency that stabilizes cultural behavior undermines forms that depend on collaboration rituals from others. After

Isla Vista in the summer of 1970, one Santa Barbara student put matters into perspective: "If you make the mistake of taking things too seriously, you're lost, for the situation is far too senseless to permit any rational attempts to deal with it. What you are left with is a kind of unpleasant study in black humor."[21] A seventeen-year-old boy, asked why he had thrown a fire-bomb into a store, shrugged: "because it was there."

"Abbie Hoffmans of the world, unite, you have nothing to lose but your hand-tailored American flag shirts and your funky brand-new imitation old clothes." The athlete, who used to be the big man on campus, was replaced by the militant radical, who has been replaced in turn by the junk-dealer. In each case, the big man on campus acted as a professional ritual figure, endowed with sacred qualities by virtue of the festival functions of his office.

GATHERINGS, CROWDS, AND POWER

Confrontation politics uses the system that Goffman calls "a focused gathering" or a "situated activity system." Because he emphasizes social communication, Goffman must grapple with the ritual, symbolic, and ceremonial dimensions of behavior. Culture is man-made and makes man, and it is constantly in a state of becoming. If persons come together into a focused gathering and stay for a time, certain "systems problems" will have to be solved: "the participants will have to submit to rules of recruitment, to limits on overt hostility, and to some division of labor." In addition, they will have to discover and create some kind of hierarchy of influence so that even a transitory group may coordinate the activities of its participants.

A focused gathering may be preliminary to the creation of a social group or it may take on some of the characteristics of a social group for a limited purpose and occasion and then dissolve. All social groups possess common organizational characteristics, including rules of entering and leaving, rules for collective action, specialization of function within the group (that is, leadership), routines of socialization, and means of satisfying some individual values, of adjusting internal conflict, and relating the group to its physical setting and to the rest of society. Whether formal or informal, these characteristics are found in all social relationships and are most perfectly developed and formalized in groups whose activity is of longer duration, frequency, and importance to the participants, whether the group consists of a relationship between two persons, an interlocking set of friends, a complex organization, a set of business men, a group of players in a game, or some other set.

Shared spontaneous involvement in a mutual activity brings the sharers into some kind of exclusive solidarity and permits them to express relatedness, psychic closeness, and mutual respect; failure to participate with good heart can therefore express rejection of those present or of the setting. Involvement and acceptance of the focus of attention and the improvised rules of behavior of a gathering in an open region, like participation in any social group, confirm the reality of the world prescribed by group unity and by the ratification of each participant's actions through the approval and reaction of his peers. Through the same processes, this reality tends to deny the reality of other potential worlds inhabited by outsiders. Participants enjoy an esoteric standing that they communicate by little signs and fragments of speech that are unintelligible to others. The bafflement of the outsiders adds a delicious quality of amusement and pleasure for the insiders who share a secret truth.

The constraints and behavior norms of a ceremonial gathering, while they generate an enhanced sense of freedom and novelty, are in fact in every way as compulsory for the participants as those of everyday private life. A gathering of strangers, held together by the magic bond of a special occasion, is capable of punishing infractions of the rules, doubts, skepticism, flagging energy, attempts to withdraw, or challenges of the norm more viciously and directly even than the brutal reprisals built into polite society. However, the elements of coercion are muted by the unanimity and high spirits of the occasion, even as the group turns on a doubter or punishes the waverer.

The gathering, the most informal and loosely constructed precursor to the social group, will be strengthened or weakened depending on the outcome of its activity, either moving toward more lasting forms of behavior or, in the face of ill-success, falling apart and rendering the participants available for reformation in other activity groups.[22] If the outcomes are favorable, forms of organization and activity emerge that are likely to be continued or repeated and the gathering will be marked by the participants as a "memorable event," retaining a call on the future loyalty of the individuals involved, and thus limiting their availability for regrouping or dividing their loyalties in other groups. It is a common phenomenon for the survivors of a disaster to feel such a strong sense of identity as to want to keep alive the cause of their group formation, celebrating it in story and song, and organizing annual reunions. One of the survivors may fall into the pathology of striving to reenact the disaster, actually or fraudulently, in an effort to recapture the sense of meaning, community, and dignity that his subsequent life lacked. Thus the survivor of a spectacular fire may become an arsonist.

Individual behavior can be understood only in relation to group values, interests, and norms. Even the anomic individual acts in reference to groups, seeking reinforcement and legitimacy for his actions. Reference-group theory has proved useful in accounting for criminal behavior. The reference group is "that group whose perspective constitutes the frame of reference of the actor" without necessarily being the group in which he is accepted or aspires to be accepted.[23] Ralph H. Turner calls such behavior role-playing; the individual, even though disoriented and socially isolated, takes the role of a member and adopts the group's viewpoint as his own.

Reference-group behavior on the part of an individual (whether he is or is not a member of the group) is often dismissed as *post hoc* alibi and rationalization. A great deal of extreme individual behavior occurs as an impulsive reflex response to provocative stimuli not fully comprehended by an excited actor. His attempts to legitimize his reflex will exploit any material he believes to be plausible to an auditor, and will therefore be of no diagnostic or analytic value. The dismissal of such rationalization, however, ignores a fundamental principle of *all* behavior, that is, its causes are always imperfectly understood by the actor who always seeks legitimacy by aligning himself with such individuals and groups as may reinforce and accept him. In other words, the process of *post hoc* rationalization is precisely the same as the process that leads individuals to identify with groups and coordinate their own behavior with group norms.

Reference-group behavior is a projection of fantasy and a ritual. It may be otherwise unrelated to organizational or purposeful behavior of group members. The hijackers of the ship *Columbia Eagle* declared that they were acting as part of an SDS-sponsored campaign to sabotage arms shipments to Southeast Asia. In fact, it turned out that neither of the hijackers had any direct contact with SDS and had been spending most of their time at sea prior to the hijacking. Through the fantasy of reference-group behavior they sought to rationalize and justify their action by the standards of legitimacy achieved by the slogans of SDS. The crew members reported that the two hijackers, who had also been crew members, were unpopular from the beginning, unwilling to do tasks that were assigned to them and spending most of their time smoking marijuana.

Durkheim argues that religious phenomena arise from the increased power that individuals feel when they are part of ritual festivities (the "great collective effervescence during periods of concentration.") Malinowski argues that the heightening of emotions is by no means restricted to gatherings and to crowd phenomena. "The lover near his sweetheart, the daring adventurer conquering his fears in the face of real danger, the hunter at grips with a wild animal, the craftsman achieving a masterpiece . . . ," all experience a sense of exaltation that could be interpreted as sacred.[24]

The classic work on crowds by Gustave Le Bon (written in 1895) notes the existence of "the law of the mental unity of crowds."[25] This unity endows the crowd with characteristics not possessed by isolated individuals and gives the crowd an identity of its own. Solely because of numerical considerations, he says, the individual in the crowd acquires a "sentiment of invincible power which allows him to yield to instincts which had he been alone he would perforce have kept under restraint." In addition to power, the crowd provides anonymity, thereby destroying the accountability that might make the use of power responsible. The individual is subject to mindless contagion: "It must be cast among phenomenon of the hypnotic order . . . every sentiment and act is contagious and contagious to such a degree that an individual readily sacrifices his individual interest to the collective interest."[26]

Elias Canetti bases his analysis of crowd behavior on the universal habit of ecological separation of human organisms: "All life is laid out in distances" for all men, "the house in which he shuts himself and his property, the positions he holds, the rank he desires—all these serve to create distances."[27] Integrity of self and elaborate manners that regulate touching and physical contact express imperatives of distance that underly the social structure. In a crowd, Canetti declares, men free themselves from this burden: "during the discharge, his functions are thrown off and all feel equal. In that density, where there is scarcely any space between and body presses against body, each man is as near the other as he is to himself; and an immense feeling of relief ensues." But the discharge is dangerous. "It is based on an illusion" and cannot be maintained against the inevitable strain of separation. Crowds run their course and then dissolve back into lonely and private individuals.

Canetti goes on to state that the crowd legitimizes itself by growth; the process of discharge can be continued only as new people are sucked up into the cortex of its action. This is seen as the main incentive for aggressiveness of crowds. Under the threat of disintegration, the crowd goes in search of victims to struggle against, thus justifying the suspension of ethics and the values of private identity. "The crowd particularly likes destroying houses and objects, breaking objects like mirrors, window panes, pictures and crockery . . ." Fragility stimulates destructiveness; "the banging of windows and the crashing of glass, the robust sounds of fresh life, the cries of something newborn. It is easy to evoke them and that increases their popularity. Everything shouts together; the din is the applause of objects." Noise is a promise of reinforcement and an omen of deeds to come. "The destruction of representational images is the destruction of the hierarchy which is no longer recognized."[28]

All rebellions against traditional ceremonial recounted in the history of religions, Canetti claims, have been directed against "the confinement of the crowd which wants to feel the sensation of its own growth." The Sermon on the Mount is enacted in the open, and "there is no doubt that it is directed against the limiting ceremoniousness of the Temple." He views Pauline Christianity as an attempt to break out of the boundaries of Judaism to become universal and Buddhism as an attempt to break out of the Indian caste system. Revolutionary crowds represent a sudden transition "from a closed into an open crowd," the result of "a sudden will to attract, the passionate determination to reach all men." This desire cannot be satiated. The crowd remains hungry so long as one human being has not been reached. Anyone who resists is an enemy and must be destroyed. The only hope of terminating the eruption lies in awaiting the natural results of fatigue or success. This end is inevitable, but it may be postponed by "the double-crowd," against which a crowd may measure itself: "The closer in power and intensity the rivals are, the longer both of them will stay alive."[29] Nation-states are crowds that have been formalized but can only survive in a world of worthy rivals.

Canetti's metaphor is simplistic. While not without power to explain the data, it carries a freight of unnecessary assumptions. His original assumption regarding individual distance and loneliness denies the content and significance of mass behavior. Such an analysis ignores the variables of ecological space in exactly the same way as do the postulations of a territorial imperative. Distance and structures are responsive to a host of social processes that must be understood in analyzing why a "crowd crystal" may lead to a crowd under certain circumstances but not under others. Crowds may expand and endure for longer or shorter times and have greater or lesser social and political impacts. The complex variables of crowd behavior cannot be reduced to the seamless and automatic dynamic offered by Le Bon and Canetti. Both of these theorists were impelled to castigate and denounce crowd behavior. Laudible as their motives may be, denunciation and exhortation will not work. The notion that sophisticated and rational men must be exhorted against the overwhelming effects of sacred rituals is futile posturing. No one is immune to the process of ritual, and a society that lacks or seeks to inhibit rituals of rebellion would be in a continuous stage of seige, internecine strife, and the very condition of mob anarchy that Le Bon and Canetti want to prevent.

Rituals of rebellion are not merely expressive and cathartic, but also innovative. They have political uses not only in conserving institutions and culture forms but also in maintaining the capability of change and adaptability. Technological societies with their high level of organization and specialization impose a protracted adolescence and a formalized educational system on their members. For centuries innovative rituals of rebellion have characteristically begun among the college generation. The students are strategically situated for taking the initiative. "Only students can do it, because they need not worry about their earnings at all." Moreover, society is prepared to grant students liberties that it allows no other group. The courts show unusual reluctance to pass judgment on students involved in disturbances. Feuer writes that the student "is perceived as society's naive child acting upon the ideas which it has been taught, and society is embarrassed by the children who quote to it its own ideals."[30] The college generation, moreover, represents the children of the elite and the privileged heirs to power. Like all insurgent power groups, they are constantly engaged in symbolic challenges and testing. They grasp the contradictions made obvious by changing social priorities and conditions, and use this understanding as the basis of a claim to ethical superiority.

Crisis and external conflict tend to legitimize existing authorities and to give certainty and confidence to existing goals and activity systems. During such periods, students find their claims aborted, rebuffed, and disregarded. Their rituals of rebellion become mainly expressive, cementing the bonds of community and friendship among cadres of future professionals. However, in times of respite from the perceived legitimacy of large national purposes, the organizing structures of the whole society become loose, and incumbent leaders become uncertain of their roles. The rituals of rebellion of students and other groups cease to be merely expressive and become political. Initially, formal authorities respond with threats combined with promises of rewards for compliance; next, they employ outright repression and retaliation. The latter tactic strengthens the emerging ritual and lends it greater currency and legitimacy. At the next stage, the existing social structure must absorb many of the proffered values, while permitting the rituals themselves to be conducted permissively. In time, the more open response tends to undermine the political momentum of the dissent; toleration for new and experimental values removes the ritual incentives. At this point, the complex process of proving and assimilating new values into the on-going private and public activities of the system is underway. The results defy forecast and can only be rationalized in generalities.

The role of the young in rituals of rebellion achieves its greatest efficacy after the basis of existing values has already changed. That change creates the vacuum and opportunity that tempts the political strategists of untempered and idealistic youth to excess. Every good movement encourages vulgarization by its very success. Success is again the father of unsuccess, as culture modulates and limits the costly events of history.

The same dynamic applies to rituals of rebellion pioneered by other groups. Every insurgent movement exploits the contradictions of the status quo as a claim to superior virtue and wisdom. Every group exploits the cost in blood and misery of every other group symbolically. As the Black Panthers became the strong arm of numerous other groups, Hell's Angels and the White Panthers sought to capture the momentum by imitation. The wave of college rebellions merely changed the rhetoric. Every spokesman for every cause turned from threatening his peers with black riots to threatening them instead with SDS uprisings. The dichotomy in 1971 between Spiro Agnew and liberal spokesmen concerned the invocation of magical authority that one side declared and the other denied. In the same way other generations quoted or refuted Freud, the Bible, Aquinas, or Aristotle.

Most of the apostles of revolutionary change who fathered the contemporary student movement have been turned off by its unanticipated success. The late Paul Goodman, anarchist and spokesman to youth five years ago, now is unread and unknown by the current crop of youth, who abhor long-winded and difficult books. He was piqued at them and attacked their "religious reformation" as lacking order and rational action.[31] Similarly, French political analyst and philosopher Raymond Aron dismisses the student movement (as does Robert Brustein) as merely "psycho-drama," a theater of temporary and fictitious solidarity into which went "a colossal release of suppressed feeling" but which produced neither a revolutionary climax nor the possibility of effective reforms.[32] Their disgust reflects the vulgarization of the culture forms, but belies the impact the youth movement had on culture and values. As a ritual of rebellion, every demonstration can become a confrontation. If all of the parties play their roles properly, confrontation is easy to arrange. The civil rights march on Washington in 1963 was a demonstration, eliciting general fear and arousing a national capability for action on part of established black leaders. The ritual of mau-mauing the Office of Economic Opportunity was built on such events.

The personal threat and response of a confrontation is the payoff and leads to a concrete exchange of social values between real persons. "You!—we are not talking about the government, we are not talking about the Office of Economic Opportunity—we're talking about you, up there with your hands shaking and your pile of papers . . ." This ritual was built into the poverty program and, as Tom Wolfe pointed out, the poverty bureaucrats "depended upon confrontations in order to know what to do."[33] Rituals of rebellion can in this way be politically significant and powerful without ever being more than symbolic.

Rituals of rebellion are a complex phenomenon, universal in organized societies, and serving many functions. They are a fit subject in the study of cultural and political change. Though ambiguous in their outcomes and responsive to the strategic interactions that rule the ritual cycle, they are more fundamental than the formalized institutions of government and representation. Like all symbolic processes, they are capable of conserving social energy while accomplishing major social purposes.

NOTES

1. The definition of hysteria contains a value-assumption: "inappropriate" and "harmful" is ascribed to the outcome of such behavior, thereby implying a *post hoc* evaluation.

2. Elizabeth Colson, "Spirit Possession Among the Tonga of Zambia," in John Beattie and John Middleton, eds., *Spirit Membership and Society in Africa* (New York: Africana Publishing, 1969), pp. 92–93.

3. Beattie and Middleton, 1969, p. xii.

4. *Ibid.*, p. xiii.

5. Richard B. Lee, "What Hunters Do for a Living, or How to Make Out on Scarce Resources," in Lee and Irven Devore, eds., *Man the Hunter* (Chicago: Aldine, 1968), p. 37.

6. Pierre Verger, "Trance and Convention in Nago-Yoruba Spirit Membership," in Beattie and Middleton, 1969, p. 59.

7. Albert Goldman, *Freak Show* (New York: Atheneum, 1971), p. 42.

8. Raymond Firth, "Forward" in Beattie and Middleton, 1969, p. ix.

9. Beattie and Middleton, p. xxviii.

10. See Charles Nordhoff, *The Communistic Societies of the United States* (New York: Schocken Books, 1965, originally published in 1875).

11. *Ibid.*, p. 54.

12. *Ibid.*, p. 209.

13. Lewis S. Feuer, *The Conflict of Generations* (New York: Basic Books, 1969), p. 58.

14. Bruno Bettelheim, testifying in the U.S. Senate Committee on Government Operations, Subcommittee on Investigations, *Hearings, Riots, Civil and Criminal Disorders*, 90th Congress, 2nd Session (Washington, D.C.: USGPO, 1968, 69), Pt. 16, p. 3075.

15. Eric Hoffer, in *ibid.*, p. 2991.

16. William Braden, *The Age of Aquarius* (Chicago: Quadrangle Books, 1970), p. 88.

17. Jim Marshall, Baron Wolman, Jerry Hopkins, *Festival: The Book of American Music Celebrations* (New York: Macmillan, 1970), p. 170.

18. Tom Wolfe, *The Electric Kool-Aid Acid Test* (New York: Bantam Books, 1968), p. 24.

19. Carl Oglesby, *New Left Reader* (New York: Grove Press, 1970), p. 62.

20. Tom Hayden, *Trial* (New York: Holt, Rinehart and Winston, 1970), p. 3.

21. Winthrop Griffiths, quoted in *The New York Times*, August 30, 1970, p. 10.

22. Erving Goffman, *Encounters: Two Studies in the Sociology of Interaction* (Indianapolis: Bobbs-Merrill, 1961), p. 14.

23. Tamotsu Shibutani, "Reference Groups as Perspective," *American Journal of Sociology*, May 1955, pp. 562–63.

24. Bronislau Malinowski, *Magic, Science, and Religion* (New York: Doubleday, 1954), p. 57.

25. Gustave Le Bon, *The Crowd* (New York: Viking Press, 1968, originally published in 1895), p. 24.

26. *Ibid.*, p. 30.

27. Elias Canetti, *Crowds and Power* (New York: Viking Press, 1963), p. 18.

28. *Ibid.*, p. 19.

29. *Ibid.*, p. 22.

30. Feuer, 1969, p. 20.

31. See Paul Goodman, *New Reformation: Notes of a Neolithic Conservative* (New York: Random House, 1970).

32. Raymond Aron, *The Elusive Revolution: Anatomy of a Student Revolt* (New York: Praeger, 1969), p. 15.

33. Tom Wolfe, *Radical Chic and Mau-mauing the Flak Catchers* (New York: Farrar, Straus & Giroux, 1970), pp. 120–21.

9 | THE DANCE OF DEATH

The constant demand for human victims to feed the solar fire was met by waging war every year on neighboring tribes and bringing back captives to be sacrificed. No more striking illustration could be given of the disastrous consequences that may flow in practise from a purely speculative error. (James Frazer, 1922)[1]

     Society celebrates a variety of deaths as contributing to the welfare and well-being of the group. It celebrates death in battle, death for the sake of another's life, death in the service of an ideal, death as an act of resistance against tyranny, and so on. The repertoire of behavior options also includes many kinds of self-fulfilling death-wishes on the part of those whom society decrees dispensable and superfluous, including ex-rulers, the aged and infirm, those whom experience has psychologically crippled and rendered useless or dangerous, and those who endure a transactional loss that destroys their hopes for any future transactions.

    Many patterns of dying are culturally prescribed rituals, evoked in certain life histories, forcing individuals to will themselves dead. Patterns of suicide, accident-proneness, panic reactions, sacrificial death, obesity, drugs, and drunkenness all may be parts of the repertoire of learned behavior made available in culture for individuals to adapt and choose. Our conscious values persuade us that psychogenic (self-willed) death is a departure from prescribed norms. This argument is far from convincing. Normatively and heuristically, we avoid dwelling on this negation of life. Our culture values appear to exhort us to choose life and survival in a wide variety of circumstances; a strong social consensus emphasizes the positive and denies that similar exhortations toward death and self-destruction are equally engrained in culture.

But in fact, psychogenic death enjoys a similar, if covert, injunction of social approval. Individuals regularly tell each other "to die" in hostile threats, rejection, withdrawal, or physical attacks. Through the power of fantasy, every option in every situation is subjectively acted out and evaluated, including the options of self-destruction by all the means available. The weight of evidence indicates a close relationship of crime, murder, suicide, and chronic self-destroying acts to status change.

RITUAL AND PANIC

The incidence of crimes acted out in public while onlookers stand by apathetic and indifferent has become appalling. A woman was pursued and stabbed repeatedly on a dark street, while her neighbors watched as she struggled for her life for over thirty minutes; no one called the cops. A twelve-year-old boy was robbed at knife point and forced to commit a deviate act on a Chicago subway while thirty fellow-passengers watched. The Montreal police conducted a survey to test citizen response to prowlers. For thirty nights, burly hoboes prowled on back porches and in apartment house corridors. The police reported: "People are so damned unresponsive, and coldly so, that it is unbelievable. They did absolutely nothing."

To some extent, such incidents are exceptional; attempts to sensationalize them by regarding them as "typical" are not entirely justified. But they did and do happen. They are usually cited by social critics as the result of selfishness, lack of legal protection for witnesses, a permissive Supreme Court that cares more for rights of criminals than victims, the death of human compassion brought on by an era of crime, violence, atheism, Dr. Spock, communism, capitalism, urbanism, sexism, or what have you. In terms of the ritualization of behavior by culture, the inability to act under stress reveals the absence of ritual definitions appropriate to certain situations. Impersonalism and privatism are ritualized defenses against the onslaught of mass technological urban society. Impassivity is a defensive adaptation against an overload of sensory inputs. Physical crowding may be less significant than the crowding of communications in the electronic media and the habit of passivity engendered by the conversion of the public into a nonparticipatory audience for the psychodramas of everyday life.

Defensive privatism is a highly adaptive culture form that protects the individual and the group against the disorienting and relentless attacks of a highly charged environment, full of cues, demands, and communications of all kinds. A sense of individual responsibility for the mutual safety of everyone within his ambit is only possible under conditions of family, group, or neighborhood identification, in which the requirements of mutual aid are more dependable, reciprocal, and *limited*. Mutual aid and defense have not been obviated in interpersonal relationships, as many charge, or even between strangers. Fear of involvement and legal complications do not inhibit personal responsibility in relationships that culturally require such behavior, as can be seen every day. However, although it may offend our sensibilities to concede it, conventions of mass society do not permit every man to be his brother's keeper in every situation.

Certain stimuli are culturally defined as unmanageable and may therefore trigger a flight reaction; in addition, certain stimuli may lack any definition at all and may therefore trigger the automatic reflex of surprise; flight or escape may follow as a form of search behavior. Panic is a ritualized culture form when the stimulus elicits flight abstractly and symbolically prior to the appearance and the action of the danger source. Nonritual panic occurs when the flight and escape reaction is triggered only by the present action of the danger. Most panic reactions are acculturated and secondhand. Once the terrible event has happened, it is often too late for flight or escape. In the future, social learning induces preventive avoidance or flight at an earlier stage both for the individual, and for others who have absorbed secondhand the individual's experience.

Search behavior is compounded of both fear and curiosity, avoidance and attraction, caution and exploration. An element of panic exists in anything strange and unfamiliar but is controlled by its opposite. That which is a continuous source of surprise, shock, frustration, or pain will sustain anxiety. The more intense these negative reinforcements, the more intense will be the avoidance tendency. The energy-saving nature of symbolic learning makes patterns of intense avoidance homeopathic, that is, subject to highly contagious group response.

Enrico Quarantelli writes that one of the most important contributory conditions "is the existence of a social or group pre-definition of a crisis as one that is likely to eventuate in panic flight. Of some crises, people have certain preconceptions of their dangerousness because of the probable behavior of others in the circumstances."[2] Fire in a crowded place is dangerous because, among other things, panic may result. Individuals in a crowd may wish to anticipate crowd behavior by acting on the merest hint of danger. Because others are doing the same, a confirmation of danger is generated, even if real danger does not exist. In this way, ordinary withdrawal can become panic flight as a homeopathic event.

The previous experience of individuals and the contents of culture create a high level of sensitivity to signs of danger. But hypersensitivity is not in itself determinative. Panic develops as a result of a sense of possible entrapment, a perception of prospective powerlessness, and a feeling of individual isolation in a crisis. Social interaction is important in the generation, emergence, and persistence of these factors. Without social interaction panic is not impossible ". . . but it is very much less likely to occur."[3] The dangers attendant on panic in this way contribute to the contagion factor.

The panic reaction is socially defined, yet may lead to nonsocial behavior. The power of blind flight takes control and shatters the most elementary behavior forms. Examples of this would be the case of the woman who, thinking a bomb had hit her house, fled leaving her baby behind, or Jacqueline Kennedy climbing out on the back of the car as if to escape the bullets that hit her husband. Such flight behavior may be personally functional. It is only in a "very rare instance that panic takes the form of a crowd of individuals trampling over one another like animals in a wild stampede."[4]

Because a social ritual encompasses and assimilates the unfamiliar, the flight-inducing potential of objects is limited, whether this is objectively justified or not. The most dangerous phase of a learning experience is not the initial actions, which are characterized by great caution, but rather the stage of inattention that comes with familiarity and mastery. The stage at which the first blush of confidence replaces caution is the most dangerous. It is well-known that driving on the same streets and highways day after day can be more dangerous than venturing into strange towns or distant highways; three out of four traffic accidents occur within twenty-five miles of home.

MORTALITY AND STATUS

The breakdown of ritual behavior, the failure of well-practiced and habitual actions, the stress of crisis and transition in private lives, both upward and downward mobility in social status, all induce the anxiety that goes with the reorganization of behavior and the fear of painful uncertainties. An excess of stress is entropic and ultimately will destroy the organism. Upward status adjustment may induce psychogenic death, accident-proneness, or compensatory patterns of chronic self-destruction through drugs, alcoholism, or eating, as easily as may abrupt downward status reversals. However, culture provides a wide variety of positive and life-preserving rituals of passage for status elevation; in addition, many social rewards tend to reinforce such outcomes.

Every upward adjustment for someone involves a downward adjustment for someone else. Negative reinforcements are part of the process by which such status loss is forced on the individual. Added to this are the psychic costs that all structures of social dominance impose on failure. While loss of status is often reversible, it often is not, and the cumulative weight of failure, aging, the loss of physical stamina, and the inability to respond in kind to new transactions or threats creates an irreversible trend. Culture contains a repertoire of rituals for those who suffer status loss. These fulfill the social functions of helping the individual adjust to change, even where it leads to the death of the celebrant. Outright suicide is both an act of retaliation against the process of status loss and the self-execution of an implicit sentence of rejection passed on the victim by his peers.

It has long been obvious that negative status values are correlated with psychogenic death. In a international study of social, economic, and medical variables in thirty countries, status integration correlated positively with homicide, and negatively with suicide and ulcers. Low-life expectancy, wealth, economic growth, wine consumption, and zinc consumption correlated with death from homicide, suicide, ulcers, cirrhosis, and hypertension, respectively.[5]

Life insurance statisticians confirm the notion that status loss is a factor in mortality. As a group, successful men listed in *Who's Who in America* were found to live longer than other men. A twelve-year follow-up of a sample taken from the 1950–51 edition contradicts the belief that "men who drive themselves during their forties to outstanding positions in their careers" are more likely to experience "broken health when they are in their fifties." The opposite appears to be true: "Age for age, eminent men enjoyed more favorable mortality" than men in the general population, with the greatest disparity at the ages fifty and fifty-nine. The mortality among the eminent and outstanding men was "only 86 percent of that among individuals insured under life insurance policies—very largely men in the middle income classes or better." Wide differences were found among various vocational groups in the sample. Scientists had the lowest mortality ratio (79 percent of the total sample, 55 percent of that of all white males, and 32 percent of that for nonlisted scientists). Correspondents, journalists, authors, editors, and critics had the highest mortality rates. The death ratio of correspondents and journalists was more than twice that of the entire sample, exceeding by more than a third that of all white males in general population. Church officials, clergymen, educators, and military men had lower than average mortality ratios. Physicians, surgeons, and government officials had higher than average ratios. Business executives, judges, lawyers, engineers, artists, illustrators, and sculptors were about average.[6]

Any change in the allocations of energy in individual behavior, even a pleasant change, produces stress. Too many changes coming close together produce grave illness, abysmal depression, and a tendency toward self-destructive actions. One psychologist devised a system of rating "life event changes" quantitatively, so as to develop a tool for the prediction of mental illness.[7] Only recently have efforts been directed at documenting indirect and protracted means of self-destruction as ritual habits shown by persons under status stress conditions. For example, why do so many otherwise healthy men in their sixties die within a few weeks after their retirement?

Too much or too sudden status change, especially status loss, is insupportable to the organism and kills. Subjective disorder and entropy induce panic. Psychogenic death may be just as highly ritualized as the rites of passage that lead to status elevation. Experiments with rats show that rats that are low in the pecking order suffer more from social instability than do higher ranking rats. They are harassed for everything they do, and become the unwitting targets for substitute discharges of the anxieties of their betters. They may become suddenly impassive, assume a crouch of catatonic withdrawal, disregard common functions of eating, fail to organize the resources in their area, and soon die a death of quiet resignation, like the proverbial Gypsy girl who drew the Ace of Spades, foreseeing death in a self-fulfilling prophecy of escape.

Psychogenic death in primitive societies is embodied in rituals of exorcism, curses, and the casting of spells. Claude Levi-Strauss writes,

An individual who is aware that he is the object of sorcery is fully convinced that he is doomed according to the solemn traditions of his group. His friends and relatives share this certainty. From then on the community withdraws. Standing aloof from the accused, it treats him not only as though he were already dead, but as though he were a source of danger to the entire group.

On every occasion and by every action the social group suggests his death. Sacred rites are held to accompany the inevitable. The victim yields to the combined effects of intense terror, "the sudden total withdrawal of the multiple reference systems provided by the support of the group, and finally, to the group's proclaiming him—once a living man, with rights and obligations—dead and an object of fear, ritual, and taboo." Levi-Strauss concludes that "physical integrity cannot withstand the dissolution of the social personality."[8]

In the tribal society of Albania, the rituals of communal expulsion include burning the man's house, killing and eating his livestock, cutting down his trees, and driving him into exile. The condemned was himself required to apply the burning brand to his property, saying as he lit the fire "on my head be the ill luck of the village and the tribe." He and his family were escorted to the tribal frontier to make sure he was not killed on the way.[9]

Rituals of passivity, slow self-destruction, suicide or violent retaliation are options for the socially outcast. All of the options are equally acts of rebellion. Each man is the hero of his own psychodrama of life. Whatever happens to him and whatever he does about it, he seeks to justify himself and his flawed nobility. He chooses ways that might justify himself to others because his human nature is a socialized product. When a man is reduced to the point where he cannot salvage some scrap of legitimacy or dignity in the eyes of someone else, then, by his own hand, he carries out the informal judgment of the world, punishing or murdering himself. This resolves the puzzle of the relationship of homicide to suicide. People who are highly socialized, who have internalized the nonviolent behavior systems by which they live, tend to commit suicide; those whose socialization is weak or divided tend to react to the same stimuli by killing others.

The rituals of nursing homes and hospital wards for the aged may be interpreted as death-inducing, whatever the conscious intentions of the actors. Death is suggested by the impersonalism, cold arrogance, or jollying indifference of nurses, doctors, and attendants. Denial of personal dignity and rejection of real mutuality are procedures that imply exclusion and death, and that only require ratification by the actual physical demise of the patient. When combined with the infliction of a brutal routine, these procedures may cause the patient to find the tasks of survival illegitimate even in his own eyes. "Chronic delirium may be initiated by defective reality testing and damaging changes in the patient's self-image. The delirium, in turn, may be followed by dehydration, exhaustion, sleeplessness, refusal to accept food, and minor injuries and infections." The cumulative effect of these stresses can build up to the point where they produce a life-and-death crisis. "Despite intensive medical and surgical care, and regardless of the specific method of treatment, the patient's psycho-biological depletion may be irreversible."[10] Many unscrupulous nursing home operators take advantage of this psychology in dealing with their patients. This is especially true in the case of patients who sign life contracts with a home.

Suicide is widely regarded as an act of contagion that taints family and friends of the victim and creates ritual imbalance in society. Suicide may be viewed as the reciprocal of murder and having similar meaning in terms of bargaining and ritual. Like murder, suicide is an act of killing—but one in which the victim is oneself. Yet taking oneself away from others can be a means of punishing them; it can be an attempt to demonstrate a threat and a means of influencing the behavior of others. Suicide and the threat of suicide are ancient instruments of political protest and demonstration. Hunger strikes and self-immolation are political acts with political motives and effects. Assassinations of prominent men in situations where the assassin cannot escape are acts that may be looked on primarily as acts of self-destruction in which the killing of others is merely instrumental.

Like all acts of escalated confrontation, a suicide is unfinished business for the survivors, if not for the victim. Anthropologists report that many tribal religions treat suicide as contagious for all who knew the dead man or had physical contact with the body and its surroundings. In Christian Europe, well into the nineteenth century, the church would not permit removal of a suicide's body except in the dead of night and by someone entirely unrelated to the deceased. The body was unsanctified and could not be buried near the remains of those who died honest deaths by pestilence, murder, or hanging. In primitive societies, it was not uncommon to sacrifice a sheep or goat to pacify the spirit of the suicide that might otherwise draw others after him.[11] In many cultures, suicide is considered unclean, and elaborate rituals are prescribed to stave off further evil. It is a common theme of literature (sometimes imitated by life) that those who feel responsible for the death are driven by remorse to take their own lives. It is not unknown in Japan for parents to commit suicide or become acolytes following the suicide of their child.

When someone commits suicide, those who sense the circumstances that drove him to it reexamine their own lives and may try to adjust the system in order to strengthen their convictions concerning the society in which they live. The suicide of an overextended installment buyer in Chicago led to efforts to reform state and national laws governing interest rates and the collection of unpaid installment debts. A suicide, apart from its real motives, will be quickly exploited by those with a social cause. In effect, a suicide resembles a resignation from a government; it challenges values and institutions, evoking in all the survivors a sense of the unresolved tensions that surround them and threaten the prospect of their own survival. As a ritual of rebellion, suicide or murder warns others that the abuse of their status advantages may force a similar dénouement. A suicide may successfully appeal to public opinion and injure the social legitimacy of any individual who profited by the status loss of the victim.[12]

It is the ritual character of suicide (or any lower-grade form of self-destruction) that accounts for the contagion factor. A suicide epidemic struck Western Europe in the years between 1962 and 1967, when the rate suddenly soared 50 percent over the previous rate. In the United States, suicide has been in recent decades the tenth leading cause of death among adults (estimated at about 44,000 a year). Suicide has been used as a political tactic throughout history, including the self-immolation and burning of Buddhist monks in South Vietnam and the sensational action of Japanese author/actor Yukio Mishima in 1971. At the turn of the century in Russia, a wave of student suicides spread through the universities following a series of sensational political suicides that attracted great attention and admiration. "Suicidalism became a theory of the truth of ideas. A man's ideas were not tested against the facts; rather, they were tested by the degree to which he was prepared to sacrifice himself for them. . . . Suicide was the ultimate test of one's sincerity."[13]

It has been noted that suicide rates fall in times of major war or in times of reorganization and turmoil even though these events increase personal stress. In times of crisis, the legitimacy of the institutions of society is emphasized, and the individual's place therein is explicitly defined.[14] The suicide rate of college students both in Europe and America tended to fall in the late 1960's as political radicalism and protest moved from rhetoric, to practice, to unparalleled success. Generally speaking, the student suicide rate in the United States has remained relatively steady, fluctuating between 5 and 7.2 suicides per 100,000 students per year. The rate does not seem to vary with psychiatric counseling services or with college-induced stresses. Dana L. Farnsworth of Harvard reported that "students who commit suicide are usually isolated or estranged, frequently for long periods of time before suicide." Hallucinogenic drugs may not be considered an independent variable, although they may precipitate preexisting disorders, he reported.[15]

Suicide as a ritualized culture response is apparent in the "many cases on record in which a man has killed himself in order to be avenged upon his foe; often he acts on the belief that his ghost will haunt or torment his survivor or that severe punishment of some kind will surely overtake the one who drove him to this extreme step." In some tribes, custom requires the one on whose head the blood rests immediately to follow suit, or else to placate the family of the suicide with money.[16] In his study of the Trobrianders, Malinowski noted a pattern as ritualized as the practice of hari-kari in feudal Japan. Trobrianders recognized three methods of suicide: jumping off a palm tree, taking poison extracted from the gall bladder of the globe fish, and taking a vegetable poison. The first two were serious, but the third was a form of warning and rarely caused death. Suicide, Malinowski writes, was used as "a means of escape from situations without an issue." The underlying motivation embraced "the desire of self-punishment, revenge, rehabilitation, and sentimental grievance."[17]

In Japan, among Samurai, hari-kari was recognized as a sanctioned and rather common form of punishment granted only to offenders of noble rank. It was his privilege to expiate the crime with his own sword instead of having to die under the hand of the public executioner. Voluntary suicide, in contrast, was construed as a protest against the policies of a chief or the crimes of a ruler although, throughout the Orient, it was a common practice for the major officers of the nobility to follow their feudal master into the next world.[18] Author Yukio Mishima conducted his ritual suicide in army headquarters, after addressing the troops in behalf of the renewal of national spirit and loyalty to the Emperor. His act was intended in the clear tradition of censor in the severest possible form, a ritual of rebellion aimed at his fellow countrymen in the cause of reviving the virtues of nationalism.[19] In much the same spirit, Thomas Newell, a twenty-year-old Vineland, New Jersey, boy had himself ritually murdered by a Satan cult involving two close friends. Newell believed that he had to die violently in order to be put in charge of forty leagues of demons, whose power he would command throughout the universe.[20]

William Graham Sumner interprets child sacrifice as arising from the same forms as do blood rituals. Blood rituals of all kinds, whether in the Mafia, in a boy's gang, or in a primitive tribe, are thought to be sacred, giving power and binding loyalty. Bleeding is universally recognized as a high priority problem. It rivets attention and forces a protective action. It achieves its ritual potency by its close practical as well as symbolic relation to life. Likewise, children are loved and cherished above all else. Their sacrifice is the greatest one possible, and, therefore, the most powerful. "All forms of child sacrifice and sacral-suicide go back to the pangs and terrors of men under loss and calamity. Something must be found which would bring pity and compassion from the awful superior powers who afflict mankind."[21]

SELF-FULFILLING PROPHECY

The slow suicides of accident-proneness, self-abuse, exposure to unnecessary risks, the use of drugs, and excesses of drink or food, are ritualized options that serve the same functions as does outright suicide. All are rituals of rebellion that seek to punish the self as well as to threaten or punish others.

The deaths in the fall of 1970 of rock superstars Jimi Hendrix and Janis Joplin from drug overdoses at a time when the rock scene was already in a state of decline may have represented a kind of ritual imperative. Janis had earlier said, "People seem to have a high sense of drama about me. Maybe they can enjoy my music more if they think I am destroying myself."[22] She was just emerging from a downturn in popularity and had formed a new group that showed great promise. Hendrix took nine sleeping pills. His friends said he was depressed over the state of his art and the demands of his audience that he continue to play and perform in his old style.[23] British rock guitarist Eric Clapton declared it the end of an era: "their deaths [were] almost necessary sacrifices. . . . Hendrix at the Isle of Wight was a mind at the end of its tether. His music was painful to hear. As a guitar player he had no equal and he knew it, but he had nothing left to say."[24]

Drugs and drunkenness have become standard ritual forms of rebellion and escape. All rituals of rebellion are structured to be a "time-out" from the normal restraints and as an apparent inversion of values. But as we have seen, this structure fulfills purposes that are deeply committed to confirming the restraints and discipline while renewing their legitimacy and adaptability. In one form or another, the ritual of euphoric transport achieved by chemicals can be found in the overwhelming majority of the world's cultures. A man "in his cups" is presumed to be irresponsible and out of control, anesthetized in his higher centers and unshackled from all of his base drives. This stereotype conceals the strict rules of behavior that govern the state of being high. Drunkenness as a ritual of rebellion is investigated with humor and insight in a recent book by Craig MacAndrew and Robert B. Edgerton.[25] The authors compare conventions of drunkenness in different societies, showing how unspontaneous is the behavior supposedly induced by drink. Even during the annual rice festival night when sexual abandon is encouraged, the Lepchas, a Mongolian tribe, enforce incest taboos of astonishing complexity. Among the Urubu Indians of Brazil, a ferocious head-hunting tribe, a drunken festival brings a highly conventionalized conciliation with enemies that is prohibited under all other conditions. The Aritama of Northern Colombia have conventionalized neurosis and self-consciousness as the effects of rum. When they drink, they sit around becoming increasingly depressed —they experience no permissive and happy effects. MacAndrew and Edgerton do not deny the physical effects of drink, but they argue that these effects are offset by behavior that is essentially learned, rituals that are embodied in culture.

The pattern of the use of socially approved drink or drugs to obtain ecstasy is reenacted in small by individuals who privately pursue the same ritual. The drunk or the drug addict is engaged in a private rebellion, whose social effect, detached and dislocated from the functions of a mass ceremonial, becomes a self-fulfilling prophecy of death to punish oneself and one's peers. The chronic drunk becomes a caricature of normal culture forms, recovering from stupor now and then to engage in an automatic and inappropriate gesture of friendliness, wit, and sentimentality that is meaningless and frightening to his audience. In the dim recesses of a partly numbed brain, the ritual patterns seem to the drunken actor to be full of grace and warmth, when they are actually dislocated cues going off automatically like the twitching of a severed frog's leg.

Saturday night rebellions have an ancient history and follow the classical form: the first act is rebellious revelry, marked by exaltation, profanation, unity and comradeship, battle with devils, enemies, and friends, and is concluded by self-immolation, insensitivity, or stupor; the second act is the morning after, characterized by repentance, mortification, and ultimately redemption, all with an aching head and thick tongue. Sunday is a day for contemplating one's sins, for church, for quiet recuperation. The disapproval of marijuana smoking may partly arise from the absence of this sequence of ritual acts. The hangover "that God intended" is lacking and there may be no repentance, and therefore no redemption.

All the sacred ritual occasions of the social group tend also to be settings for escalated conflict, aggression, intensified behavior of all forms, and a heightened incidence of death. More old people die during holidays than otherwise. Assaults, rapes, and murders tend to follow the ritual calendar. There is an increase in homicide during the hot summer months when social interaction and street life are facilitated. The incidence of riots in warm weather is probably less related to irritation and discomfort caused by heat (which is only increased by strenuous action) than it is related to the incipient festival atmosphere that is created by the centering of activity systems out-of-doors, rather than in the isolation of rooms and houses.

Murder is significantly associated with the weekend in general, and with Saturday night in particular, especially the hours between 8 P.M. and 2 A.M. During a five year study, almost twice as many criminal homicides occurred during the forty-eight weekend hours as occurred during the whole balance of the week.[26] Men kill and are killed most frequently in the street; while women kill most often in the kitchen but are killed in the bedroom. Most cases of black males who kill black males involve a stabbing in a public street; most cases of white males who kill white males involve a beating in a public street. Eighty-four percent of all female murderers slay males, 87 percent of all female victims are slain by males.

It may be argued that the incidence of heart attacks among middle-aged men is a self-inflicted form of psychogenic death induced by the dynamics of culture ritual and not by somatic causes. Like suicide, heart attacks tend to be subject to social contagion. A well-known comedian falls dead of a heart attack, and a number of lesser-known comedians within a few weeks reenact the scene. A respected neighbor is afflicted, and a number of men in the neighborhood of similar life situations fall victim. The culture is infinitely suggestive in encouraging repetition of the ritual through the constant media warnings of "the seven danger signs," and the use of the heart attack cliché in soap opera as a way of removing a character no longer needed in the plot.

The syndrome works like all rituals of culture. Every individual identifies with and learns from others' experience. One man struck down by sudden death generates incipient panic and patterns of heart-stopping self-consciousness. Any jarring shock or passing angina is immediately interpreted as the fatal attack and the panic that ensues, indeed, makes the attack fatal. The psychogenic heart attack deserves greater examination as a medical problem. The tendency of wives and doctors to treat every apparent heart attack as a grave and dire portent is a powerful means of suggestion. It constitutes cultural reinforcement of the syndrome and may account for many psychogenic heart stoppages. The primitive pagan curse that kills by suggestion and self-fulfilling prophecy has not been expunged from the panoply of culture rituals in advanced societies.

NOTES

1. James Frazer, *The Golden Bough: A Study in Magic and Religion* (New York: Macmillan 1956, originally published in 1922), p. 506.

2. Enrico Quarantelli, "The Nature and Conditions of Panic," in Duane P. Schultz, ed., *Panic Behavior* (New York: Random House, 1964), p. 52; see also Alfred Lindesmith and Anselin Strauss, *Social Psychology* (New York: Dryden Press, 1949), p. 332.

3. Quarantelli, 1964, p. 53.

4. *Ibid.*, p. 41.

5. Gerald V. Barrett and Richard H. Franke, "Psychogenic Death: A Reappraisal," *Science,* January 16, 1970, pp. 304–06. In a study of psychological disorders and social status, the Dohrenwends finds that the culture values of the middle classes lead them to psychiatric help. Middle class disorders are therefore more likely to be recorded and studied, throwing doubts on efforts to correlate status and mental illness. (See Bruce P. and Barbara Snell Dohrenwend, *Social Status and Psychological Disorder: A Causal Inquiry* [New York: Wiley, 1969].)

6. Jules V. Quint and Mrs. Bianca R. Cody, article in *American Journal of Public Health,* July 1970, reprinted in *The New York Times,* July 26, 1970, p. 60; see also Curtis M. Hames, "Heart Attacks in Evans County," *AMA* (Washington, D.C., 1972).

7. See Thomas Holmes, "Rating Life Changes," paper presented at AAAS meeting, reported in *Time,* March 1, 1971, p. 54.

8. Claude Levi-Strauss, "The Sorcerer and His Magic," in John Middleton, ed., *Magic, Witchcraft and Curing* (Garden City, N.Y.: Natural History Press, 1967), p. 23.

9. Margaret Hasluck, "The Albanian Blood Feud," in Paul Bohannan, ed., *Law and Warfare: Studies in the Anthropology of Conflict* (Garden City, N.Y.: Natural History Press, 1967), pp. 398–99.

10. A. D. Weisman and R. S. Kastenbaum, *The Psychological Autopsy* (New York: Behavioral Publications, 1968), pp. 24, 29.

11. Paul Bohannan, *African Homicide and Suicide* (Princeton, N.J.: Princeton University Press, 1960), pp. 110–14.

12. See H. L. Nieburg, *Political Violence: The Behavioral Process* (New York: St. Martin's Press, 1969), pp. 122–23.

13. Lewis S. Feuer, *The Conflict of Generations* (New York: Basic Books, 1969), p. 102.

14. Louis I. Dublin, *Suicide: A Sociological and Statistical Study* (New York: Ronald Press, 1963), p. 68.

15. See *The New York Times,* October 11, 1970, p. 71.

16. Dublin, 1963, p. 90.

17. Bronislau Malinowski, *Crime and Custom in Savage Society* (New York: Harcourt Brace Jovanovich, 1926), p. 5.

18. Dublin, 1963, p. 99.

19. See *The New York Times*, December 16, 1970, p. 6.

20. *Ibid.*, July 6, 1971, p. 29.

21. William Graham Summer, *Folkways: A Study of the Sociological Importance of Usages, Manners, Customs, Mores, and Morals* (New York: New American Library, 1940), pp. 460, 464; see also Bruno Bettelheim, *Symbolic Wounds: Puberty Rites and the Envious Male* (London: Thames and Hudson, 1955), especially pp. 30–36.

22. Quoted in *Time*, October 19, 1970, p. 54.

23. See *The New York Times*, November 3, 1970, p. 26.

24. Quoted in *ibid.*, October 18, 1970, p. 28.

25. *Drunken Comportment: A Social Exploration* (Chicago: Aldine, 1969).

26. Marvin E. Wolfgang, "A Sociological Analysis of Criminal Homicide," in Hugo Adam Bedau, *The Death Penalty in America* (Garden City, N.Y.: Doubleday, 1967), pp. 79–80.

10 | THE ARTS

A voice from the back, calm, sweet, and patient: I just embraced eight members of the Living Theatre. I embraced them with love. And one of them took my wallet. You can keep the money, but would you kindly return the cards? (Robert Brustein, 1970)[1]

Culture is the glaze over chaos. It is the warehouse of arbitrary inventions of behavior, meaning, values, and operational procedures for doing and making. As a collection of arbitrary abstractions, it imposes clarity and form on the turbulent blur of existence. Culture is an artifact, that is, a work of art.

The word *art,* as it is commonly used to denote the fine or practical arts, is a narrow and status-conscious segment of the arts that constitute the whole body of culture. All culture forms are infused with fantasy, culture learning, paradigms of action, and expressive rituals and ceremonies of all sorts. Most of culture has been assimilated into social institutions, attitudes, and behavior, and is so familiar as to be virtually unnoticed. For this reason, the vast frame of culture belongs to the profane realm. Art, in contrast, is surrounded by magic and presentiment; it is highly conscious and carries a prescribed set of ritual observances that give it a character sacred and apart.

SACRED PROTOTYPES

By virtue of the conventions of attention, concentration, and special significance, the subject matter of art (and the role of the artist) is enshrined with a special legitimacy and regard; it represents the isolation of form and meaning from the mundane flow of everyday things. Like Plato's Essences, the sacred arts constitute a gallery of "pure forms," a rotating exhibition of original models of culture. Styles, forms, and values that acquire this technical esoteric status become sacred prototypes.

The notion of beauty is a human endowment that represents a quality of sacredness. "Beauty is truth, and truth beauty," expresses the high field of concentration and sensitivity in the worshiper. Beauty is another expression for legitimacy, flowing not from inherent form, but as a convention of attitude. The words of John Keats provide a definition of trust that can be used for political office as well as for art forms: "That's all we know and all we need to know." Anything can be endowed with sacral intensity, surrounded with special observances and ceremonies, enriched in significance and set off in a high field of concentration, whether a soft construction of a toilet, a Campbell soup can, or the Sistine Chapel.

Legitimacy is a political fact and reflects an allocation of status values to serve the purposes of organized groups. Art, therefore, cannot be separated from social power and the political process. This is not to say that taste must subserve political movements; it is rather a matter of the individual's place in the process of culture change, and one does not quickly surrender to the assertion of new culture forms that storm the bastions of prevailing values. But no one escapes the process of strategic interaction and competitive collaboration that reinforces and sorts out the new inputs of values and forms, allowing some to rise and others to fall.

The realm of art reflects dynamic social forces whose claims to legitimacy are authenticated by social power. "The power to write the songs of an era is greater than the power to write the laws." Any social group able to assert the sacred authority of its own culture forms and values can indeed forecast and make the future. Trotsky made the point, "Art, don't you see, means prophecy. Works of art are the embodiments of presentiments. . . ."[2] For saying this, he was later accused by his political enemies of supporting the notion of "art for art's sake," which in Stalinist Russia meant art for anti-Stalinism.

As culture is an artifact, so the frontiers of culture lie in the sacred realm of art. Life imitates art in that some of the paradigms and values at the frontier acquire legitimacy as social learning, even as their assimilation into everyday life tarnishes their sacred character. The power to determine what is art prefigures the power to determine the good life, who should rule, what the social goals and policies should be, and priorities and values in every realm of private and group activities.

Herbert Read makes "the immensely presumptuous claim" that art is "the patient fixation of what is significant in human experience," a crystalization "from the amorphous realm of feeling" of forms that make possible all symbolic discourse, including religion, philosophy, and science. Art invents reality, leading the inner eye "toward the light, discovering an opening in the veil of nothingness and becoming aware of significant shapes." The specifically "aesthetic act" is to take possession of "a revealed segment of the real, to establish its dimensions and to define its forms." Reality becomes "what we thus articulate, and what we articulate is communicable only in virtue of its aesthetic form."[3]

As Nietzsche understood, art is a ritual form whose social function is to create boundaries. The absence of boundaries is not liberty, but madness and impotence. Without form and organization, energy devours itself. When the old forms die, enormous energy is liberated; it immediately craves form, whether regressing into the elemental and the infantile, or reforming into a new and stable synthesis. T. S. Eliot states, "The poet dislocates language into meaning. The artist smashes open the doors of perception."[4] The frontier of art is a self-contained ritual of rebellion, a crowd of infinite possibility that erupts as a random mob, looting the psychic storehouse of images, toppling identities and monuments along the mental streets and squares of sensibility.

Culture is stylized and learned—it is the trail left by art. It is limited to the range of possibility provided by the cumulative technology, resources, and energy that is available; it builds on already established forms, even when it negates them. Art is an anti- or counter-environment through which man can perceive the environment itself. As antienvironment, it is a means of developing perception and judgment. McLuhan goes a step further and holds that art is at once a step behind the present and a probe of the future. Existing environments are always taken for granted and embodied in un-self-conscious behavior. Only as the environment changes does it provide materials for art. McLuhan holds that the subject matter of art is already dead when it arrives on the scene.[5] The self-conscious artist is a curator of the dusty past. He becomes respectable and recognized only when his work and his life style have become relics and museum pieces. The real, innovating artist as a future probe will not be recognized until it is too late, unless, of course, he is Marshall McLuhan.

Every form, in its own time, tends to be raised to the highest level of sophistication and variety. It is, as Read notes, a mistake to compare the graphic art forms of the prehistoric cave artist with those of a kindergarten child. Conventualized forms are not distortions, but rather styles and paradigms of social learning. Their conventions are taken for granted—they communicate their social meaning rather than their concrete size, shape, weight, and so forth. Like many art forms, cave paintings were "not intended to be looked at or seen, but rather to exert influence at a distance, as though by ESP." Just as soon as the conventions of form are ritualized and are no longer merely the exploratory, idiosyncratic products of a single artist, they become, in McLuhan's words, "not means of private but of corporate expression. They are vortices of collective power, masks of energy."[6]

The cave artists were perfectly capable of naturalistic drawing as some of their work demonstrates (for example, that in the cave at Lascaux); the schematic and simplified form, which some might compare with the drawings of children, represents a culture choice. Picasso can draw representational and photographic figures, yet he prefers to experiment with conventionalized distortions in order to intensify the sacred character and significance of his work. He chooses to assert the legitimacy and reality of unfamiliar and astonishing forms. Furthermore, there is evidence that the graphic representations of children are stylized and learned rather than spontaneous. The conventions of children's art are absorbed by the child, whether he draws free forms or stick figures. Emphasis on liberating the child's own creative forces, in practice, means merely that cues and reinforcements that transmit culture become more covert.

Art generates myth.[7] All works of art exist in and create mythic ambiance. The arts of a period embody the great legends that arise historically in periods of crisis and cultural transition, when great prophets and artists redeem the values of the past and the present in symbolic form, transposing their historic transitoriness into permanent promises. "Art," says master poet W. H. Auden, "is our chief means of breaking bread with the dead."[8]

McLuhan sees tribal myth resurrected as the unique product of electronic immediacy and the syncretic simultaneity of historic and spatial forms. He sees it as the end of the linear conventions of form based on type-setting and print. Surely he exaggerates; the mythic dimension with its unifying and integrating functions has never been very far below the surface. The analytic and linear did not destroy the mythic and the integrative functions performed by theory, concepts, and meaning. The tendency in modern literature to revive myth and mystical forms, as in Joyce, Kafka, Sartre, Cocteau, and Faulkner, is merely a convention; the elements of the mythic and the archetypal can be just as clearly seen in all prosaic, naturalistic communications and in preelectronic systems.

Similarly, Daniel Bell diagnoses the collapse of rationalism in contemporary culture:

We see in all the arts a breakup of the rational cosmology: foreground and background in painting; sequence, beginning, middle, and end in narrative; melody and harmonic tonalities in music. Against the classical theories of distinguishable disciplines, we find the break-up of genres and an emphasis on total environment, i.e. so-called antiart movements which erase the distinction between art and everyday experience.

The criticism is misformulated. We are confronted by syncretism and a deliberate opening of the range of materials entitled to the sacred realm. Rationalism as the conceit of the special values marking the middle-class revolution of the nineteenth century does not possess any monopoly on clarity, objectivity, and authority. Rather, rationality is a convention of communication and symbolic structure. It is universal, ubiquitous, and inherent in the structure of language. The primeval, the tribal, and the fantastic are as rational, in the technical sense, as the logistics of corporate administration. Every sectarian group claims unique rationality for its own metaphysical preferences. Like beauty, truth, and sexual prowess, it is just another term for the claimed legitimacy of social values.[9]

RITUAL DRAMA AS THE HUB

Writing a century ago, German philosopher Conrad Fiedler stated, "Artistic activity begins when man finds himself face-to-face with the visible world as something immensely enigmatical. . . . In the creation of a work of art, man engages in a struggle with nature, not for his physical, but for his mental existence."[10] The bringing of experience into consciousness through art is not fortuitous, but necessary; its products are not secondary nor ornamental, but absolutely essential to social life.

Kenneth Burke makes the same point. Art, he wrote in 1931, enters when "revelation is ritualized, when it is converted into a symbolic process." He notes the sacred aura that surrounds the formalities of art: "We treat with ceremony a fact considered of importance. If we consider a thing distinguished, we surround it with other things which we consider distinguished. We touch a pure object with clean hands." As eloquence, ceremony, and ritual, art is "nothing other than the principle of consistency, of matching the important with the important." Once a metaphor, a truth, is asserted, the artist confronts the problem of symbolic extension. A creative writer does not "state facts," but rather frames his revelations in ritual. Savants who seek to catalog the thoughts of stylists like Milton or Mao are in error. Art may be factually "insincere" and yet embody truth in a deeper sense, as a fusion of revelation and ritual.[11]

Burke sees all art as spokes on the *hub of ritual drama.* All art, whether a painting, *object d'art,* style of dance, detail of dress, religious or secular ceremony, whatever its concrete and specific subject matter, implies and gains significance as part of a complete ritual drama. Art is the apotheosis of an event in the form of a myth in which the dramatis personae are the forces of good and evil locked in relentless combat, as highly stylized and artificial as an Arthur Murray samba, with set-backs, perplexities, and problems, but with a programed and inevitable outcome. The underlying ritual drama celebrates the victory of the good guys, the values, and the forms, whose assertion of legitimacy is reduced to practice by culture.[12]

Every age and every stage of culture implies an underlying set of ritual dramas; all of the specific forms of art are but details, turnings, ceremonial practices, relics and crystals that imply the whole drama. Burke proposes the notion of ritual drama as the hub of art and culture, not necessarily as historical interpretation, but rather as a calculus, "a vocabulary or set of coordinates, that serves best for the integration of all phenomena studied by the social sciences." He proposes the study of ritual drama as the logical alternative to the study of the mechanistic metaphor of human acts and relations that later became the chief metaphor of the behavioral sciences.

James L. Peacock made a pioneering study of folk drama as "a ritual of modernization" in Indonesia. Assuming that art expresses underlying conflicts of social values and the direction of social change, he attempts to reach the subjective dimension of a social order through a systematic study of popular art forms. His work is illuminating and suggestive.[13] Focusing on the underlying ritual drama of a given cultural setting provides an approach that is still bold and innovative. Social scientists often fail to interpret adequately the meaning of symbolic forms because they are blinded by the content and context that they abstract from form. They ignore Burke's, McLuhan's, and Gluckman's injunction that form itself is an independent variable that may determine the expressive range of the content, that content cannot be interpreted merely as an inventory or a mirror, the folk equivalent of a projective test. All of the forms and disparate elements of a culture constitute a symbolic dialectic of traditional and innovated forms. The traditions, exigencies, and logic of symbolic vehicles are combined with all the motives of the changing social order.[14]

Art may be seen as archetype or prototype event, apotheosized to the sacred realm by conventions of form, whether in the high or low arts, the practical or the fine, the transitory or the enduring, whether style or artifact. Ritual drama expresses collective revelations, "the social structures of meanings by which the individual forms himself."[15] The ritual drama is never wrong, because it contains within itself the legitimization of truth and reality. "Even the most superstition-ridden tribe must have had accurate ways of sizing up real obstacles and opportunities in the world, for otherwise it could not have maintained itself." Every element of art, as an item of the ritual drama, is surrounded with dramatic and dialectical significance. Every item is related as response or rejoinder to other items, and as such each item carries meaning as a strategy of action that can be reduced to practice and applied to real human relationships by individuals living within the culture.

Fantasy, we have seen, is the internalized process by which the subjective life of the individual participates in the archetypal life of the culture. Fantasy enacts and reenacts, swiftly and multitudinously, all of the rehearsed sequences of behavior and their outcomes that lie latent or active in the collective experience. It is like an infinite number of computers racing their tapes and scanning their memory banks instantaneously in search of the appropriate sequence to be telegraphed to the muscles as electromotive energy. Art is a projection of the fantasy-life of the artist, and as such collectively represents the fantasy-life of the whole society. Projection and symbolic display of such fantasies elicit a responsive chord from the audience and in this manner test reality. The audience response is the ultimate reality check that gives closure and versimilitude to stylized offerings of creative fantasy that are capable of holding an audience.

Art implements fantasy by making it actual and by providing new conventions and behavior modes to express new values. The underlying rationalization of social meaning, which is embodied in a ritual drama, provides a common touchstone of fantasy that joins together all members of a given social group, maintaining their capability as common audience and as mutually reinforcing actors. In this way, the ritual drama achieves subjective linkage and congruence between private fantasies that support and facilitate all of the culture forms, values, and activities of the group. Linkage and congruence of sensibility may never be fully communicated or evoked in collaborative behavior among group members, yet it is there, and may be implemented fractionally as the life of the group requires. Only in the ceremonial rituals of mass assembly and celebration is the full congruence of sensibility evoked and made palpable and concrete; the word becomes flesh in mutually reinforcing ceremonial activities more fully than in the secular activities of everyday life.

Any detail of the profane social process may be abstracted and cast into the sacred realm by conventions of form. Herman Nitsch and the *Aesthetics of Butchery* elevate blood and guts into art. The "happening," the participatory and spontaneous Living Theatre, the celebration of "found objects" as sacred are other examples. To be elevated to sacred art, a form must achieve recognition from an audience that must confirm the inherent claims and values of the ritual drama against prevailing notions of legitimacy. The abstraction of form universalizes and sacralizes the essence of a thing. The artist is like the man who burned down the golden temple (in the words of Yoko Ono): "He couldn't stand the idea of its falling apart as it got older; and now the golden temple exists in perfect form—forever; it became a myth." Art starts by counterfeiting reality (that is, the existing conventions and clichés of the culture), but the counterfeit soon becomes the reality—if it serves a social purpose and achieves for itself legitimacy. Yoko Ono says,

You know, creating or destroying something is easy; but changing the value of something, that is where art comes in . . . art changes values; you don't even have to touch anything, you just change values so much that the establishment doesn't mean anything anymore. Look at Marcel Duchamp, just by putting a toilet bowl on a stage he made it into a completely different thing.[16]

DECLINE OF GENTILITY

The prevailing definitions of art represent the values of class, caste, and the social dominance hierarchy. Emerging forms always attack the genteel and respectable as dead and bankrupt. In the postwar period, all kinds of new forms have emerged into respectability after prolonged development in the underground: pop and rock music, automobile customizing, stock-car racing, demolition derbies, every element of the teenage subculture, all the plastic, stiffened, painted, epoxied, and sandblasted day-glo products of the industrial process, obscenity and pornography. Syncretism in popular culture and pop art was inevitable; it can be seen in media forms, industrial products, entertainment, television and films, romantic novels and mysteries, the whole sentimental sawdust-among-the-sequins maudlin heartache of soap opera, and all the manufactured culture of the great middle classes.

Until the 1960's, the cultural forms of the 1930's dominated everything, a whole generation whose time was consumed by war, diplomacy, production, and prosperity. Art became stuffy and closeted, the monopoly of an educated elite; in their service the media men and communication experts learned to despise their own products of popular culture. The mission of this elite was to complete the nineteenth-century democratization of culture, a mission that largely succeeded in this period of fading legitimacy. The period ended in the 1960's; the structure of inhibiting pressures of national security and values imposed from above collapsed not only under the weight of failure in Vietnam, but also under the satirical lashing of warning signals like the success of Mort Sahl and the box office smash of *The Russians Are Coming, The Russians are Coming.* The old order died when the nation laughed at nuclear destruction portrayed in the film *Dr. Strangelove!*

Goldman calls the collapse "a colossal failure of sublimation." His generation had been "launched like a flight of rocket-driven missiles straight up into the highest heavens of ambition and aspiration; but just as we reached our apogee, we ran out of gas and came tumbling down on the meadows of our childhood." The old culture generation was congruent with the explosion of the mass media. Talkies, electrical recording, radio, the comic book industry, the music business, fashions, fads, juvenile journalism, teenage commercialized culture, none of this existed when the parent generation were children. "It rose into being as we grew up." Then came inevitable cultural anemia: "our paintings turned black, our plays absurd. Our composers took to extolling the mystic joys of silence. The high culture, the official culture, the culture we admired, extolled, and revered, began to stultify in a dreary atmosphere of middle class piety." As classic culture shriveled up in the middle of the twentieth century, the "great pop bubble began to rise from the lowest depths of our civilization. From the minds of the Lumpen-puerile came the sounds of rock, the cackle of the sick joke and the lower comic book shapes of pop art."[17]

One indicator of the decline of genteel culture is the slide of classical record sales during the past decade. Before the Second World War the consumers of classical records were a small but loyal elite; in the decade after the Second World War, the LP and the universal spread of record-playing equipment brought a phenomenal popularization of classical music. At its height in the late 1950's, classical recordings held a significant share of the total music market, at least 20 percent. Then came the movement to serious rock; the pop music field held its own, along with the chewing-gum rock market for the teenyboppers, but classical music fell to 3 to 5 percent of the market. Success always leads to excess and overproduction, and the offerings of classical music are enormously redundant and competitive. How many recordings of Beethoven's Ninth will the market bear? "Bernstein's Greatest Hits" replaces Beethoven and Mahler, as the record companies seek to renew the saturated market by pushing the star system.

Bell claims that bourgeoise culture in the postwar world had no intellectually respectable art of its own, no major figures in literature (the best is James Gould Cozzens), painting (except perhaps Andrew Wyeth), or poetry, to counterpose the adversary culture.[18] The new syncretic forms (in spite of their revolutionary pretensions) are already in fact the prevailing cultural establishment. The publishing houses, museums, gallerys, major new weeklies, theater, film, and the universities are all celebrating the new forms. The insurgency of the 1960's was an accomplished fact simultaneously as it happened. Much of the syncretism came from Hollywood films. *Dr. Zhivago, Bonnie and Clyde,* all were integrative vehicles of style and manners. Every new historical romance or melodrama revived the totality of customs of a period, adding to the mix of culture forms that included not merely the improvisations of youth, but the commercialized products of the great couturiers and the massed production lines of the garment industry as well. Fashion is everything and the latest Sears-Roebuck catalog offers an inventory of pseudo-funky, pseudo-underground, pseudo–Catholic Charity styles for male and female, ages three and up. Film-making has become a primary input of new ritual manias.

Today, we have arrived at a point where nothing in pop culture is so tawdry and cheap as not to find serious critics to extol its virtues. From Russ Meyer nudie films to the exploitative whimsies of Andy Warhol, from the garbage of shallow voyeurism to the fine distillations of experimental films and Musique Concrete, art has become syncretic, open both to snobs and antisnob snobs, excitement for the yahoos and camp for the cognoscenti. Western civilization is in the throes of an Augustinian period of fusion and confusion of forms, of experimentation that presses the limits and threatens the apotheosis of formlessness. Adolescence has become a sacred state, and children become the bearers of culture forms. History and tradition are rejected as culture contrives an uncritical and blind plunge into syncretic invention.

With the legitimate theater in collapse and the arts in disarray, Goldman notes, with fascination rather than alarm, that the fashion/rock/film axis controls the scene, its power arising from a universal longing to commune with images and become as one with the bright skin of appearances. Culture shifts frenetically from place to place, age to age, person to person in a kaleidoscopic spin that continually revises all shapes, styles, colors, tunes, and dramatic themes. An enormous appetite exists for continuous entertainment and novelty. Our wealth and technology provide the opportunity for an unlimited number of variations. "We are fast becoming a society of private projectionists."[19] Custom cars, stretch pants, dayglo colors and psychedelic images, decal eyes and pornographic knee patches mark the emergence of the values of proles, peasants, petty burghers, gangsters, and teenagers into serious art and culture. The mission of democratization, the Fabian Society schools for workingman, have succeeded beyond the wildest dreams. The old aristocratic celebrities must now compete with twelve-year-old groupies as leaders of art and fashion. The jet setters follow the acne set, making overnight sensations out of some raunchy discothèque or hamburger drive-in, outdoing the kids in outlandish dress and profaning the proprieties by wearing tie-dyed blue jeans to opening night at the opera, or exposing a bare nipple through a transparent body stocking at Lindy's.

THE PROSCENIUM ARCH

In his 1970 book, *Revolution as Theatre,* Robert Brustein writes eloquently about the spurious pretense of white college militants. In an impassioned and effective diatribe, Brustein seeks to insult the young Maoists by positing a dichotomy between *theater* (playing around just for fun) and *revolution* (a real attempt to grab power and smash the regime). He assumes that successful revolutionaries of the past had nothing in common with contemporary militants. This assumption of dichotomy is invalid. It is ahistorical, a sin for which he attacks the young. All revolutions are theatrical, and the art of revolution must always be that of dramatization and imagination. The real difference may be between that which succeeds and that which fails. He overlooks the very great success the young revolutionaries have had in loosening up values and opening the way for social change. Nowhere in his book does Brustein make clear what Yale street-fighters need to do to qualify as real revolutionaries, except that he calls on them to study hard and not to disrupt the campus, so that his theater group may get on with its work. Yet, the actual collapse of the revolutionary movement at Yale later in the year tended to confirm Brustein's criticism. Ultimate legitimacy must be won by accidental success, not by plausible and consistent analysis. Revolutionist theater can be real revolution, just as pure theater can be highly significant in maintaining and challenging values.

Both Eric Bentley and Brustein place the role of theater at the hub of the arts. It demands concentration and attention and it has a sense of mission that the media cannot fulfill. "A sense of this fact underlies all that has happened in radical theater in the 1960's, from Grotowski to the Becks, and from the playwriting of Hochhuth to the non-literary guerilla and street theaters." Those who remain loyal to serious theater seek to recall people from Muzak passivity to the great intensity of making ritual drama. The flesh and blood encounter of the theater can penetrate "that elephant hide of resistances" that all of the patterns of established ritual serve to thicken and maintain. "Cerebral persuasion is beside the point or at best grossly insufficient. . . . What is usually implied in the words *touching* or *moving* is but a passing sensation or mood, as soon forgotten as last week's orgasm."[20] Good theater must be visceral and must penetrate the whole psychophysical system.

While entertainment is a dimension of all of the arts, and passive consumption a legitimate function, the sacred in arts is a projection of collective fantasy and has to do with the ultimate destiny of the national group, as well as the temporary assuagement of pleasure and pain. The legitimate theater is the sacred realm par excellence, partly because the conventions of the proscenium arch elevate the actors to supernatural status as symbols of universal mythic forms. Theater also is bound by the discipline and structure of concentrated and economical story-telling. The mythic must be rendered in concrete personalities and relationships. From ancient times to the present, theater has been a condensed form of social meanings, and the sparse economics of story-line and dramatic detail maintain its special role. Films and television can be secularized by familiarity and the toughening skin of the audience, but the voluntaristic nature of theater attendance, the immediacy of mutual response between actors and audience, the necessity to encompass a total myth structure while maintaining the concreteness of real life, endow the theater with a central role in the making of culture. While the media become forms of secular theater, theater retains its sacred character against all of the formidable panoply of electronic and celluloid offprints. Theater fleshes out fantasy in a face-to-face encounter that maintains the sacredness of the forum in a way that mechanical and impersonal media, faced with the dulling effects of saturation and familiarity, cannot.

Fantasy in the theater is encapsulated experience, separated from the implementation and embodiment in the subsequent behavior of the audience. Not all fantasies are acted out; rather the sequences of action are highly edited samples of the infinite options of the cultural repertoire. That is why, during a particularly moving performance, everyone in the audience is transported and full of love and exaltation. While the show is on, everyone is willing to give his shirt to his brother. Yet once the show is over, how many are willing to give their neighbor a lift back to town?

Peacock sees the folk theater of Indonesia as "a sort of X-ray machine" that lays bare aspects of Javanese existence that cannot be seen with the naked eye.[21] Julian Beck, the founder of the now-defunct Living Theater saw the role of his troupe as that of breaking down stage conventions as precursor to a period of national culture in which all of the conventions and barriers were to fall. He sought to pioneer spontaneity, nudity, a relaxation of physical constraints in the sacred theatrical mode. "Coming attractions, coming attractions!" he cried as new patterns, including violence and disruption sparked first by the police and later by actors and audience, eventually made it impossible for the group to perform. By 1970, the group was dead, its former members seeking new forms and stages. Mark Estrin, a Beck protégé, one of the leading practitioners of guerilla theater, sees the actor as activist with a function to "create scenes in the midst of real events." The future of theater, he holds, lies in its shedding "the protective mantle of being art." It must become coterminous with reality in the sense of incorporating risk, uncertainty, and participation. It must play in the streets, factories, parks, subways and, in the words of Julian Beck, "close to the places and means of production." The Living Theater, Beck declared, "doesn't want to perform for the privileged elite anymore." But alas, no other audience appeared and the street people preferred Abbie Hoffman, Jerry Rubin, and A. J. Weberman. The Becks were caught in too many contradictions. Could one perform a play in a theater and pretend it was an antiplay? Could one invite spectators to participate and then insult those that did? Could one talk of freedom and charge admission? Could one raise the slogan "the streets belong to the people," and then take the audience only as far as the lobby? Could a theatrical production be mixed with the unprogramed contribution of the audience and still be artistically valid?

REBELLION AND ENTERTAINMENT

It is curious how frequently the arts embody the theme of Hamlet, Dionysus, and Jesus. The theme is ritualized rebellion, embodied in an attack on authority represented by the father and the ultimate tragedy of the son's punishment, in the name of which everyone involved is both punished and redeemed. Through the hero's punishment, the audience punishes their own unconscious tendencies: "the catharsis has to be regarded as a means of objectivization."[22]

Everyman's fantasy is full of oppositions and openness. In fantasy, all men contain each other as options. The specific projected fantasies of art offer values, arguments, and points of view. Hamlet may be seen as the victim of illegitimate authority struggling for a higher truth; or he may be seen as a pampered, power-grabbing postadolescent who exploits the sensible and legitimate attempts of his elders to restructure order in an ambivalent world. The greatness of Shakespeare lies in the breadth and universality of his vision, which permit a variety of conflicting value systems to be projected through the same material.

The arts may also employ laughter as a ritual of rebellion, although laughter is not always rebellion or release from servitude. The uneasy laughter of the ferret-faced clerk at his supervisor's unfunny jokes is servitude and a ritual of humiliation. A great deal of laughter is of this nature, including laughter at jokes, situations, and pratfalls in the media and on the stage. The clichés of "laughter as rebellion" are mistaken. They are only relevant when the comedy or satire represents, in our own scale of values, a protest against illegitimate authority. Not everyone who laughs is proclaiming freedom and independence; quite the contrary. The conventions of the funny and the laugh-worthy are ritualized as are all forms of social behavior. Laughter is a release of energy closely related to automatic defense reflexes, crying out for help to release anxiety or to express pain. The delicate counterpoint of laughter, responsive intakes of breath, and grunts of approval are essentially a means of continuous feedback and communication, capable of expressing the whole range of attitudes possible in human relationships. In this regard, there may be little difference between the laughter of a free man and that of a slave. Cataplexy is a disease of laughter, in which the urge to laugh gags in the throat and cuts off the blood supply to the brain. The victim, seized with the impulse to laugh, instead falls helpless and unconscious to the floor. Panic and death may follow. Laughter may be dangerous to your health!

But laughter frequently does express rebellion and criticism of authority. The underlying impact of most entertainment is similar to rituals of rebellion in function and form. Like a formalized rebellion, humor displaces hostility and aggression. Comedy achieves its effect not only by a cathartic release of repressed emotion, but also as a symbolic warning whose message softens and moderates the use of authority, thereby helping to maintain the legitimacy of prevailing institutions. Turner writes that "nothing underlines regularity so well as absurdity or paradox. Emotionally, nothing satisfies as much as extravagance or temporarily permitted illicit behavior . . . . By making the role mimic the behavior of the high, and by restraining the initiatives of the proud, [rituals of status reversal] underline the reasonableness of everyday culturally predictable behavior between the various estates of society."[23]

In modern culture, the immemorial role of the clown remains as salient as ever. Countless versions of the clown are found in the arts and in the media. The artist plays his role not only by producing culturally defined "works of art," but also by playing an outsider role, challenging social values by his style as well as by his work. The timeless, harmless, wandering clown plays an ambivalent role. In heroic times when social values are rigid and powerful, he is the opposite of the cultural hero, and his barbs of attack are humorous, pathetic, and not always welcome. In times of social confusion and uncertainty, the antihero, stripped down, egoless, and wondering, becomes a real culture hero in the positive sense, and he is treated as saint or rebel.

In Javanese folk drama, the clowns have only fleeting commitments to anyone and will betray their partners in an instant. They mock all of the conventional rituals, imitating gestures and words out of context. Clowns are reductionists: "a clown begins to say something in a high-pitched voice, using cosmopolitan and intellectual Indonesian language, but suddenly drops to the low growl in Surabaja dialect. By compulsively revealing his low side, the clown becomes invulnerable; no one can reduce him lower than he reduces himself."[24] Television comedian Steve Allen states, "the funny man is the man with a grievance." McLuhan notes that the clown is an artist-priest, and vice versa. "Whether it is Al Capp or Walt Kelly or Pat Paulson or the medieval jester, the clown attacks power. . . . The clown is merciless, without conscience, yet he gets our sympathy because he is a scapegoat."[25]

The artists of the counter-culture are the heroes/antiheroes seeking to impose on national culture their own surrealist psychodramas as the ritual hub of emerging culture forms. When Abbie Hoffman calls for a politics of ecstacy to combine the life styles of Fidel Castro and Andy Warhol it is not so much guerilla warfare as monkey business. "Revolution is in my head. I am the revolution. One learns reality from subjective experience. It exists in my head." He warns the politicians of the New Left to beware the power freaks: "People who take themselves too seriously are power crazy. If they win it will be hair cuts for all."[26] He has been proposed as the Shakespeare of the era. Lenny Bruce has already been canonized as the patron saint of the American nightmare, which he saw as full of crazy judges, tribal chieftains, lepers, jazz musicians, irreverent priests, and naked prophets. Ancient Greek comedy originated from improvised invective dramas of tribal ceremony. Similar dramas, like the comedy of Jack E. Leonard and Don Rickles, can be found in folk cultures throughout the world, in a market square in rural Mexico, or as a means of settling interpersonal disputes among modern Eskimos. Gestures of provocation are part of the trick of getting attention and audience involvement. Brustein says, "no apologies need be made . . . the improvised drama of invective has always been an alternative to violence." Abbie, his antecedents, and his imitators express the choice of "effective action as being between comedy and martyrdom."[27]

Yippies and other put-on political groups actively invent dramatic comedy routines, such as their attempts to hijack the Staten Island Ferry or to turn a Billy Graham rally into a pot party, the money destruction in the Stock Exchange, the levitation of the Pentagon, the Grand Central Station massacre, the Chicago confrontation, and the "Great Conspiracy" trial, a metaphysical farce in which the defendants played complex roles as devil-martyrs. Enhancing these productions were the collaborative contributions of Vice-President Agnew and the Nixon administration's own Abbie Hoffman, Martha Mitchell. In his *Revolution for the Hell of It*, Abbie's *Mein Kampf*, every page shows his total dedication to theater: "Life itself is theater." Actions should be invented that are "total information." It is, he writes, "a mistake to tell people what they already know. We alienate people. We involve people. We attract-repel. We play on the generation gap. . . . We tear through the streets. Kids love it. They understand it on an internal level. We are living TV ads, movies, yippie!"

Ritualized direct action, the strategy of the absurd, demonstrates rather than preaches and creates vignettes that force people to take sides, while traditional propaganda is designed for those already convinced.[28] Abbie sees his work with aesthetic objectivity: "I never accuse the cops of being brutal. That was not my role. There are plenty of Liberals around to do that. I applauded the police performance."[29] Many of the most successful theater productions of recent seasons have been edited versions of judicial transcripts involving the Berrigans, the Rosenbergs, the Chicago Eight, and J. Robert Oppenheimer. But what infinitely better theater was the actual Chicago conspiracy or Catonsville Nine trials than the Off-Broadway interpretations.

The canonization of Lenny Bruce is a subject that no student of American culture can ignore. Comedy as rebellion was his forte, although his career was transformed as he became a cult-leader, hunted and persecuted by those who sought to quiet the tremors of the cultural revolution. By legal persecution, they helped to bring on the very thing they sought to avoid, apotheosizing Bruce as mythical giant and saint. The life, death, and resurrection of Lenny Bruce reenacts the Dionysus-Hamlet/Christ theme in the context of the mid-century crisis of Western culture. In real life, Bruce began as a classical clown, the saloon entertainer who is the champion of common sense, putting into proper and hilarious perspective the insanity of all around him. But as Walter Kerr noted, "Lenny Bruce somewhere along the way lost his cool, lost his place on the brink, toppled right over into the quicksand. . . . He became as compulsive, as single-minded, as insistent, finally as boring as a Tartuffe. . . ." As he neared his tragic end, he became "the victim of a passion rather than the parodist of fashion."[30] Brustein writes that in his role as nightclub comedian, Lenny "taught us to see all of American life as a venal extension of show business, with politics, religion, justice, even history itself, functioning as façades for commercial exploitation."[31] Lenny's doomed conflict with the law ultimately helped to lay the groundwork for the unprecedented cultural and artistic freedom that followed. Without Lenny, there would probably have been no X-rated films, no *Futz* or *Tom Paine* or *Hair*. There is value in uncensored theater, in spite of the tendency toward vulgarity, puerility, empty posturing, and fashion-mongering.

The transformation of the Broadway hipster into the bearded hippie saint mocks reality, but embodies salient ritual realities of the era. Lenny's decline as a self-conscious artist coincided with the surfacing of the cultural revolution in the early 1960's. One sensitive observer, Albert Goldman, noted that after his first arrest in 1961, the once-cheerful comic began to resort to "shock tactics in an effort to communicate his new mood of earnestness and anger to jaded nightclub audiences." He abandoned the elaborate comedy routines, his tricks of vocal mimicry and mugging, and developed "a new image and delivery as an underground man: beat, raffish, and satanic. Slouching on stage in a crumpled black raincoat . . ." he would exploit his arrest and his sudden notoriety as the central theme of his art. Growing physically fat and ever more dependent on drugs, he affected a crazy fantasy of hate, vulgarity, and shock, transforming it all with his humorous invention into a ritual of struggle. Goldman writes, "He had become a black-garbed shaman pursuing an archetypal pattern—summoning up the demons with words and noises, joining them in mock combat and finally vanquishing them, while the tribe sat around in fearful absorption, empathizing with his struggle and breathing easier only after he had returned, all smiles and little boy animation, from the land of the boogies."[32]

POP ART AND SONG

Pop culture and participatory theater is a response of the mass audience. It protests against passivity and anonymity. Saturated with art and entertainment, the audience mills about awaiting the next coming, its expectancy inviting a vast variety of pretenders of all sorts, mostly unequipped and untalented. The archetypal image of pop art is the fun house with its distorting mirrors, spooky vistas, traps, tricks, and surprise attacks by puffs of air. Sounds and images have been torn loose and scrambled in a frantic mix. The electronic maelstrom shapes our sensibility with all the modalities of syncretism.

Andy Warhol creates pop art by focusing all the attention and reverence due to the sacred on the most banal and familiar objects. His *Campbell Soup can, 1965* frames and elevates as sacred object something that can be found in anyone's pantry. There is no contagion of personality, no special vision, no idiosyncratic style. What remains sanctified, framed, and elevated in a field of intense concentration is the flat, mute face of the thing itself, a soup can, a dollar bill, a movie star, an ESP sticker. Because of existing conventions, it was deemed improper to find art objects among the decadent, ephemeral, popular, and trashy; therefore, it was assumed that Warhol was being ironic. His films have the same characteristics; the legendary entourage of drag queens, juvenile models, and human parrotfish are arrayed in vacuous and plotless pirouettes. Whether he is being ironic, critical, or radical, or whether he is in truth merely celebrating Brillo cartons and Del Monte peaches, is irrelevant. Warhol's historical importance is beyond question. His impact on other artists, his use of multiple and serial images, mechanical reproduction, and systematic banality as an absolute, his command of all of the latest techniques of calligraphy and printing, have changed the balance of our senses and the nature of art in our culture. To enter a supermarket today is to feel the reality of Warhol's forms. The monstrous hallucination of repetition and meaningless abundance creates a landscape as real and ineluctable as the country scenes in French romantic painting. The landscape of American artifacts, the newsphoto, the whole range of experience, has been lifted from the secular and the unconscious and given theatrical immediacy.[33]

The popular song as a brief excursion of rhythm, melody, and lyrics has been a culture form of significance for several hundred years. The power of rhythmic repetition and the augmented tonalities of speech have a tremendous ritual power. Song involves the slowing down of speech, and the singing styles of each culture reflect conventions of language and voice.[34] The artificial structure of speech in song gives it an elemental and primitive intensity, transforms it into sacred utterance, like prayer or incantation. Rhythm and dance embellish this intensity in the same way as a frame ritualizes a photograph, or the proscenium arch the stage. Separating prosaic items of speech from their practical context and framing them in a sacred form gives them holy significance and intensifies their elemental and universal meanings.

The song is ideally suited for its ritual function. It leaves a memory trace of melody, rhythm, and lyric that reverberates in the mind as a kind of spontaneous and collective vibration. Further, the conventions of simple melodic structure and brief duration make it available as a perfect commodity for selling records, for providing a vehicle of entertainment, and for serving as a staple of the mass media. The possibilities of variation, musically, lyrically, and rhythmically, are infinite. The song becomes for the sacred realm a form of currency, like money, combining convenience, portability, producibility, and versatility, and bearing an unlimited range of content. It constitutes the pocket change of social ceremony and communication.

There is a constant turnover of song cycles in every style from country blues, to rock, to folk, to the art song, the purest currency of social ritual and interaction. As jingles, through Muzak and ubiquitous transistor radios, in seances of musical hypnotism in bachelor apartments or nightclubs, this universal small change of social ritual is available in convenient carry-home packages for everyone to evoke and program at will. The supply of songs is constantly renewed by the professional mints and the weekly crop of hits is announced by a thousand holy disc jockeys on a thousand local radio stations to a world hungry for private ritual transactions. The replenishment of the petty cash accounts of social ritual is a necessary function. Value is maintained only by freshness and evolution. The necessary functions that the small bits of magic accomplish in private lives and interchanges is dependent on a steady flow of value. Pop songs are desacralized rapidly by exposure and the currency must be replenished by a constant stream of new songs.

War songs, political songs, songs of unrequited love, songs of harvest and of season, songs of the stages of life, songs of universal dilemmas and conflicts, songs of the times of sorrow and the times of joy, songs of birth and death, songs of courage and shame, even the rituals of the "Top Forty" and the "Hit Parade," have ancient roots that long preceeded the burgeoning of the mass media. Songs were communicated spontaneously through the oral tradition, by amateur performance on street and highway. Such usage spread the currency of the song in much the same way in preindustrial societies as it does today with added technology. As the small change of social ritual, the song transmuted any private emotion, any minor response, any message into a brief magical performance, whether an argument, an assertion, a demonstration of loyalty, revenge, or rebellion, the reflective pause of self-awareness and self-examination, the pensive gaze on nature, or the genuflection of awe or respect; songs were the arias and soliloquies of the common people. The bare prose of work-a-day life is through song elevated into a self-conscious art form endowed with meaning, importance, and style. The song survives more powerfully than ever, a small paradigm of ritual invention, sacred form, and succinct ceremony.

"Do you believe in rock-and-roll?" Rock music as a system of religious faith and sacred rites is clearly understood by its adherents. Even the outsider can see the earmarks of theological seriousness and high moral purpose in the 1968 "Paul is Dead" cult ("God is dead/Paul is dead/Rock is dead/Turn me on, Deadman!") or in the teeny bopper mini-exegetics that surrounded the 1972 hit by Don McLean, "Miss American Pie."

The impatience of the young with the cerebral and the courtly is not necessarily a change in cultural meanings, but in the conventions of culture forms. The symbols by which meanings are transmitted are in the process of change, but the hunger for legitimacy of form is as strong as ever. Sexuality and sensuality may be symbols of legitimacy and conventions of theatricality just as are the stage whisper, the sigh, the pregnant pause. The issue is not whether the change of convention expands the range of communication and meaning, but whether the available range is used by the artist to communicate values and behavior models that validly reach the audience through the power of fantasy, thereby changing the repertory of ritual patterns and values, and creating new possibilities of invention and discovery.

Pornography as an art form must serve an artful purpose or it will die. Pornographic films, especially the sexploitation variety, are increasingly dull because they have nothing pending, nothing at stake. Even the most vulgar and inept strive for some redeeming significance or gloss of story and plot to dissemble movement and development, and thereby maintain some level of involvement with the audience beyond mechanical and empty masturbation. Religious symbols can be used as shallowly as pornographic ones. The invocation of Christ, godliness, or patriotism can be equally dull, because they have nothing pending, nothing at stake.

A ritual action like a spectacle, a race, sex act, the clichés of violence in children's cartoons, all have a superficial and initial ability to attract attention. Movement itself arrests the eye and holds the focus until the line of action is completed. However, automatic and mechanical processes, empty of meaning, full of dreary and predictable clichés, cannot be redeemed by sex or violence. Movement does not occur *in vacuo;* the prostitute who depersonalizes her performance completely has few repeat customers. A ritual action must have moral dimension, interpersonal meaning, action/reaction all of which may point the way toward paradigms of value, learning and invention, the constituents of ritual drama, without which no symbolic materials can retain potency. If it has these qualities, the least symbol, the flick of the finger or the turning of the head, can be charged with emotional significance and communicative power that transforms an audience. Pornography and obscenity, like religion and ideology, exploit pre-existing social potencies. Such exploitation inevitably steals the luster and meaning of sacred symbols, briefly, but the process generally runs in the other direction. Banality soon pervades the symbols and destroys their brightness. Their power is extinguished.

Whatever legitimate power sex retains must go underground once again to preserve itself against the onslaught of public office and banality. Voyeurism and exhibitionism are grim levelers that soon destroy the fragile illusions of our culture conventions. The geek is a carnival performer sunk so low that he will entertain morbid audiences for a bottle of booze, cutting off the head of a live chicken with his teeth, or doing any nastiness the audience can invent for him. Geeks are plentiful on the American cultural scene and in the arts. But they do not create legitimacy and their function is largely to destroy existing and discredited forms and symbols. The pure geek cannot hold an audience in spite of his efforts to outdo himself in the disgusting and pathetic. When he finally falls senseless in his own vomit, the audience laughs and turns its back. There must be compensations of meaning and audience involvement for a culture form to soar and survive. The correctives are built into the system.

Art was defined in industrial England of the nineteenth century as "the quickest way out of Manchester." Eric Bentley notes that the counter-culture movement in America of the 1960's, "was the quickest way out of Westchester or Elmira." The counter-culture has become establishment culture. Its actions and frauds have been widely and instantly applauded and believed. Bentley notes, "if I were to criticize the Beatles or the Stones *in the establishment press itself*, the editors and I would be bombarded with outraged letters." Most rock, like most art of all kinds, Bentley says, is mediocre, and "quite a lot of it is atrocious." The people who created the rock scene are "exactly as revolutionary as the directors of General Motors." Antiestablishment culture has its own ties with big money and its own snobberies—generally forms of inverted snobbery like pseudo-proletarianism or, traditionally, bohemianism. Bentley laments the counter-culture's "sheer lack of esthetic standards" and, most disastrous, the lack of interest in "what any art essentially is, lack of contact with what each art is actually doing." Even rock is perverted into a new form of Muzak, background music to other activities that are more important, such as getting high on drugs, seduction, making the scene. The rock festival, political demonstrations, the films of the counter-culture, all are transformed into a gentle consumers' mush, background and surrogate activity, containers for essential passivity. Like Muzak, peanuts, and popcorn, products of the counter-culture "scarcely even demand what in former times was thought had to be demanded: attention."[35]

The discontinuity in Jean-Luc Godard's films and the flow of images without story in the whole experimental genre make vanguard films another form of sensuality bath like drugs and superamplified bass rhythms. Passive entertainment and conformity are the opposite of cultural activism. The latter demands that the prestige and legitimacy of innovation at some point begin to create meaningful activities and rituals that are self-sustaining without artificial aids. The collapse of the counter-culture into Jesus revivalism, evangelical antidrug movements, and renewal of middle-class values marks the shallowness and conceit of much of the culture change of the 1960's. Culture as distraction has little future and ends in tyranny.

Excesses in any direction beget extravagances in response. The theater of violence, the theater of the absurd, the theater of horror, Antonin Artaud's theater of cruelty, the excremental sculptures of Sam Goodman molded from polyethylene plastic, Robert Whitman's filmed triptych of scatological toilet facts, all that is the vulgar and dirty and perverse and revolting, including the fervid mysticism of filth and solipsistic squalor, all are symbols in a dialog of culture forms that are caught in the tightening vortex of a storm. But this holocaust is only a state of furious becoming and must be judged as such. The claims of anything as art must not grant immunity from evaluation. The sacred authority is not automatic and self-justifying. It must serve the goals of the broad audience and must be tested by the reality principle of all ritual—whether it dramatizes the themes of underlying meaning while limiting waste of energy and optimizing the craving for stability.

At the beginning of the 1970's all the components of the pressure-cooker media-madness of the cultural revolution, including the mystic chant of Om, the orgiastic writhing on a theater floor, the sensitivity acrobatics of encounter therapy, the touch and grab of Essalin, and the Living Theatre of the streets and of the people's parks, seem to be losing their vigor. The culture pauses, jaded and weary, waiting for the next wave of apocalyptic invention. It is symbolized by the image of an old and tired-looking, over-thirty Abbie Hoffman haranguing an audience: "We are America's youth."

Pornography for the sake of masturbation and rebellion, without closure or purpose, has no cultural future. Obscenity that desacralizes words and objects, and strips bare the cupboard of symbols available to serve special purposes, has no cultural future. What will take the place of the four-letter word when the last one has lost all of its sacred shock value? How will we express vulnerability and intimacy if nakedness and sex become species of public ceremony and political rally? Obviously, man is resilient and inventive. He will fashion substitute means of communication, or may even, after a suitable period of transition, renew the old values and symbols to serve their immemorial purposes.

NOTES

1. Robert Brustein, *Revolution as Theatre* (New York: Liveright, 1970), pp. 41–42.

2. Leon Trotsky, *Literature and Revolution*, tr. by Rose Strunsky (New York: Pioneer Press, 1925), p. 100.

3. Herbert Read, *Icon and Idea: The Function of Art in the Development of Human Consciousness* (New York: Schocken Books, 1965), p. 18.

4. Quoted in Marshall McLuhan, *Culture Is Our Business* (New York: McGraw-Hill, 1970), p. 44.

5. Marshall McLuhan, *Understanding Media: The Extension of Man* (New York: New American Library, 1964), p. ix.

6. McLuhan, 1970, p. iii.

7. Harry Slochower, *Mythopeosis* (Detroit: Wayne State University Press, 1970), p. 15.

8. Quoted in *The New York Times Magazine,* August 8, 1971, p. 36.

9. See Daniel Bell, "The Cultural Contradictions of Capitalism," *The Public Interest,* March 1970, pp. 18–19.

10. Quoted in Read, 1965, p. 17.

11. See Kenneth Burke, from *Lexicon Rhetoricae,* in *Terms for Order,* edited by Stanley Edgar Hyman (Bloomington, Ind.: Indiana University Press, 1964), pp. 20–21.

12. See Max Lerner, "Constitution and Court as Symbols," *Yale Law Journal,* June 1937, pp. 112–34.

13. James L. Peacock, *Rites of Modernization: Symbolic and Social Aspects of Indonesian Proletarian Drama* (Chicago: University of Chicago Press, 1968).

14. During the arid period of quantitative behaviorism, anthropology preserved the humanistic strain, with its ties to folklore and literary criticism, and provided the seeds of a humanistic revival in the 1970's in all of the social sciences.

15. Burke, 1964, p. 124.

16. Quoted in *Village Voice,* June 24, 1971, p. 65.

17. Albert Goldman, *Freak Show* (New York: Atheneum, 1971), p. ix.

18. Bell, 1970, p. 23.

19. Goldman, 1971, p. 47.

20. Brustein, 1970, p. 121.

21. Peacock, 1968, p. 237.

22. Theodor Reik, *Ritual: Psycho-Analytic Studies* (New York: International University Press, 1931), p. 164.

23. Victor W. Turner, *The Ritual Process: Structure and Anti-Structure* (Chicago: Aldine, 1969), p. 176.

24. Peacock, 1968, p. 73.

25. McLuhan, 1970, p. 288.

26. Quoted in William Braden, *The Age of Aquarius* (Chicago: Quadrangle Books, 1970), p. 254.

27. Brustein, 1970, p. 125.

28. See Eleanore Lester, "Is Abbie Hoffman the Real Shakespeare of the 1970's?" *The New York Times,* October 11, 1970, p. D-3.

29. Abbie Hoffman, *Steal this Book!* (New York: Grove Press, 1971), p. 3.

30. Walter Kerr, "Lenny Lost His Cool," *The New York Times,* June 6, 1971, p. D-1.

31. Quoted in Stanley Kaufman, "Lenny," *The New Republic,* July 17, 1971, p. 26.

32. Albert Goldman, "What Lenny Bruce Was All About," *The New York Times Magazine,* June 27, 1971, p. 20.

33. See Robert Hughes, "Man for the Machine," *Time,* May 17, 1971, pp. 80–82. For a more jaundiced view of Warhol, which attacks his self-

conscious put-on of the artist as public figure, see Harold Rosenberg, "Art's Other Self," *The New Yorker,* June 12, 1971, pp. 101–05. Rosenberg charges that Warhol sees himself as an enameled cliché like those of his silk screens: "I am recognized, therefore I am"; the artist becomes a trademark.

34. Marshall McLuhan and Quentin Fiore, *War and Peace in the Tribal Village* (New York: Bantam Books, 1968), p. 136.

35. Quoted in *The New York Times,* August 30, 1970, p. D-1.

11 | THE MEDIA

It took me a long time to discover that the key thing in acting is honesty. Once you know how to fake that, you've got it made.
(John Leonard, 1970)[1]

The media transmit a wide variety of acts that are designed to get attention, to dramatize and display value patterns of conflict groups. They extend the range, scope, and speed by which the symbolic and ritual dimensions of behavior are communicated. Real and pseudo-events blend in an omelet that cannot be unscrambled. The moon landing, the funerals of John F. Kennedy and Martin Luther King, Jr., an eclipse of the sun, a campus riot, all blend and merge to become indistinguishable as culture forms from a sports match or a St. Patrick's Day Parade.

Man has always needed something to watch over his environment and report to him on dangers and opportunities; something to circulate opinions and facts, to help a group make decisions, and then circulate the decisions; something to help pass on the lore and wisdom and expectations of society to new members; something to entertain people on a broad scale; something to broaden trade and commerce.[2]

Simpler societies met these tasks with watchmen, tribal leaders, parents and teachers, bards and jesters, and itinerant traders. These roles are still intact in advanced nations and continue to operate informally both through the traditional person-to-person networks and through the media. These simpler media can be seen more clearly in the primitive nations: the Yoruba talking drums, the custom of reading the newspaper to illiterates, the interchange in the coffee house, the village square, the schoolhouse, or any other place where people congregate. The bazaar, where for centuries people have exchanged information, still serves this function. Puppet shows, story-tellers, poets, ballad-singers, and dramatic groups continue to play their timeless roles.

THE PROBLEM OF CREDIBILITY

The public arts solicit the favor of the entire public because the power of communication rests not only on physical reach and scope, but also on something more tenuous and fundamental: the credibility (or legitimacy) of the communicator. To the extent this quality is earned, the public arts become common carriers for all kinds of social functions, including expressive ritual, individual and group conflicts, and exchanges of values and outcomes.

The public arts focus audience attention and close the gap between private attitudes and public morality, providing a symbolic amphitheater for all processes that constitute a complex pluralistic society. The power of publicity is a kind of cosmic energy transformer that can shift the focus of public attention, and thus the availability and responsiveness of social energy, to this or that person, activity, or issue, conferring status and reality on public issues, persons, organizations, and social movements.[3] Just as a bank concentrates social credit of individual savers and confers on a borrower the power to command resources, so the public arts lend their credibility and legitimacy to any reportable subject. The attention-getting capability may even operate in the absence of credibility; in which case, discredited media may have an inverted affect on the audience, conferring discredit on those whom they treat sympathetically, and raising the respectability, by reverse contamination, of those they discredit.

The media are under considerable pressure to maintain credibility. In some cases, this means noncommitment to sectarian or factional values (where the media have the most legitimacy to protect), or pluralism and balanced advocacy (where audiences are already resistant to influence and media power is low). Newspapers long ago made the transition from the first to the second state; radio went through the same transformation from sacred to profane in the 1950's; television continues to have great efficacy, but in the last decade it has also begun to move from the sacred to the profane realm.

Scale, speed, and availability of modern technology create differences in kind between modern and traditional communication networks. In McLuhan's words, "Today electronics and automation make mandatory that everybody adjust to the vast global environment as if it were his little home town."[4] The instantaneous electronic global village ties all its members into a single web of interacting, vibrating hearts and souls. The poor, the young, and the black are no longer invisible to the great middle majority, and the closed lines of communication of the old printed media (which tended to follow and maintain caste and class structures) no longer exist to exclude anyone. "You are there, and they are here!" The most scabrous cold-water tenement, lacking books, newspapers, or print of any kind, has television sets going day and night in every flat. Ghetto teenagers have transistor radios glued to their ears. The black child wonders why his skin is not "flesh colored," to match the Bandaids.

There are sixty million homes in the United States and over 95 percent of them are equipped with television. (More than 25 percent have two or more sets.) In the average home the television is turned on some five hours and forty-five minutes a day. The average male viewer, between his second and sixty-fifth year, will watch television for over three thousand entire days—roughly nine full years of his life. During the average weekday winter evening nearly half of the American people are to be found in front of the set. The census bureau reports that 87 percent of nonwhite households have television sets; 94 percent of white households have them. In contrast, a *Washington Post* survey indicated that black readership of newspapers is only half that of whites.

When millions of people follow the same communication at one time, the cosmic amplifier has the potentiality to summon qualitative changes of a significant order. The infinite replications of comic books and records, the velocity of radio and television, the availability of the motion picture, and the way the various entertainments support one another create a highly centralized marketplace for culture transactions of all kinds, channeling symbolic processes into a single stream that requires a continuous flow of manufactured images and information to serve as content. The mass audience must be held in a mobilized state, as much as possible, in order that the media can maintain contact in the competitive struggle for credibility.

The media perform a ritual function merely in keeping the channels of communication open and in a regular periodicity. The music and idle chatter of a radio station provide security by their very presence, like the predictable appearance of newspapers and magazines on the doorstep. The sudden silence of the radio station, the blacking out of a familiar video channel, the disruption of the habit of newspaper and coffee at breakfast, disrupt the ritual balance of society and thereby endanger the patterns of stability, making energy available for redirection, anxiety, and confusion. The stabilizing ritual function of the media invites interruption by those engaged in revolutionary or counter-revolutionary action aimed at obtaining the disorganizing effects resulting from the attack on a well-chosen symbolic target. The fact that communication blackouts may be highly effective accounts for the tendency of mass media to take a high priority in a revolutionary order of battle. The United States had a faint foretaste of this in newspaper strikes "whose impact, though dampened by the presence of radio and television, creates the sense of malaise, of something wrong, but adds a touch of anxiety (and of emptiness), especially among the educated classes."[5] In a highly articulated mass society, the maintenance of open channels of communication is a significant hedge against panic reactions of all kinds.

A circular dynamic exists because the technological potential of media demands constant use. The social need for latent availability of communication channels results in a continuous exercise of the dispensing function, quite independent of the legitimizing value of individual transmissions. The permanent crises of the Second World War developed an unprecedented appetite for news. Diplomacy and war became the biggest show in town, even after the war had ended. Just as nations find it difficult to return to prewar budgets, the usages of wartime news-gathering and reporting survived. To maintain legitimacy, the news media were forced to treat all kinds of esoteric political conflicts as though they were critical confrontations involving the life or death of the republic. The ritual drama of the Second World War (democracy versus Naziism) was easily changed to fit the Cold War (democracy versus communism). The tremendous national prestige that attached to strategically minor disputes was at least partly aggravated by the wartime habits of the news media.

Like a mother listening to the infant breathing in the cradle, or the constant search for vital signs by a soldier in contact with the enemy, the media are relentlessly turned on, filled mostly with idle chatter, hungry for meaningful crises and threatening facts that will renew their legitimacy. Conversely, the individual who has been trained by the media remains turned off continuously, listening without hearing the background noise of his existence, the machine-gun presentation of news, weather, and music. He is programed by the media who want to keep the hot lines open, ready to mobilize attention for the announcement of a football score, a battle lost, the end of the world.

Although they generally serve the status quo, the media must first of all safeguard their credibility. Thus, they cannot indefinitely resist the challenge of new images and values. The pluralism of their structure introduces a competitive element that makes them vulnerable to all kinds of claims by innovators, whether serious or merely eccentric. Any individual or group who can force a reportable event can gain media-attention, and thereby can help shape the ritualized reality or culture. All of the ambivalences of the social process are projected into the media. Critics who would make a scapegoat of the media are grasping at a partial truth. New technology does modify the functional significance of certain kinds of behavior by providing new routes and means of expression. Street theater may become an institutionalized ritual of social conflict. Stylized violence in front of a television camera may have an augmented and amplified effect in changing attitudes and bargaining relationships throughout the country. But media-attention generally serves to limit and control dangerous escalations. Ritual violence is a safety valve and a catharsis. If it is too much feared, it is because the legitimacy of formal institutions is already insecure. Public authority must accept the inevitability of the challenge; it must seek to dramatize its legitimacy by using the media as effectively as do the challengers.

IS THERE A SANTA CLAUS?

In a recent documentary film, French movie-producer Frederick Rossif comes to the conclusion that the violence in America in the late 1960's was culture ritual, not political action: "Everything in America is a spectacle, everything answers to a profound and original rhythm—strikes, music, a presidential election, baptism of blacks in the Mississippi, crazy speculation in Wall Street." Everything in America is transformed into art, entertainment, and music. "The Charleston, Jazz, assembly-line work, hunger marches, billionaires and public enemies—everything is animated by a vital sense of growth that left Europe a long time ago. In American brutality, there is less underhanded egotism than in the apparent gentleness of European life."[6]

The presence of ritual drama as the hub of culture is manifested more clearly in the media than in the arts. While the latter are exploratory and inventive, the former are standardized, stereotyped, and unambiguous as cues to responsive behavior. The ritual drama of the mass media embodies the prevailing ideological content of the social and political order—the clash between good and evil, the accepted myths of history that explain and justify existing institutions and behaviors, the self-righteousness and cultural chauvinism of the moment. The clash between American ethical superiority and European decadence in the nineteenth century, the drama of the innocent bucolic mechanics, farmers, and woodsmen put upon by Eastern merchants and conniving railroads, the Wilsonian period of American idealism pitted against corrupt European imperialism, the image of the world as a stage for the contest between democracy and communism, are recent versions of the U.S. ritual drama, the universally acknowledged and ubiquitously repeated formulas for rationalizing the self-righteous claims of an age.

By and large, the mass media purvey expectable images, reading all the cliché variations and categories of the ritual drama into the infinite variety of actual events. "News" becomes a means of elaborating the underlying mythology by projecting it into the concrete images of daily happenings, anecdotes, pictures, and parables. Robert E. Park says, "News story and fiction story are two forms of modern literature that are now sometimes so like one another that it is difficult to distinguish them. The *Saturday Evening Post* writes the news in the form of fiction, while the daily press frequently writes fiction in the form of news."[7]

The method is what Boorstin attacks as "the manufacture of pseudo-events," that is, events created by and for the purpose of its creators. The pseudo-event is distinguished from a "factual" event, which reveals the "real world" (something that Boorstin fails to define). Boorstin is overwhelmed by the phoniness of the media. He cites P. T. Barnum as the classic "master of pseudo-events." When Barnum's winter circus quarters burned, he pyramided the news by announcing that insurance had covered only a fraction of the losses. When Jumbo, the African elephant, was killed in a railroad accident, he put out the story that "Jumbo died sacrificing himself to save a baby elephant." He imported a female elephant and exhibited her next to Jumbo's stuffed body as the bereaved widow.[8]

Boorstin's ire is misplaced. His inability to distinguish pseudo from real events betrays the shallowness of his critique. Virtually all events are pseudo in that they enter the mainstream of culture as symbolic communications surrounded by ritualized significance.

The assimilation of events into culture is what makes them real, in terms of the notions of legitimacy that they challenge or support. It is difficult to imagine an event that is not culturally distorted, except perhaps the proverbial tree that falls unseen and unknown deep in the forest, setting up vibrations that no one can interpret as sound. Every natural event that occurs in a social setting is quickly encrusted with acculturated definitions and responses. Every action of man or nature projects an entirely secondary reality through symbolic forms.

Boorstin recognizes this process and describes it well, yet he is forced to postulate that a world of pure forms and events outside of culture does exist and should be the primary source of undistorted information. Pseudo-events, he writes, "spawn other pseudo-events in geometric progression." Being planned, each tends to become ritualized "with a protocol and rigidity all its own." Pressures arise to produce other derivative forms of pseudo-events that are "more fluid, more tantalizing, and more interestingly ambiguous."[9] This is a useful description. All events contain a strong element of cultural contrivance and ritual drama. Whether arranged with the convenience of the media in mind or merely exploited by the media for their own or for a social purpose, all information, the very power to isolate and define "a fact," depends on preexisting symbolic categories and culture values. Whether anything is "factual" depends on how convenient it is to believe it, and whose interest it serves. Provisional versimilitude is the nature of truth, and it is not unrelated to the methods, ideologies, and interests at stake in its impact on existing social relationships.

The role of contrivance and purpose in making "news" should not be despised. President Sadat of Egypt called off his war with Israel in December 1971, because, he said, the India-Pakistan War over Bengla Desh broke out and made the timing unfavorable. One event may inhibit another. The impact of an event may be different if it does not compete for attention with other events of a similar magnitude. This fact reveals something about the causal factors underlying events, factors not related to the dynamics of the event itself but rather to the availability of a stage in the psychic theater of world attention.

The popular media mediate between the ideology of the community and the stream of events.[10] Lasswell points out that the ideological framework "affects the recognition of an event as newsworthy." Ideology provides a set of fundamental expectations about future developments and their meaning. "When set-backs have come, the interpretor's task is to use them to strengthen the ideology rather than to allow disappointments to militate against faith, belief, and loyalty."[11] The ritual drama provides the basic set of stories that dramatize and legitimize the values of the ideology, making "the present and the future relatively intelligible." Ideology contains the explanatory categories, permitting the goals and objectives of public policy to be clarified and rationalized.

Boorstin's criticism implies that social analysis based on pseudo-events does not provide "problem-solving guidance" to the community. Were this the case, obviously the underlying ideology would suffer a loss of credibility along with the institutions that specialize in interpreting events. The issue is one of values in conflict. Boorstin thinks his values are *more real* and therefore more problem-solving than those he criticizes. His problem is intellectual parochialism. Underlying ideologies of the social order *are* problem-solving in the sense that they reflect the social order itself, its ability to mobilize its resources, its empirical learning through trial and error, and the basic self-fulfilling prophecy of its behavioral unity. Obviously, culture embodies a cumulative process of social learning and reinforcement.

McLuhan aphorizes: "Reality tends to conform to the pseudo-event."[12] There is clearly no socially desirable, professionally agreed-on definition of "news." Theoretically, news is information concerning changed conditions in the social and physical biosphere that may require appropriate adjustment of social values and behavior. Culture forms embody the cumulative outcomes of adjustment that, so long as they remain in steady state, may be safely taken for granted. There is no fascination in steady state conditions, but only in changes that jeopardize the equilibrium. News, therefore, is anything that requires cultural assimilation, whether a change in technology, a change in scientific knowledge, a change in the weather, or a change in a political regime.

News is a report from the adaptive frontier of the social order. However, there are no hard-and-fast standards that determine which changes are news and which are not. The perception of change is relative to existing culture forms, stereotypes, and interests. The fact is extracted from a welter of events. It is the product of attention as well as an objective situation. Societies are structured hierarchically and the distribution of values and influence is always relative to perceptions of legitimate social purpose. The discovery and acknowledgment of change is therefore dependent on the hierarchical structure of social purpose. In short, the ability to discover "news" involves a recognition of social values and an assertion of what constitutes reality. The discovery and reporting of facts are political acts and constitute claims on the body politic. There is no absolute empirical test to choose between the discoveries of mystics and those of economists. The bad dream of a witch doctor may be significant news in a tribe that endows the dreamer with legitimacy and his notions for restructuring the social order with temporal authority.

Editor Charles A. Dana stated, "News is anything that will make people talk." Hearst editor Arthur McEwen countered, "News is anything that makes the reader say *Gee Whiz!*"[13] After losing his fight to Frazier, Mohammed Ali declared, "News don't last too long. Plane crash, 90 people die. Presidents get assassinated, civil rights leaders assassinated. World go on. You got children to feed and bills to pay. Got other things to worry about. You'll all be writing about something else soon."[14]

News is an expression and projection of the ritual drama of a period (which includes the social structure, the perception of legitimate authority, and changes that command attention) and the resources invested in collecting information.

The basic legitimacy and unity of the group, the efficacy of its collaborative and communicative systems, constitute problem-solving characteristics of a high order. These are embodied in the myths of ritual drama and ideology, however baffling, absurd, and implausible these may appear to a visitor from a small planet. This is what V. O. Key calls the "latency of opinion," which he holds to be "a sovereign explanation of fundamental aspects of the governing process."[15] Such latency rests on "engrained sets of values, criteria for judgment, attitudes, preferences, dislikes—pictures in his head—which reflect the social myths and ideologies of the time." Walter Lippmann uses the term "social fictions," by which he means representations of the environment "which are in lesser or greater degree made by man himself." The range of fictions extends "all the way from complete hallucination to the scientist's perfectly self-conscious use of a schematic model." The alternative to the use of fictions, he writes, is "direct exposure to the ebb and flow of sensation. This is not a real alternative, for however refreshing it is to see at times with a perfectly innocent eye, innocence itself is not wisdom, though a source and corrective of wisdom."[16] The wisdom of culture form and ritual, like a skin over raw nerve-endings and tissue, saves the energy of the organism and protects against entropic processes.

The prevailing myths of a culture are not seen as bias because of their universality. It is only when they are in the process of significant challenge that they are seen as fictions, and attacked in the name of new truths and realities (made of exactly the same ritual and symbolic materials) that have assumed greater legitimacy. The succinct and uncritical clichés of newspaper headlines are part and parcel of the ritual drama that convinces us that what we already know is true. During periods of social unity and confidence, the media play to the galleries, projecting a grade B movie of the mind of America. The news is the story of everybody's life. It is a true sacramental ritual celebration. Every individual in all the details of his existence is immersed in the main chance, the developing ritual drama of his times.

Even in the cultural revolution of the 1960's, despite the loss of confidence in the old fictions, all the new candidates for legitimacy tend to be as vulgarized by clichés and archetypal stories as are the forms they challenge. Sentimentality, maudlin self-love, and self-righteousness provide the ultimate legitimacy to which even revolutionary values must appeal. Adventure and romance still outsell sex and social criticism. Despite the wide variety of innovative movies, the biggest box-office hits of recent years were *Airport* in 1969, and *Love Story* in 1970, both traditional romantic forms. Lamentable as may be the prospect of a host of imitations, the fact is that tastes in ritual drama have not essentially changed, even during a period of culture storm.

There is a hard core of conventional wisdom in the public's distaste for intellectual verbalisms and preference for dramatic stories with a poignant moral dimension. The public senses that the ideological hair-splitters who compete in theoretical issue-mongering and iffy proposals for solving all of our problems, are really pitchmen and schlock-dealers posturing as experts. They sense the ambiguous and insubstantial nature of cheap talk, and hold it suspect. Their sense of what is legitimate is far more fundamental. It arises from the symbolic ritual roles that political personalities strive to satisfy. It arises from the existential psychodrama of the body politic. Campaign strategist Jerry Bruno saw New York Mayor John V. Lindsay as the John F. Kennedy of 1972. His scenario for the campaign aimed at "creating excitement." Keep the candidate in front of the public in every conceivable setting, especially where crowds form. "The press sees crowds—the crowds sense that they are part of something exciting and important, and that's what goes on TV and in the press, while the intellectuals debate the last sentence on the first page of the speech. But the average voter, he sees excitement and enthusiasm, and that's what he wants to be a part of."[17] It didn't work for him for larger reasons.

If the media are strongly shaped by the demands of ritual drama, neither can they escape the conventions of form and expressive range that arise from the technology of communication itself. The mark of modernization is the lengthening of communication channels. Centralized government, roads, schools, literacy, and the mass media roll back the horizons of the individual's social world. First-hand experience and interpersonal communication coexist with the stream of information in which the individual recognizes nonlocal events as dangers and opportunities. These changes fundamentally transform his psychological world, extending and redefining perspective. The tendency of the mass media is national and centralizing but it does not replace the immemorial world of personal interrelations and firsthand observation that continues to play a powerful role within the umbrella of information technology.

The political order is a web of symbolic transactions and events. As city-centered mass media envelop the information process, access to media-attention becomes a political fact of tremendous importance. Those who have such access are in the unique position of projecting their private interests and fantasies into the mainstream of national ritual drama and ideology. It follows that emerging political constituencies and newly self-conscious groups should seek access to the mass media by whatever means are necessary, from direct action political tactics to imaginative self-promotion and behavioral invention. By achieving access, they may challenge the legitimacy of existing culture forms and institutions by exploiting the contradictions, failures, and old wounds of prevailing power groups. This is the underlying basis of political change. New leadership cadres seek to capture the ritual leadership of culture forms and values, the essential prerequisite to winning formal political office. Would-be contenders look for ways to enact the struggle that will credit themselves and discredit their adversaries, by the same process that Goffman describes in mental hospitals as looping: each error and failure of strategy by rivals become new reasons for their eventual downfall in a ritual drama designed to embody the new values and anoint the new leadership with legitimacy.

A recent study of the Chicago slums described the network of interpersonal communications and its operations among those who have virtually no mass media access. Rumor and gossip create the realities of perceived common interest and conflicts: "The mere inception of a rumor seldom progresses exactly as a self-fulfilling prophecy. Once such a rumor has started, it is neither believed nor disbelieved in the strict sense. Instead, it is taken as *likely* and people begin to prepare just in case. When people begin to alter their own behavior to suit the rumor, it gains credence and moves on toward being a *certainty*. . . . Each party to the potential confrontation is faced with the problem of denying or corroborating the rumor." Reciprocal defensive maneuvers produce additional rumors that incite further maneuvers that implicate more people. In this way, the nexus of rumor becomes a symbolic process of political interaction and bargaining entirely through informal media.[18]

The media develop well-defined conventions, whether those of gossip and word-of-mouth or those of television. The rule of expressive range applies: the energy of the communication varies directly to resistance and noise. The conventions of overacting and extravagant gesture arose in the unamplified theater and were carried to the silent screen. Any individual trying to communicate amidst the clash and din of a noisy background, finds himself engaging in extravagant gesture, slow and deliberate mimicry, and explicit acting-out of the meaning of his words. He imitates the conventions of the theater of Sarah Bernhardt and the films of Harold Lloyd. When speech and sound were added, film became intimate and background noise was considerably reduced. This made the earlier conventions of overacting appear absurd and primitive. It is cultural chauvinism to think that the changes in acting from Bernhardt to Brando are a progress of taste and art; rather, they are change in the requirements of technology. When the technology does not require it, any convention of style becomes grotesque, humorous, or camp. The difference between what McLuhan terms hot (hard-sell explicit, analytic concreteness) and cool (soft-sell, casual, and integrative) should be understood as related to the conventions of technological form in terms of the rule of expressive range.

In every medium, there is a tendency to preserve the repertoire of styles of all the other media in order to combine them in new and surprising combinations, as a way of achieving contrapuntal depth of meaning and surprise. However, the widespread imitation of a certain style can quickly lead to a loss of media effectiveness. The conventions of the rock festival are the same as those of a television spectacular like the film academy awards or the "Ed Sullivan Show." Staginess, Busby Berkeley production numbers, vacuous patter, announcements attempting to outsuperlative the last, are typical: "And now, straight from their sensational European tour, let's hear it for The Who!" They are extravaganzas of bobbing guitars, weaving bodies, and pas de deux between vocalist and microphone, characterized by staginess, contrived excitement rising to shrillness, occasional slow and reflective interludes like acts of repentance, and returns to shrillness that try to achieve dramatic form and climax by the simple expedient of blasting, tearing, and ripping vocal chords, loudspeakers, and emotions.

A continuously high level of excitement and stimulation leads to a high threshold of response. Media overload leads to media insensitivity. Hard-sell leads to no-sell, and excessive appeals for emotional response lead to impassivity and withdrawal. The saturation effect of modern mass media has succeeded not only in bringing the moon landing into every living room, but also in making it dull. What a paradoxical climax!

The media cannot replace face-to-face interaction, with the latter's richness of information flow and facilitation of immediate feedback. The social norms that regulate copresent behavior also develop conventions that reflect the rule of expressive range. The intensity of a communication varies directly with the physical distance separating the communicants. Goffman states, "On Shetland Isle, during cold nights, mainland visitors walking together along the Bay in apparent isolation who laugh loudly could cause Shetlanders an eighth-of-a-mile away to raise their eyebrows. Conversely, when an individual whispers or uses eye expressions, the body acts as a focusing barrier, effectively restricting the usual sphere of propagation of sense stimuli, so that reception is limited to those very close to him."[19] Lovers holding hands can communicate a whole delicate range of responses by pressure and finger movement with hardly any energy-waste at all; a rich dialog of assertion and rejoinder is clearly understood even though the communications are barely perceptible.

The apparent lack of spontaneous feedback in the electronic media is not crippling. All kinds of feedback mechanisms develop through market surveys, audience inventories, critical journalism, the politics of FCC regulations and control, the economic marketplace of programs and commercials, the competitive interplay among members of the industry themselves, and less important, the use of live audiences, interview and talk formats, and audience participation in the studio or by telephone.

THE MEDIA FALLACY

It is argued that the media, particularly television, create a stage that actually controls events, often fraudulently. Jack Gould asks, "How to get access to the television screen?" It is going to be the dominant issue for years as evidenced in Senate hearings on the right of Congress to have automatic television time for reply to the White House, in questions of equal time for nonserious third and fourth party candidates, in questions of controlling television campaign expenditures, and in issues of the credibility of the media and monopoly control raised by Spiro Agnew and others. "Everyone from the president down to the militant activists knows that the name of the game in the arena of opinion is television. If you want to make a point quickly, and reach everyone everywhere, the tube is almost a government in itself."[20]

Abbie Hoffman, the Yippie leader of the 1968 Chicago riots, was explicit in his strategy of image-making, applying all the lessons of Madison Avenue as methods of packaging and selling confrontation: ". . . I fight through the jungle of TV, you see . . . . It's all in terms of disrupting the image, the image of a democratic society being run very peaceful and orderly and everything according to business."[21] The elaborate array of grandiose threats (to dump LSD in the city's water supply, for example) was part of the script, designed to condition authorities and demonstrators for the parts the leaders hoped they would play. Chicago's Mayor Richard Daley, in the city's television special designed to defend police actions (entitled "How Many Trees Do They Plant?"), argued that the police were not to blame if the demonstrators sought to incite certain reactions and were accommodated.

In its vulgar form, this theory of the active role of the media in creating events has been offered in connection with almost every major violent event in the last decade. The mayors of Birmingham and Selma both blame the unblinking eye of the television camera for massive and provocative demonstrations against prevailing authorities. In Chicago, a number of newsmen observed how quickly a throng of demonstrators gathered when a television camera came into sight. One cameraman exclaimed, "Give me enough cameras, and I'll take over the world!" As a result, the violence of the police is often directed not only at peaceful or violent demonstrators, but also at reporters and cameramen and their equipment.

Violence is held to be a kind of energizing human electricity, the link to electrical signals and current.[22] The television screen, McLuhan says, has changed the balance of our senses. Unlike the theater, the printed word, or the movie screen (the latter being merely a variety of theater), the television tube minimizes the communicator's programing and predigestion of experiences. In all the older media, the editor, writer, actor, and director can structure the communication of experience to make it conform to images that reflect his own ways of reacting and absorbing, ways that usually are consensualist and tend to reinforce the status quo. Consequently, the older media tended by and large to maintain social distance and insularity in the vision of reality they transmitted differentially to social groups.

"The medium is the massage" expresses the fact that the *forms* of communication themselves have a central and primary effect on the kinds of things that are communicated. The intrusion of television, especially documentaries, news, and live coverage, makes us suddenly and distressingly aware of realities for which we lack insulation and prescribed social images. There is no literacy gap to reinforce existing institutions; every watcher sees all kinds of things not intended or prepared for him. The commentator, the film and the videotape editor, the cameraman who points the electronic eye, the director who selects the product of many cameras, all strive to do the filtering traditional of the older media. But television fails to achieve the same effect as the older media because their efforts to program and structure the experience in accord with yesterday's clichés and norms is imperfect.

Television, with its immediacy of news coverage, transmits a vast amount of raw, undigested experience to which people react, not according to safe and recognizable categories, but in direct and wholly unpredictable ways. The world becomes a tribal village. The picture is not on the screen; rather, the beam of light goes to the very brain of the viewer as a kind of firsthand experience, identical in effect to his face-to-face experiences. Tribal immediacy, spontaneity, and highly personal reaction to everything that is happening throughout the world extend the group and the self in unprecedented ways. The entire locked-in audience reacts to far-flung events, including wars, riots, and assassinations, with untutored nakedness. Geographical distance and perspective, the buffers of human relations in complex societies, disappear, and all things everywhere reach, involve, and threaten the entire audience.

Government policy, McLuhan suggests, can no longer separate killing for policy reasons abroad from murder at home. Overseas wars become impossible because the whole nation experiences them simultaneously and completely. The viewer looks into the face of a wounded Viet Cong and sees a man. He looks into the face of a president and reads a message entirely different from the man's words. Whatever official policy does in faraway places threatens and justifies similar behavior at home in every context of personal relations and domestic politics. Television, McLuhan proclaims, has eliminated the possibility of making careful separations and distinctions, as previous ages did, in order to specialize behavior norms to serve differentiated social functions. Now everyone is in on everything; all respond to all kinds of events in clusters of meaning that have nothing to do with official purposes and often conflict with them. A riot, demonstration, or act of police terrorism in Chicago has the same effect in Birmingham as if it had occurred there. Any provocative event creates a simultaneous and epidemic reaction throughout the country. Social excitement and panic in the New York subway becomes social excitement in subways in Chicago, energizing and precipitating not only home-town muggings but also overreactive prevention and retaliation. The very simultaneity and sensitivity of the extended tribal village generate every variety of extremism, and predispose extremists to seek exposure and an audience through the media in order to generalize and propagate their own acts.

In its hyperbolic form, the thesis holds that electronic media are directly responsible for the incidence of personal and political violence, quite apart from all other kinds of factors that may predispose individuals toward tactics of confrontation. The dynamics of the electronic media compel individuals and groups to seek exposure and attention by doing something different or new. They are forced to dramatize themselves by escalating sensation and inventing new tactics to maximize shock values. Four-letter words, nudism, public fornication, and the like are justified as forms of political protest in the competition for attention. Ersatz events and manipulated happenings assume political significance and power that they never had in the rationalistic, linear clichés of prevideo media. The least inhibited youths become the dominant innovators because they are the freshest and most spontaneous product of the video age. Everything becomes possible as those who are least programed by the clichés and inhibitions of the past respond to and exploit a new possibility of instant revolution in every area of life and in all institutions. Even the advertising men look to the innovators in seeking to market goods and ideas.

This doctrine of the capability of the media to incite violence attracts not only beseiged public officials who require a scapegoat, but also the media men themselves, for whom it tends to confirm and inflate their claims of importance—and their revenues. If the thesis were valid, the solution to confrontation politics, extremism, and violence would lie in more perfect control of the media in the interests of public policy and, conversely, more attention to the example set by public policy. Interview shows, documentaries, and news would have to be more competently tailored to avoid unintended communications that arise from the simultaneity, rawness, and immediacy of the tube. Situation comedies, old movies, and straight news broadcasting might deprive us of what little breath of reality now comes across the airwaves.

Fortunately, the problem is not that simple, and the power structure would have nothing to gain by trying to suppress the pluralistic nature of present media coverage. One of the most important facts militating against this theory is the existence of the contagion phenomenon. Imitation, fadism, and mimicry are fundamental to the process of socialization. They are how we learn from each others' experience, how we test and prove new values and new behavior. A violent march anywhere tends to generate violent marches elsewhere. This was true not only before television but also before radio and even before newspapers. Channels of communication gain their credibility not by their mere existence or ubiquity but by the immemorial test of confidence and trust that arises out of the satisfaction of the individual's needs. The real coin of communication is validated by the old fundamental usages.

Word of mouth between people who serve each other's needs remains the most powerful and sometimes the most rapid form of communication. Under McLuhan's hypothesis, it is incredible that Christianity could revolutionize the Roman Empire, or that the American, French, and Russian revolutions, with their awkward handbills and posters, could have occurred at all. The receiver of electronic communications edits the content of the message in accordance with his own structures, images, predispositions, and needs, just as he always has edited the editors, the commentators, and the Madison Avenue boys. Even the best-conceived propaganda and the most delicate soft-sell can be edited out by the viewer as the electronic beam scans his retinas. What is transmitted to the mind is meaningful only in terms of what is already there. Interest, attention, and the predisposition to react in certain ways are not spontaneously affected or locked-in equally to every communication.

The immemorial human relations of individual and group experience, affiliation and loyalty, and identification with social values and perceptions of self-interest are commingled in that vast complexity that underlies all political reality, the modern as well as the ancient. People have always reacted to events in terms of their own needs and problems and their own social identities, not in terms of the self-serving construction placed on events by those who may communicate them. Receptivity to certain kinds of experience and a predisposition to interpret and react in certain ways are much more basic than the precise form or vehicle of communication. When violent demonstrations proliferated in response to the assassination of Martin Luther King, Jr., it was not because of the televised funeral; it was because of what Martin Luther King's life and actions meant to the lives and actions of those who loved and hated him. Events that reflect conflict tend to be generalized when others identify with the conflict. When this condition does not exist, there is no automatic generation of imitative behavior.

The media managers have a feeling for the kinds of experience that will arrest the attention of large groups of people. While educators and churchmen may disapprove of the attention given to sensational acts, while mayors and police chiefs may not be pleased by scrutiny of their treatment of minorities, the news media are attracted to these frontiers of social change for the same reasons that the general audience is interested in them. All people select and abstract from the noisy buzz of communications the categories that serve their individual purposes. Society has a more urgent need to know about one person killed crossing a street than about thousands who crossed safely. Newsmen and editors are as much a part of conflict groups and have as much stake in the changing institutions as anyone. Where people are willing to take grave risks, where social institutions are threatened, where disruptive or self-destructive behavior proliferates, there are the real frontiers of social change where values are struggling to be born or to die. Human relations, conflict, situations that embarrass or compromise the powerful, the character of men, and the universal comedy and tragedy of real lives are the things closest to all people. Reports of crime and criminality, suicide and murder, strikes and divorces, are real. All the rest are self-serving abstractions and ideologies that buffer and conceal the dimensions of trauma in society.

News of the Columbia University revolt in the spring of 1968 was transmitted to other campuses throughout the country not only by Huntley and Brinkley. Personal couriers, working through student and church groups, in letters and newspapers communicated rumors, lies, and the imaginative constructions of all sorts of individuals to many kinds of audiences. Imitative outbreaks proliferated because many people with related problems could use the information in some way. The outcome of any high-risk bargaining engagement is interesting to all engaged in similar situations, since the engagement may provide a model for both tactics and outcomes. A powerful model, in fact, tends to influence behavior and outcomes symbolically, making unnecessary the repetition of escalated risk-taking. Thus, S. I. Hayakawa and Governor Reagan sought a showdown at San Francisco State College in order to create a new model that could refute the symbolic efficacy of the Columbia and Berkeley models and thereby discourage future tactics of disruption.

When someone goes over the edge at one place, his act tends to excite conflict elsewhere and to force others over the edge. Fads of suicide, of lynching, of demonstrations, sit-ins, and so on reflect adaptive reinforcement of behavior. Communication is the link, but the content of the event and its adaptability to other situations are what cause some kinds of faddist behavior, but not others, to achieve epidemic proportions. In addition, the same process causes the proliferation of built-in correctives and counterforces by those who are threatened by a specific wave of mimicry. Not the media but the substratum of bargaining among individuals and social groups has always been the chief factor in shaping and changing human societies. One fad peters out in a few weeks and another becomes a permanent way of life, while the media sometimes help, sometimes resist, and sometimes tag along for their own purposes.

Violence may, under certain circumstances, prove an adaptive method of inducing political action. Television through its coverage of violent encounters may encourage extremism, but it may also, in contrast, discourage it by providing a forum at less risk. Were the common forum of the nation's psychic life to exclude certain social groups or values, political change might be forced into even more extreme tactics in the search for attention and audiences. (Here we see the wisdom of the Bill of Rights, which guarantees the right to petition, hire a hall for a meeting, or demonstrate peacefully in the public streets, however unpopular the occasion may be.) It is universally evident that the deft use of political symbols is always and everywhere superior to the bludgeoning escalation of real conflict. The media may facilitate communications; they may also have just the opposite effect. When they are misused, they sacrifice their credibility in the interests of the advertising dollar, entertainment, or the propaganda interests of government or powerful economic groups. People then may not believe even what is communicated honestly and may not respond to it. The debasement of the coin of public communication is a much more dangerous and subversive tendency than is exuberant confrontation politics.

Censorship or voluntary agreements to suppress the news serve only to discredit the media and to drive communications underground. They do not discourage rebellion. People have never been fully dependent on any single medium of information. The raising of artificial barriers to information forces greater risk-taking as a means of obtaining public attention, entrains a vast proliferation of all the informal means by which people and groups customarily communicate and concert their reactions to events, and prompts futile and self-defeating attempts by the powerful to impose the same control on informal media. As a link between social groups, television is preferable to underground committees of correspondence and courier networks that serve to deepen alienation. Insurgents willing to take risks have considerable freedom of action in defining the issues at stake and in projecting their own self-serving rationales of conflict to the public. This advantage is the very nature of direct action techniques; it gives them whatever efficacy they have. Efforts to deny this advantage by controlling information can serve only to undermine the legitimacy of formal authority and thereby to enhance the advantages of the dissidents.

Since informal communication networks cannot be eliminated,

formal authority has more to gain by accepting media coverage as an opportunity to demonstrate its own viability, countering the insurgents with their own weapons, setting an example by not playing the demonstrators' game. In a study of insurrections in underdeveloped countries, Lucian W. Pye writes, "Government's behavior is usually the test people employ to judge the credibility of insurgent's claims. A government can expect to be judged according to its grasp of reality, its capability of coping with the threat, its chances of controlling the future—in sum, its ability to act as a sovereign authority should in preserving its authority."[23] Because the dissidents hold the initiative, it is an exceedingly difficult task for public authorities and the police to act as they should. But it is not impossible. Adequate force can remain passive, meeting force with force in kind and degree, and never escalating the conflict above the degree of risk imposed by the demonstrators.

Beyond the confrontation itself, credibility and legitimacy must be sought by all the forces of the community through constructive political leadership. All the routes of democratic access should be widened to ensure the transmutation of conflict from "street theater" to every kind of social and political forum that can be made available for the conduct and management of social bargaining. If television and radio are indeed the significant forums of our times, more coverage, not less, is required to contain destructive violence. Indeed, public attention should be served by all the ways that are available to the competing centers of media control; such competition prevents the much greater danger involved in blanketing the information channels with the wishful thinking of beseiged and anxious men in television studios, city hall, or the White House.

SECULARIZATION OF THE MEDIA

The dichotomy between sacred and profane applies to the process of communication via the media as it does to other symbolic acts. The fine arts are sacred by cultural definition and function; the public arts are more ambivalent. The tremendous technological innovation of the last seventy-five years has created revolutionary means for mobilizing audiences. The tendency of news media has been to begin their careers as sacred and ordained offices in the communication process, surrounded by taboos and restraints designed to safeguard their sacred state and to control their magical powers. Gradually, through familiarity, omnipresence, better understanding of both their limits and potentials, and the subsequent rise of competing media, each medium has tended to become secular and profane, to be stripped of sacred functions, and to be reduced to a work-a-day instrumentality that deserves no special regard or purification rites and holds no threatening magical powers over the audience, but is still useful and beneficent in its own way.

The tendency of the media to move from sacred to secular is a recurrence of the pattern seen in primitive societies by which a sacred ceremony like a funeral provides the site and occasion for the exchange of information. The first institutionalized marketplace was an extension of such rituals. *What begins as a shrine ends as a forum,* with accompanying changes in the definitions of appropriate ritual behavior. The classical period of any public art (that is, the period of exploring all the new possibilities implicit in a new medium and mastering its forms) is sacred, whether in the manufacturing crafts or in communications. Once the learning phase is completed, the form is assimilated; some aspects may retain a technical sacral status, but most of its uses become secular.

In the last century, prior to the electronic media, political oratory and public meetings retained a sacred regard, comparable to collective religious rites and ceremonies of rebellion. The audience was sensitized to the conventions of oratory as a species of the fine arts embodied in theater. The Lincoln-Douglas debates as a traveling minstrel show could not be repeated today. James Michael Curley notes that even the most "magnetic silver-tongued orator" can no longer attract a crowd.

The old-time rally has gone the way of vaudeville and the hurdy-gurdy man. Impromptu speeches, prepared gesticulations, histionics and other oratorical displays are as dated as an old-fashioned melodrama, like Bertha, the Beautiful Sewing Machine Girl. Daniel Webster would have difficulty holding an audience unless he took time out every ten minutes to give away a frigidaire.[24]

The age of newspapers has the longest history and represents a formalized secular mode as compared with the sacred character of books. Newspapers and magazines belong also to the profane realm of controversy, pluralism, and prose, holding their own as a source of entertainment, service information, and news. The magazine may be looked on as an attempt by a periodical publication to achieve some of the sacred status of the book. Newsweeklies and photojournalism in the early days of the Luce Empire succeeded, but when the classic phase was over, magazines fell into the realm of the secular prints in spite of their glossy, long-lasting paper.

The revolution of film captured the highly charged sacred trust and social function of theater. Today, film can be both sacred and secular: as theater and ritual drama it retains its sacred character; as documentary, it is secularized. However, the ritual of assembly in a darkened theater tends to maintain the sacral dimension of film, whatever the content. The use of old films to feed the hungry eye of video has had an interesting effect. As television becomes increasingly secularized, films of all kinds, whether dramatic or documentary, are tending to lose their special status as classical culture inputs.

The first electronic medium, radio, was a powerful influence and created a highly charged sacred shrine. Controversy and the ad lib were banned and stuffy self-important forms of speech (for example, funereal-ministerial style of the most successful announcers) prevailed during the sacred period of the sound box. Originally, classical music was thought more appropriate than jazz, and moral uplift more appropriate than comedy. Even as programing became more eclectic, the overall tone was portentous and dignified. McLuhan says, "Radio was a disaster for a goal-oriented America. It inspired multiple goals and a multiplicity of new images, depriving the country of a simple visual-mindedness." Both Roosevelt and Hitler were products of the radio age.[25]

All of these traits were later transferred to television. In the early 1950's, radio completed its classical phase and joined the periodical press as a profane medium. Controversy, talk shows, interviews, public services of all sorts, music, weather reports, news, relaxed and casual styles, permissiveness in spontaneous nonscripted performances, a relaxation of standards as to profanity, the mention of rival networks, open discussion of previously unmentionables, all came into use and are all characteristics of the secular. Radio abandoned theater presentations, drama, and variety shows and became instead a vehicle of work-a-day communication, "a tribal drum," like the webs of rumor, gossip, and information in preliterate societies. The family no longer gathered after the evening meal to listen to the archetypal evening radio program of the 1930's. However, radio is far from dead; in fact, it is stronger than ever, but in an altogether different form. People listen to the tribal drum while they are doing something else—getting dressed in the morning, driving to work, sorting mail, working in a manhole. The religious catatonic observances in the evenings now occur in front of the television set. Radio has become an automobile accessory.

The 1950's marked the classical period of television, which still maintains a considerable degree of sacred power. Much television programing is lapsing into the profane realm, but not all. Before

1963, surveys revealed that people said they got most of their news from newspaper; after that date, the balance was reversed, leveling off in 1971 with a 15 percent for television over newspapers. In a comparison of source credibility of news, newspapers led until the early 1960's; in 1971 more people termed television the most believable than chose the other three media combined.[26]

The size of the television audience is itself a revolutionary fact. A book that sells a few hundred thousand copies is considered a best-seller. A recording becomes golden at the million mark. A very successful film may attract tens of millions over a period of a few years. The ordinary television program commands the attention of tens of millions simultaneously almost any evening of the week. But audience size is not the major characteristic of the sacred state, rather, audience sensitivity, intensity of attention, and responsiveness to media content. To maintain the magic of the sacred state, the television medium masters feel the necessity to maintain a taut control of programing.

During the classic phase, anything that appeared on the tube gained a monumental mythic quality in the collective mind of the nation. The televising of the Kefauver crime-investigating hearings in the early 1950's became a religious morality play that transformed all of the participants into towering ritual figures of good and evil.[27] The Army-McCarthy hearings of 1954 similarly created a ritual landmark in the history of the period. Early quiz shows, comedy shows, variety shows, and dramatic shows, also gained mythic proportions. Jack Paar's late-night program became the universal language of greeting throughout the land the next morning. The sensation of the 1958 quiz show scandal revealed the religious character of television; the nation recoiled in horror on learning that the instant culture heros of "The $64,000 Question" had been coached. The reaction was as if a temple had been defiled, Mt. Vernon vandalized, or a sacred trust brazenly betrayed.

In 1971, the fracas over a CBS documentary ("The Selling of the Pentagon") led to a Congressional investigation and an intensely critical reaction by the Vice-President and a congressional spokesmen. The incident demonstrated the still sacred role of television. The CBS documentary was undoubtedly strong television but, as television critic John J. O'Connor pointed out, "in the overall context of the mass media, it was relatively tame journalism." If precisely the same story had appeared in a newspaper or magazine (as it had frequently during the previous few years), it would have stirred little response. The profane status of newspapers permits them to engage in crusading journalism without the requirement or pretense of balanced objectivity. In contrast, television has a special power and therefore a special responsibility to conserve its impact.

The sacred status of television leads to blandness and a narrow expressive range. Sports scores are given a weight exactly equal to that given the crisis in the Middle East. Everything and everyone is reduced to the same level. Vietnam is brought vividly into the American living room, settling comfortably alongside "I Love Lucy" and "Hee Haw." Carol Channing and Stokeley Carmichael appear together on the "Dick Cavett Show." Carol, in hot pants, smiling and laughing a lot, plugs a new film. Cavett says, "Why, how very interesting!" Stokeley, in sharecropper overalls, explains why Hitler was the greatest white man and why blacks should tear down the country. Everyone smiles and laughs. "How very interesting!" says Dick.

Television is changing rapidly now and becoming more flexible and interesting. But the transition is incomplete and the medium still is a national shrine as well as a marketplace. Exposure on television becomes the incentive for much behavior, political and otherwise. Politicians accept speaking engagements merely to provide a hook for news stories and video clips that they hope thereby to generate. The Rolling Stones plan a new U.S. tour to be confined to a few live concerts, but with national closed-circuit television simultaneously in at least one hundred and fifty theaters around the country, "all of them with large screens, full stereo and color," a concept pioneered by the Ali-Frazier championship fight. The cost of a ticket to the video performance will be as high as the live performance. The closed network makes it possible to offer the advantages of instantaneous national television without giving it away free. The live performance becomes a mere technical original staged primarily in order to be televised to its major market.

In the same way, the forms of sacred video have a tremendous impact on national political conventions, which become merely technical theatrical events staged for the national audience. The result is that programing, drama, concision, and interest must be controlled in the interests of entertaining and holding the audience. Floor struggles that might hurt the party have to be eliminated or resolved off-camera. What happens on screen becomes the only reality and must be stage-managed, like "The $64,000 Question."

When Senator Edmund Muskie returned from a long interview with Russian Premier Kosygin, he went on the "Dick Cavett Show" to report to the nation. During the SST fight in Congress, the White House was in constant negotiation with Dick Cavett to obtain equal time to defend the supersonic aircraft against critics who had appeared on earlier shows. Dick Cavett has an audience that the government does not. In March 1971, President Nixon allowed himself to be interviewed informally by Howard K. Smith as a means of overcoming charges of inaccessibility and remoteness. The President would have been better-advised to go on the "Dick Cavett Show," because he succeeded in attracting only 11 percent of the available audience, while an NBC movie won 42 percent, Doris Day 25 percent, and Carol Burnett 32 percent of the audience.

Television as icon and shrine is an energy source that captures light and movement and irradiates them like a principle of vital force into the room. It glows with the eerie blue crown of the godhead. "While other media sell content, television sells a pleasing experience with content as a byproduct. The object is to make television-watching as comfortable, reinforcing and reasurring as possible." In front of the television set something is always happening. It is a closed system of gratification, a flow of fantasy in which the ego of the viewer is submerged and dissolved.[28] But desanctification is now well-advanced.

After a generation of viewers, television has lost its novelty, and its classical period of new forms and discoveries is drawing to an end. The task of being entertaining, informative, and innovative for eighteen hours a day, seven days a week, begins to tell. Television ennui and audience resistance are mounting. All the clichés of comedy, drama, talk shows, and news have been seen and heard too many times. "Turn on any dramatic show tonight in any dramatic series—any dramatic show—and I promise you that from the first three minutes' viewing, you'll know all the character relationships, all the plot convolutions to come, and half the dialogue. Whatever the conflicts, there will be no catharsis, no dramatic relief, because network fears and government pressures smeared the tube with chicken fat."[29]

Adding to the desacralization of the medium is the economic recession of 1970–71. A great shakedown of programing and profits, the first since the start of the industry, coincided with the loss of magic. Following the end of cigarette advertising and the general decline of business profits and employment, a ruthless price war embroiled the sale of commercial time. In addition, Vice-President Agnew achieved celebrity by attacking the networks, revealing the growing disillusionment and alienation of the national audience from their old security blanket. As a result of economic retrenchment, commercial television was forced to do all the wrong things, to fall back on reruns, fewer new shows, and more old Hollywood movies, while cutting back on public service shows, documentaries, and high-quality cultural offerings.

The medium becomes less shrine and more forum, opening the way for greater casualness, variety, controversy, and spontaneity. As television loses its unique authority, it can, like newspapers and radio, fulfill the more enduring functions of work-a-day service and pluralism. It can escape the role of oracle and begin to talk in a multiplicity of normal voices without the necessity for theatricality and playing by sacred clichés. Cable television and educational television have stolen a march with public service shows and how-to presentations, along with experimental presentations of the fine arts. In essence, the direction is toward services to specialized audiences, without the paralysis of will that prevented earlier attempts to fractionalize the audience. The universal audience is fast disappearing anyway. There is nothing to lose by breaking down the standard formats regionally or by interest groups. It is no longer necessary to provide a uniform mush within the categories of morning show, children's hour, housewife's program, and prime family viewing time.

The inevitable secularization of the medium can be positive. Obviously, if the top fifty markets simply revert to reruns of syndicated material and old movies, the decline of the medium will be hastened. For better or worse, television has nothing to lose in exploring all kinds of new materials that are not homogenized into the old major program categories. The expansion of the spontaneous talk show is a symptom of the trend as are human interest features, local coverage of people and community life apart from crime and government, increasing opportunities for young artists to bring to the tube their cinemagraphic experiments, the breaking down of the thirty-minute segment format, greater pluralism of channel ownership and operation, ranging from commercially owned private and network stations to NET, cable-originated programing, and public access. It is impossible to forecast the changes of direction that flow from the desacralization of video. The time of controversy and a continuing loss of legitimacy is likely to continue. Jack Gould says,

For both commercial and noncommercial TV, the future choices will not be easy. Ideally, the current turmoil will yield a generation of TV leaders and producers who will demonstrate what a healthy diversity of outlooks in entertainment and journalism can be achieved on both network and local facilities, with due regard for different tastes and philosophies.[30]

Dr. Peter C. Goldmark, one of the leading statesmen of the electronic media and chief CBS scientist, is convinced that the whole structure of broadcasting and communications is headed for a kingsize shakeup and that within another generation American television will hold more potential for diversity of service than human ingenuity can use. The heart of his concept is the ultimate marriage of domestic satellites and cable television. The union, he believes, will outmode the monopoly of existing networks and stations and provide for a profusion of coast-to-coast and local services cutting across entertainment, culture, information, instruction, education, business, and population dispersal. He envisions the end of what has been the backbone of the Federal Communications Act of 1934—the element of scarcity of airwaves on which the whole evolution of American communications has been legally based—and the junking of the artificial allocations table that has given one city ten stations and another two.[31]

The role of the media in providing models for antisocial behavior is highly overrated. The fantasy life of the culture is replete with all of the possibilities of action, including the antisocial, the self-destructive, the perverted, and the merely obnoxious. The projection of fantasies of one kind or another on the screen of the mass media does not change the process of individual editing and evaluation of behavior options. The process by which selections from fantasy are translated into motor responses is not well understood, but it is related to the existential interaction of personal relationships. Explicit pornography leads mostly to a facilitation or a channeling of individual erotic fantasy; it does not show any relationship to sex crime or deviance. The amount of pornography consumed by respectable family men in one covert form or another is probably enormous. Similarly, the glorification of crime and criminals in the media merely reflects an incipient trend already in the culture that challenges the legitimacy of prevailing values.

The media are merely expressive and are generally sanitized and emasculated compared with the fantasy capabilities of individuals. A rash of imitative antisocial actions cannot be stopped by censorship or media blockage which only accentuates the disorientation, panic, and loss of legitimacy that leads some individuals into antisocial behavior in the first place. It does no good to beat up the messenger to insulate oneself from the realities of the social process.

Pop man, the transfigured archetype of the mass media, has been stripped of all the essentially incorrigible human qualities. He is an empty abstraction, incapable of any feedback, programed for nothing but abject adoration. Sexless, mindless, physically vigorous but emotionally infantile, he "sustains a precarious existence at the breast of the media which provide the measured routines, the soothing sights and sound, and the benignly looming presence of the nursery."[32] This Pop man is a lie! He does not exist. The critical habit is not the property solely of the estranged intellectual, but of all men. All men are sensitized to the media only in proportion to the latter's earned legitimacy. The overwhelming fact of the cultural revolution of the 1960's has been its spontaneity and pluralism. The media acted at first as pillars of gentility, ignoring the innovations and surprises beginning to flow in a constant stream from below. When the dynamism of these uncontrolled inputs began to sweep all before them, the media began to imitate, to placate, to patronize, seeking to avoid isolation and irrelevance, seeking to capture some of the dynamism and force, seeking to avoid entrapment in the collapsing temple of old culture forms. Far from controlling national values, the media, as processes of social ritual and human incorrigibility, contrive to save us from our own nightmares, affording us no escape from moral judgment and the mysteries of self.

NOTES

1. Quoted in *The New York Times,* November 26, 1970, p. 17.

2. Wilbur Schramm, ed., *Mass Communications,* 2nd ed. (Chicago: University of Illinois Press, 1960), p. 115.

3. See Paul S. Lazarsfeld and Robert K. Merton "Organized Social Action," in *ibid.,* p. 497.

4. Marshall McLuhan and Quentin Fiore, *War and Peace in the Tribal Village* (New York: Bantam Books, 1968), p. 11.

5. Harold D. Lasswell and Satish K. Arora, *Political Communication: The Public Language of Political Elites in India and the United States* (New York: Holt, Rinehart and Winston, 1969), p. 11.

6. Quoted in *The New York Times,* April 13, 1970, p. 13.

7. Robert E. Park, 'The Natural History of the Newspaper," in Schramm, 1960, p. 18.

8. Daniel J. Boorstin, *The Image, or What Happened to the American Dream* (New York: Atheneum, 1962), p. 210.

9. *Ibid.,* p. 33.

10. See David E. Apter, ed., *Ideology and Discontent* (New York: Free Press, 1964).

11. Lasswell and Arora, 1969, p. 7.

12. Marshall McLuhan, *Understanding Media: The Extension of Man* (New York: New American Library, 1964), p. 293.

13. Quoted in Park, 1960, p. 19.

14. Quoted in *The New York Times,* March 14, 1971, p. E-5.

15. V. O. Key, Jr., *Public Opinion and American Democracy* (New York: Knopf, 1964), p. 264.

p. 476.
16. Walter Lippmann, "The World Outside," in Schramm, 1960,

17. Quoted in *Sunday Press*, Binghamton, N.Y., June 6, 1971, p. D-1.

18. Gerald D. Suttles, *The Social Order of the Slum: Ethnicity and Territory in the Inner City* (Chicago: University of Chicago Press, 1968), pp. 197–98.

19. Erving Goffman, *Behavior in Public Places: Notes on the Social Organization of Gathering* (New York: Free Press, 1963), p. 17.

20. Jack Gould, "The Opinion-Makers Battle for the Screen," *The New York Times*, August 16, 1970, p. D-13.

21. Quoted in *Milwaukee Sentinel*, December 2, 1968, p. 3.

22. As this huge new arm—electronic communications and computers —reaches out into the community, "it is inevitable that it will proliferate spastic behavior for some time to come. The attempt to adapt the new computer to the diversity of older technologies creates a great deficiency of feedback." (McLuhan, 1968, p. 95.)

23. Lucian W. Pye, "The Roots of Insurgency and the Commencement of Rebellions," in Harry Eckstein, ed., *Internal War: Problems and Approaches* (New York: Free Press, 1964), pp. 157–59.

24. James Michael Curley, *I'd Do It Again* (New York: Knopf, 1958), p. 340.

25. McLuhan, 1968, p. 134.

26. Survey by the Roper Organization, 1970, reported in *The New York Times*, May 27, 1971, p. 72.

27. See Bernard Rubin, *Political Television* (Belmont, Calif.: Wadsworth Publishing, 1967), p. 12.

28. See Jeff Levine, "Are You Hooked by TV?" in *The New York Times*, June 27, 1971, p. D-21.

29. Tom Gries, "I Escaped from Television," in *ibid.*, December 6, 1970, p. D-25.

30. Jack Gould, "The Party's Over, The Pinch Is On," in *ibid.*, November 29, 1970, p. 19.

31. *The New York Times*, August 5, 1971, p. 59.

32. Albert Goldman, *Freak Show* (New York: Atheneum, 1971), p. 336.

12 | LAST RITES

The kids today are demanding not revolution, but revelation.
They say "we want a whole new set of values," and what are they?
The values are "love, peace, justice, security." These are words
we have had with us for centuries. But man being what man is,
you start from where you are! (Saul Alinsky, 1971)[1]

PRINCETON PLAN, R.I.P.

James Cunen recorded the revolution at Columbia in a thin volume
titled The Strawberry Statement, *where he testified to his deep*
alienation from American values. He was immediately lionized by
the TV talk shows where he bristled fiercely over the capitalistic
ethic. Then MGM bought the movie rights and asked Cunen to
play one of the roles. Cunen pondered the morality of collaborating
with the system. His conclusion: Making movies about revolution
and making money from revolution is really the same as making
revolution, isn't it?

O deathknells! O end of eras! O cascade of culture change!
O cooling avalanche! The major transactions of values of the last
decade seem to be closing. All social exchanges follow the sonata
form, ending with a restatement of the beginning—a restatement
that is charged with the ritual power of hurts and triumphs, of
mortifications and short-lived prides, of memories, oppositions, and
convolutions, various and poignant, in short, charged with the
power of total recall, of hope and anguish locked in a climax of
energy and survival.

Culture is supreme! But it is acted out in the fantasy and action
of the culture hero and the artist. Experimentation, search behavior, and pretensions of art in all their infinite variety reflect the
impulse for change. The deepest and most profound crises arise
from culture. Changes in moral temper and social forms, the fusion
of imagination and life styles, are not amenable to social engineer-
ing or political control. They are the sea in which the latter may
die or flourish. Conflict is an essential aspect of growth, one that we
can neither fully control nor prevent, nor should we wish to do so.
Social life only strives toward humanizing power and dampening

extreme oscillations of change. The ultimate sources of legitimacy of a society cannot be artificially contrived or fraudulently promoted. The most sophisticated promotional campaign cannot sell dog food that dogs refuse to eat.

At a time when old authority structures are collapsing and new priorities are yet to be discovered, the imagination searches for a new sensibility, new culture forms, social values, priorities, activities, structures, and purposes. In times when the universal subconscious dances in the streets, when everything is up for grabs, and every madness is conceived as superior truth, moral and philosophical eras are born and die in weeks and months. An epoch, with a well-defined and relatively fixed set of culture forms, may last as long as five years.

As the storm subsides, we can chart its path. Since the beginning of the industrial revolution, business and corporate power have been busily involved in reorganizing society under the constant pressure of war and diplomacy, geographical discovery and mobility, invention and augmented mastery of the physical world. The aristocratic modes of earlier eras were busily cannibalized by entrepreneurs and political leaders of the bourgeois revolution, just as the bourgeois modes are being cannibalized today.

Lorenz compares this process with what he calls pseudo-speciation (the development of group mannerisms and discrimination against outsiders) in the animal kingdom. The cultural norms and rites of human groups endure in "much the same manner as inherited properties evolved in phylogeny of subspecies, species, genera, and greater taxonomic units." The history of the pseudo-speciation of culture forms can be reconstructed by much the same methods of comparative study. As values and behavior forms are sorted out by some reality principle, they begin to channelize and diversify. They standardize as features of enduring groups, much as historical development within a species leads to diverse ecological specializations in different physical environments. For animals, as we have seen, ritualized behavior is subject to more rapid change than are physical forms. The elaboration of behavioral responses gives "the character of inviolability" to the norms and rites of a group, enabling them to be propagated for a considerable time.[2] However, pseudo-speciation also includes an immeasurable number of abortions, false starts, maladaptations, and dysfunctional climaxes.

Nature provides a mechanism for unlimited cultural pseudo-speciation in order that natural selection will have a greater amount of material and options with which to work. The process goes on continuously. Times of stability (related to the perception of high-priority social purposes) conceal the ebb and flow in art, literature, dreams, and private behavior. As the imperatives of existing structure lose their saliency, the process of cultural pseudo-speciation suddenly rises from the depths to employ a vast amount of social energy. Demanding attention and imitation, it struggles toward formalism and legitimacy through a complex and unconscious process of selection.

The reality principle cannot be stated in advance. Every interest group offers its own, claiming special authority for itself and its own proffered culture forms. Easy preachment and exhortation from books and pulpits uses the turbulence and unrest to argue the special credibility and problem-solving magic of its own values. The eventual definition of reality will depend on the process that creates legitimacy and political truth.

THE FRISBEE CONSTITUENCY

Contemporary syncretism, fads, forms, and life-styles are an expression of pluralism and pseudo-speciation: a surplus of images, of fantasy, of richesse, of culture spawned, generated, used up, and discarded at an incredible rate, in such an even-handed way as to permit every contribution to have provisional legitimacy for some group in society providing it is fresh and imaginative. A phrase that arises from a new television program and goes the rounds soon becomes common coin, a ritual incantation by which individuals prove themselves tuned-in to the source of culture input. Yet within a few months, the phrase is stale and has been replaced by so many new candidates that only a complete square or a child will be found guilty of using it. Later, the phrase might evolve into a new stage of freshness in which it becomes a deliberate malapropism deriving brief freshness by inverting its meaning.

In much the same way, the flower children movement evolved in the brief span of five years through all the change of political tactics, from throwing flowers to throwing dung and bombs. All that free-floating anxiety needed was a name and an enemy. These it soon acquired. The gentle mods and the tough Rockers in Britain or the hippies and the Hell's Angels in the U.S. evolved apart then joined, then grew apart again. Rejecting every institution, the culture rebels were reduced to believing in traditions only five years old. John Lennon said "I'm sick of all these aggressive hippies or whatever they are . . . either on the street or anywhere or on the phone, demanding my attention, as if I owed them something. They frighten me, a lot of uptight maniacs going around wearing peace symbols."[3] Historyless, "they will commit an infinite number of blunders, including submission to the very forces that they oppose—when they use violence, they are submitting to violence, when they use drugs, they are widening the scope of the drug industry."[4]

The overload of inputs and the rapid exhaustion of culture forms are aspects of ritual in a society undergoing vast and important changes. Such a swift current of culture consumption, uncomfortable to some, exciting to others, is a necessary means of experimentation, leading to the emergence of new groups and constituencies, new value systems and systems of behavior. Some of these may be assimilated into enduring forms and institutions while other are discarded as a transitional phase of growth.

An industrial society based on high-level production and consumption makes novelty itself a positive value and an object of much social behavior. The parameters of our lives are changing rapidly, due not only to social and political factors, but also to the unrelenting pace of technological change. This requires a constant replenishment of new values and behavior forms. Through a process of testing and competitive group formation, some of these forms may survive in cloistered confines of this or that special activity or interest group, while others may be generalized for a longer or shorter time as an approved value with prescribed behavior patterns for the whole society. That this process should be transformed into symbols and rituals is not surprising. Symbolic and ritual behavior is a low-risk, energy-conserving method of experimentation, learning, social choice, and consensus-building. Artificial constraints or the use of state authority to staunch, limit, or channel the flow of new forms is part of the winnowing process, but hardly determining. Attempts to use state power in a controlling fashion are bound to lead to a variety of protective responses, resistance, concealment, challenge of the legitimacy of state power, and other such forms to safeguard the need for a continuous and pluralistic input of new values, patterns of behavior, and group loyalties.

An understanding of the dimensions of ritual in political behavior may buffer the affronts of the cultural revolution. If you do not like the forms this year, to quote Casey Stengel, "wait until next year!" Understanding the process of ritual and its essential functions may serve to quiet our premonitions. After all, efforts to quash rebellions only feed the fires of dissent; the chief factor that can arrest the tide of culture experimentation is the overreaction of those vested with formal authority, seeking to obliterate the challenge of change and collect all of the strings of power from above. To do so validates the sense of community and united purpose that some of the most extreme agents of rebellion hawk in the streets.

Such a reaction tends to revitalize the ritual Woodstock nation and its variants and to delay their inevitable fragmentation.

Uncivil and disruptive behavior, stylized as ritual, must be looked on as not merely pathological or erratic, but adaptive and practical, at least in some sense. Saul Alinsky claims that today's youth cult, like superpatriotism, has become "the refuge of the ignorant and confused." Examine the self-justifying rhetoric of the youth cult: the proclamations of everyone else's guilt and hypocrisy and shrill claims that the values of Western civilization are daily corrupted and contradicted by war, atomic weapons, police brutality, ethical ambiguity, reliance on force and raw power, and the dalliance and relativism of middle-aged liberals. The fathers have cheated the children, they cry, creating an impossible world overshadowed by nuclear missiles, ugliness, and unspeakable stupidity, invoking in them a sense of anxiety, helplessness, and rebellion. All nations, but especially the rich and powerful, are rotten; their leaders have lost the way and are unable to cope either with injustice, racism, and environmental despoliation or the challenge of the poor, the blacks, and the young. This is the current ideology used by some to justify the most extreme tactics, including those of Charles Manson or a Greenwich Village bomb factory. But what is said about the hypocrisy and sham of the youth,[5] the put-ons and manueverings of left wing politics, the discredited leaders of last year or last week's rebellion, the process of transition as older youth fall away from political activity and go back to whatever it is young people do when they are not demonstrating, and the continuous recruitment of dewy-eyed youngsters, each year younger, seeking to be blooded by the celebrated puberty rites of last year?

Many radical activists are power freaks and ego-trippers. They are mirrors of all that is brutal, brainless, and greedy in modern culture as a whole. While claiming to defend human values and individuality, they act as though people were puppets to be manipulated. Alinsky states, "To any revolutionary, the action is in the reaction. If as a consequence of your action you are strengthening the enemy more than yourself, then you are really a counter-revolutionary."[6]

The young have a short attention span. Spectacle and sensation need constant renewal. One may doubt whether the young really care about environmental pollution, the problems of the ghetto, or even Vietnam. When these slogans are not available to elicit the breast-beating guilt of the establishment, the young readily exploit whatever guilt can be found to undermine the powers of the prevailing culture, while they are seeking to create their own sense of ritual community out of the welter of experimental values that characterize the zone of transition of youth in a rapidly changing society.

Despite these unpleasant factors the ritualization of politics during this troubled period is serving the same function that apolitical culture forms serve—as rites of passage, courtship rituals, rites of spring, and so forth. There is the example of the black civil rights movement and the success of the black constituency and that of virtually all its imitators, including the antiwar movement, and the mobilization of Indians, homosexuals, and women. There is the unique historical sequence of the last few years when the pressure of international crisis suddenly disappeared. Anticommunism and the dangers of war receded even as the morass of Vietnam deepened, wrenching loose all the priorities that had so rigidly commanded our values and institutions for thirty years. There were the accumulated deficits of domestic problems, and the unrecognized new groups demanding their place in the sun. There is a breakup of old coalitions—nationality groups that finally took their place as "real Americans" through the dynamics of the labor movement, crime, and politics. The coalitions of the power establishment that conducted the Second World War and the Cold War collapsed when success and power eliminated their reason for vigor and unity. This establishment, the tired and aging revolutionaries of the New Deal, reached a turning point. The end of the Cold War, the breakup of communism, the breakup of the regional ghettos of Jews, Italians, Poles, and others as a base of political power in American cities, the loss of credibility and self-confidence in the face of Vietnam and black uprisings, all such factors made the time ripe for new groups that were more dissatisfied and more unified by geography and inequality to march, to manifest their unity, and to force the established groups to admit them as full partners in all institutions, from television networks to political offices.

The blacks are a real constituency. The question is no longer black power or white power, but how to orient, relate, and use the tremendous power that blacks have already acquired and to which whites now defer in many areas where previously white supremacy ruled with impunity. The black success has spawned a host of imitators and claimants within and without the black community. As for the middle-class white youth, the frisbee generation, the question arises whether or not they are in fact *a constituency*. Certainly in numbers they have a potential far more awesome and overwhelming than that of the blacks. But are they a constituency? Do they share a deep sense of common grievance? Do they really crave the responsibility of power and the drudgery of administering the complex and thankless tasks of public policy and government, sewage treatment, mail delivery, or educational planning and scholarship? Are they united by overriding interests? Or are they divided by the same pluralism that divides their elders?

If an observer puts slogans and clichés aside, it soon becomes clear that among the youth themselves there are deeper cleavages and gaps than those between the generations. Recent events and numerous studies reveal that youth are fractured, fractious, and various.[7] They are not a constituency. In fact, much of the troublesome rituals of political violence arise from this fact. Irrational forms of extremism and the counter-productive, unpolitical and self-destructive tactics of the period 1969–71 demonstrate this point. Even with all of the help from Attorney General John Mitchell, state legislators, and police departments (who through persecution, intimidation, and repression tended to foster a degree of political unity among the young), the youth are too divided, disparate, and politically indifferent to provide the kind of constituency that can lead to positive and constructive reintegration and sharing of power in reformed civil institutions.

The guilt of the establishment, the disillusion with great causes, the traditional apotheosis of youth (which characterizes a society that refreshes itself every new television season) encouraged the claims of the youth movement. Six years ago on the Berkeley campus, a segment of the free speech movement adopted the slogan "Filthy Speech." Now filthy speech has succeeded while free speech falters under the pounding of both left and right; reactionary forces seek to stifle dissent, and the ritual of ceremonial profanation becomes a feature of the left. Young racists at the University of Alabama shout down George Wallace, their hero of the previous year. A Tarzan film festival is stormed by militants who object to Tarzan as the black man's burden. Militant conservationists shout down a speech by life-long conservationist Arthur Godfrey in much the same way that elements of the black militants, in the name of black power, turn against any black who acquires any power.

The children of the middle classes in great numbers have adopted the tradition of the slums that jail is not only honorable but a necessity for personal development and peer recognition. They picked up on drugs as blacks rejected drugs, on violence as blacks found power and put violence aside. When the young revolutionaries discovered that confrontation creates community, they set about creating confrontations. When the authorities would not react with overwhelming force, the method no longer worked and the militants were forced to initiate the use of force themselves in order to reenact the past. The Weathermen who conducted a destructive three-hour binge of window-breakage in Chicago described their arrest as "a continuation of fascist repression of dissent." The critical difference about who initiated the first violent escalation, the all-important question in the moral evaluation of conflict, is conveniently expunged from memory.

After two years of enormous success, SDS dissolved into a melange of factionalism and futility. Having aroused the sleeping giant of American college students as it has never been aroused in American history, the promoters and organizers fell into disarray. Some of them began experimenting with tactics that alienated vast uncommitted groups. The rituals of guerilla tactics (à la Che Guevara), the bombing, vandalism, anonymous hit-and-run tactics, the anonymity of the leaders, the demand in advance for amnesty, the refusal to negotiate demands, all of these stylized rituals represented not principled testing of authority, but rather catharsis, trauma, and action for its own sake, or for the sake of solidifying a remnant of a faction by high-risk commitments.

While revolution must be built in the hearts and minds of people, the latter stages of the cultural revolution became instead attempted rape. The momentum and dynamism of general approval and attention tempted the revolutionary strategists into taking foolish advantage, thereby discrediting their motives and creating resistance and opposition, rather than inspiring consent. It might be said that the surrender of the larger society to the rampage of the youth was a wise method of control. Western society acted very much as did Communist China. Allowing the youth to act out their infantilism throughout the nation was costly and difficult for the Chinese, but it finally discredited the youth and reconfirmed the power and authority of the Communist leaders. Divided among themselves, they battened down the hatches and prayed that the storm would soon blow over. They avoided overreacting too soon in ways that would legitimatize and corroborate the moral significance of the challenge. But in the United States society also went a step further; what infuriated student radicalism at the latter stages of its success was not the affluent society, but the stable society, which, even as it celebrated and lionized them, coopted their values and undermined their impetus.

The youth cult has indeed been coopted. Corporation executives wear long hair and side burns, some sporting bell-bottom multi colored trousers and brilliant waist sashes. The leading fashion designers have adopted hippie styles, while suburban wives are furnishing their homes with psychedelia. Even Spiro Agnew has longer hair. The new culture forms and rituals provide the season's most popular television series. The so-called underground is now so far above ground that middle-aged investors are signing up rock groups and building strangely incongruous lines of latrines across the countryside where the youth tribes may reassemble. AM and FM radio stations across the country have donned the "underground" style, and the *Village Voice* is as respectable as *The New York Times* and has been purchased as an investment by a conglomerate holding company. Abbie Hoffman has franchised a shirt manufacturer to produce his American flag shirt.

In a concentrated period of less than a year, the parable of Woodstock was travestied in the destruction of Zap, North Dakota, the financial exploitation of Miami, Florida, or the ugliness of Altamont. In less than a year, the parable of woodland elves and Campfire Girls was transformed into a dread morality play featuring the Marquis de Sade and the ritual death of Che Guevara at the hands of Hell's Angels. And Nixon and Mao exchanged toasts. *Woodstock* became a highly successful film playing at the best downtown houses. In the film, the new collectivists look and sound alike, whether they are paranoid (like the young man who is convinced that fascist pigs in helicopters are dropping poison from above), happily skinny-dipping in a nearby pond, making love, or just grooving on the music and telling the cameraman how "beautiful" it all is. The insistence upon "how beautiful everything is" comes through as an automatic response as mindless as a bulletin from Vietnam. The sequel film, *Gimme Shelter,* blasted the same values and was also a great commercial success. Both movies were transformed into industries in the same way that every Walt Disney film extended its life through merchandising the logos in every possible sphere of manufacture. *Woodstock* and *Gimme Shelter* licensees include the makers of ponchos, T-shirts, capes, serapes, suede vests, tote bags, plastic laminated medallions, bracelets, pendants, and sunglasses.

The youth today are a new leisure class. They are not only a larger fraction of the whole population than ever before, but are also in constant communication with each other through the media. The youth in many respects qualify as an emerging counter-elite. They have the time, the energy, the wealth, the numbers, the self-consciousness, and, in some cases, the will to rule. And the times are propitious. All the old power elites are caught in the throes of historic blunders, unresolved conflicts, environmental decay, and discredited policies. They seem to have lost their mission and their sense of purpose. They no longer can find a substitute in world wars or struggles against personified evils. The times are propitious for the counter-elite to emerge and ring in the new. They are doing so ritualistically in terms of culture invention in a melange of syncretism.

The prospects for the future are for continuous evolution. Violence appears on the way out in favor of practical political action. In 1970, we witnessed the disintegration of street politics in the desperate actions of isolated groups acting in a dream-world full of Blue Meanies no longer communicating with their peers—the fights on Moratorium day between smashers and marchers and the running berserk of small groups after large peaceable demonstrations. These trends bespoke the desperation of a movement that could not sustain its roots in the face of repeated capitulation to its demands. Hysteria is a form of ritual behavior that seeks to recapture an event of the past by reenactment under wholly inappropriate and self-destructive conditions. The decline of the street movement into hysterical exercises was symptomatic.

The student radicals not only have failed to create a youth constituency, but have failed in their efforts to align themselves with the black militants and with the "working class." All of the recent studies of the disaffected groups in our country indicate a trend back to "working through the system" and looking for ways to bring influence to bear through the political process. The 1972 Democratic Convention and the McGovern campaign are evidence.

There is a self-limiting quality in ritual rebellion and high-intensity tactics of protest. It is impossible to sustain the level of excitment at the same high pitch because people respond to persistent disorder by raising the threshold of sensitivity. A higher degree of disorder becomes bearable, thereby denying the instigators of disorder the fruits of their efforts. The failure to achieve constituency appears to motivate many extremist claims by radical leaders. As the Yippie ploy of 1968 was validated by the overreaction of Chicago police, many other would-be leaders adopted the pattern, called press conferences, promised sensational tactics. But after public fornication and the ubiquity of Viet Cong flags, what is there to do? There is always oneself. There is privatism and creativity. There is pleasure, discovery, and friendship. There are useful and fulfilling work, skills, and tasks. There is, in the words of Jerry Garcia, of the Grateful Dead, "clean-up action."

THE STORM SUBSIDES, THE WHEEL TURNS

Understanding the process of ritual in behavior should not make anyone overly sanguine about the thrill of living through a culture storm. Exhortations of optimism are whistling in the dark, and doomsayers and salvationists are equally without credentials. The ambivalences of life and death, of victory and defeat, of growth and disease are intensified during a period of ferocious pseudo-speciation. Excursions of joy are more intense, but also more fragile, subject to a sudden plunge into horror or catatonic rigidity. "Letting it all hang out" can produce the same results as "holding it all in." Instead of Salem witches there may be Hell's Angels; instead of the KKK, the Weathermen. Rituals are not quick cures for civilization's discontents. They are instead the question and answer dialog between life's energy and mortality, between order and chaos. "They are the new compact that man tries to make with reality after the death of his illusion that he is God."[8]

There is no special virtue in understanding that you are trapped in a storm. Escape is not available and the magic of books and learning is no protection against vulnerability. However, there is pleasure in being able to recognize when a storm is coming, and also in knowing when it ends. There are many signs in the changing temper of the driving gale that indicate that the present disturbance is in its final stages. Many things are winding down. The cycles of rapid change are virtually complete, and most of the values and culture forms that a few years ago seemed irresistible have devoured themselves and been discredited. Many traditional values are beginning to emerge from storm shelters everywhere, tentatively and cautiously at first, then with greater confidence. The generation bred by storm is aging and learning new reality principles, many of which redeem the past, while at the same time opening new possibilities for the future. The cacophonies of the storm pass down the generation ladder to become mimicked by ever-younger groups, marking the further discredit and demise of the forms and rituals themselves. Elementary school children do not have great legitimacy for other age groups, especially those immediately ahead of them in the march of generations. Such rituals as fall into their hands are practically dead. The cry, heard from now weary and discredited college revolutionaries ("wait till my kid brother gets here!"), is an empty and futile threat.

As the storm subsides, we attempt to chart its course. Many analysts point to the ever more protracted period of adolescence in highly industrialized societies. Erik H. Erikson has noted that each society and culture institutionalizes a moratorium for its young that coincides with post adolescent apprenticeships and adventures. The moratorium is a time for horse-stealing and vision quests, a time for wondering, going back to the people, academic life, military service, a time for self-sacrifice and pranks, and a time for mental illness and delinquency. He described this psycho-social moratorium as a sanctioned delay of adult functioning, the preliminal state described by Ralph Turner.

It is a period that is characterized by a selected permissiveness on the part of society and by provocative playfulness on the part of youth, and yet it also leads to deep, if often transitory, commitment on the part of youth, and ends in a more or less ceremonial confirmation of commitment on the part of society.[9]

As William Braden writes, the parents, in effect, tell the young: "We'll pretend to be shocked and dismayed. Just stay out of jail if you can, and don't get pregnant. And when we're ready for you, we'll let you know."[10] You cannot grow up if there are no walls to push against. But you also cannot grow up if the walls give way too readily when you push against them.

While our culture protracts adolescence and increases the numbers of adolescents in our midst, the turnover of culture forms has also weakened the legitimacy of old adolescent institutions, including those of the threshold state: the football rally, the fraternities, the dances and mixers, the visit to the forbidden red light district, secret sex, and booze in the shrubbery outside the chapel, the drunken weekend party or the college homecoming celebration. In addition, the affluence of the age has given middle-class youth the means of implementing their fantasies as never before, with cars, airplane tickets to anywhere, food and clothing improvised or taken for granted, and mutual help and communes when in some cases the home subsidy is cut off. The traditions of leisure, the floating fantasy, the good health and vitality of youth, make them available and eager for the agonistics of conflict that mark commitment, growth, and responsibility. The aggregation of youth in mass cities around the country near all the great universities provide a setting for the birth of new culture forms and experiments. There exists a vast floating audience in the country that can respond to outdoor gatherings with an insatiable appetite. The potential crowd exists not only in summer and in warm climates; but it is only the sun that provides occasions for this sizeable audience to demonstrate its collective existence, will, and self-conscious power. In Newport, the audience was 40,000 in 1963, 70,000 in 1964, 80,000 the next year, until by the end of the 1960's, every effort was made to limit attendance, and competing festivals of enormous romanesque size were transpiring in cow pastures throughout the world.

By 1972, Newport was moved to New York, and the whole future of these ritual occasions seemed threatened by their popularity. The circus could be another such event but the circus is near death in America. After twenty years of circus on television once or twice a week, the audience is not available. Audiences at outdoor sporting events are getting smaller and older. Baseball and football games, once the weekend rallying excuse for jubilant student festivals, are sparsely attended. Professional football remains strong on television, but college sports are dying and professional baseball is moribund. Boy Scout Jamborees are not the answer. Summer "field days" sponsored on the Fourth of July in thousands of communities have been despoiled by money-grubbing. Parades are fading fast. The Olympic Games and World Fairs have increasingly become competitions of nation-states and corporations, less human than mechanized, products of the commercialized mass media, bearing the mark of distance and manufacture.

Media overexposure is not the central cause; there are a variety of factors contributing to the demise of traditional events. Overexposure and loss of credibility are marks of institutions suffering not only from lack of imagination, but also from lack of the sense of the grand occasion that may tender and confirm their authority. The pause in the national purpose and the collapse of old priorities are a more fundamental cause. This generation has not had a war with a worthy opponent. This generation has seen the ritual drama of anticommunism fall into desuetude, repudiated not only by youth, but by events and by old political leaders as well. The general crises and calamities that might draw the nation back together again and command the priorities of private lives do not exist. The whole era is one of respite and release from the tensions of control that galvanized social energies throughout the world for three generations. A worthy diplomatic opponent, a real peril, like that faced by the Jews of Israel, might well have preserved the legitimacy even of the trite and cliché forms of the mass media. The content of the mass media is not an independent variable.

Nor can we endorse the diagnosis of "the obsolescence of youth." Bettelheim says, "Vietnam and the bomb serve youth as a screen for what really ails them—their feeling that youth has no future because modern technology has made them obsolete, socially irrelevant, and as persons insignificant. . . . If a young man does not feel that he is sorely needed to bring it [social justice] about, then the feeling is that he has no future."[11] In itself, generational imbalance might have been an asset for war rather than a contributor to culture storm. This has been the case for the last three generations. Certainly this factor intensified the power and scale of youth as a political force seeking to aggrandize itself in the face of a shattered establishment. But this feeling of purposelessness afflicts not merely the youth, but the whole society, from feather-bedded labor unions to ghost payrollers at City Hall, from over-heavy staff contingents at corporate headquarters to underemployed professors at universities. What causes protracted adolescence is the existence of material abundance without work. The young are most exposed and sensitive as indicators, standing statuslessly between protected childhood and the shocks of postadolescence. Middle-aged parents bound to their jobs, mortgages, responsibilities, obligations to their children, and old dreams and fears are purposeless too. They demonstrate it in their hunger for entertainment, novelty, and social meaning. They express it in a willingness to tolerate and even encourage experimentation.

The folklore of youth resembles a body of myths in search of membership and activation. Now and then, some of the myths have been fleshed out by an event of expressive value, leading to ritualized reenactments. Nakedness, feigned or real poverty, squalor and passivity, drugs, the transport of a multimedia mass ceremonial, worship of leather and wood as ritual objects to replace plastic, vegetarian and macrobiotic food cults, the return to nature and the earth, all are embodiments of perennial themes of transition states of culture. They exist somewhere in the interstices even in rigid and purposeful societies. They emerge as mass culture forms and capture the mass media when there is a vacuum of purpose.

There has been in the 1960's a terrible loss of location in culture. When the conditions are present that maintain the unity and coherence of societies, culture becomes homogeneous for the activity group; private experience and public wisdom coincide. "One can go inward and discover, in ecstacy and experience, the shared sources of power and knowledge; culture myths bind together and create a web of felt-meaning." Instead, we have come, old and young together, to a terrifying and exhilarating period in which our myths wear thin and we see through them into the immense existential universe of emptiness and possibility.

We drift, disconnected in a country of demons and delights. There is nothing to ground or hold us, imagination reigns, and we begin, haltingly, confusedly, to doubt our dreams. There is both a loveliness and terror to that, for we seem to be flying and falling at the same time, moving through ourselves toward the raw stuff at the heart of being itself.[12]

The unmediated raw experience demands the quick development of culture rituals. The direct and brutal coupling of the individual to experience, without the mediation of culture, is entropic and cannot be borne. It need not be borne, because the process of ritualization is ineluctable. Even in a time of loss of location, the process persists. However, it is fragmented into a thousand glittering explorations and discoveries that seem to defy reintegration and consistency. Even in times of turmoil, the symbolic dimension of conflict reigns supreme. All experience is ritualized and transformed into culture—sectarian, cultish, and often destined for rapid demise, but culture and symbolic action nonetheless. The giant panoramic screen of the mass media raises to a special power and popularity all the experimental life-styles once limited to tiny elites.

During the culture storm of the 1970's these experiments have been almost incredibly various and evident. The use of drugs provides a form of surrogate activity, demonstrating the need for meaningful purpose to organize group life and providing a dramatic ritual to give content to subjective values. The exhilaration of uppers is a standing-still form of activity, releasing the fantasy process while immobilizing motor responses. The Japanese insist that it is not the tea but the ritual that gives meaning. In the same way, drug-taking is meaningful as a procedure of group participation and sharing, implemented by the surrogate action of the drug itself. A further contribution is accomplished by the aftereffects, which are like those of work completed, fatigue and a present sense of satiety. In primitive societies, circumcision and initiation rites that bind age-mates together perform the same function, creating latent political structures. The ritual bonds between age-mates, like all social ritual, create sets of obligations and commitments that can hold the latent political structure intact until such time as the succession of generations brings it to fruition as an organizing principle for the whole society. Education, apprenticeship, social and work mobility, all the dynamics of culture inputs, facilitate the upward ascension of new political forms, the process of renewal, a continuous greening of society. Nor does this process necessarily imply a revolutionary transformation of values. The results may eventually reconfirm old values, albeit superficially disguised by new names and transitory styles.

In the 1930's, the influx of culture from below was a reaction against the machine, urbanism, and corporate power. This cultural revision was aborted by the Second World War and the mobilization of national fantasy for the purposes of war. In a sense, the cultural revolution of the 1960's was a continuation of the prewar period, but with some major differences. The upward mobility of European minorities, including Poles, Slavs, Italians, and Jews, was embodied in the political coalition that came to power under Franklin D. Roosevelt. The intelligentsia, labor movement, professional groups of all sorts, the lower middle classes, and all the imperfectly assimilated national minorities completed their insurgent phase and became the establishment. It was their children who constituted the revolutionary generation of the 1960's. All of the myths of insurgency and national unity that played so rich a part in the upward mobility of the great mass of middle Americans during the previous generation was transformed into a target for profanation by those seeking ways to formalize their own power, latent political structure, and values.

Old Western liberals are appalled at the return of fascist symbols and the recurrence of mass ceremonials full of aggressive exuberance. Love, love, love in general and in your own group! But hate everyone else in particular! Goldman observes, "The current generation seems like an army of doppelgangers, chanting love and peace as they march to the most militant strains ever blared from the horns of war."[13] Peter Pan may once again become Peter Panzer, as happened in interwar Germany, except that the contemporary cultural revolution lacks a persistent political interest.

Readers of Daniel Bell's *The End of Ideology* were astonished to find youth going back to Marx and Lenin, Trotsky, Mao, Che, Regis Debray, and Frantz Fanon. Perhaps it was an attempt to hold together by the rituals of ideology the remnants of a movement for which the rituals of political action were collapsing. To the culture storm we owe the repudiation and discredit of old self-serving ideologies. Many considered the rebirth of ideology an enduring trend, but today, ideologies appear even deader than before.

Most political movements show a tendency toward severity and discipline in their ranks, reflected also in clothing and taste. The culture storm started out imitating poverty and simplicity, but elaborated and embellished these cues into a new form, a funky baroque, a high style of fashionability. Similarly, every imitation and repetition has tended to modify and soften the original model. Rock music quickly lost its revolutionary potential as it achieved preeminence. Elvis started out hot, but quickly cooled down. Dylan ended by sounding the way Elvis started. Some groups have maintained the hard rock style, but soft rock and the inventive subtleties pioneered by the Beatles and Simon and Garfunkle everywhere came to dominate the style. Music for its own sake, for its structure and musical qualities, has become the object of the serious groups.

The Maharishi Mashesh Yogi, the white-clad, garlanded guru with the beatific mien was discovered by the Beatles. With Madison Avenue help, he parlayed this association into countless theater tours with rock bands, until rejected by the Beatles, he came to be considered a rip-off by the radical youth. However, the monument to his brief celebrity still thrives, the International Meditation Society, which has groups throughout the United States and claims

60,000 members, all of whom subscribe to the Maharishi's inspirational newsletter.

Long hair has become a cliché, is taken for granted, and is no longer a political issue. One night sometime in the late 1960's, the long hair and sideburns fairy struck the middle-aged and middle class. Presidents of the Jaycees and all kinds of reputable professional men sport beards and striped flare trousers. Even the armed forces now permit longer hair. Obviously, the symbol is vulnerable and has already been attacked by "skin heads" in London and Liverpool and frizzled naturals elsewhere.

Out of the welter of experiments, the work ethic is being resurrected and reconfirmed. The failure of love-oriented leaderless communes has demonstrated that much more is required for successful group life. Rejection of drugs and a new sacred regard for work and discipline is coming into vogue. The Jesus freaks provided a place for alienated youth within what is essentially an authoritarian structure, based on self-sustaining farm work and handicrafts, alleviated by mass rituals.

The so-called sexual revolution continues to shock and astonish, but has lost much of its energy. The tendency of private sexual behavior has not changed. Once sex ceased to be a public flaunting for effect, it returned to its traditional role. The new freedom moves toward stable interpersonal relationships, seeking mutual responsibility, and providing the basis for children, marriage, and family life, whether licensed or not. Permissiveness and promiscuity are increasingly seen as antisexual, unstable, and unhappy. Casual sex remains the domain of the impressionable young seeking recognition by a sexual calling card, and for all age groups, a reflex of depression, fatigue, chemical euphoria, and interpersonal unsuccess. The sexual revolution desacralized sex, threatening its small and fragile value in human relations. In the name of sex, people are really seeking friendships, community, and associations. It is a substitute for church clubs and bowling leagues. The abstract sexual act without responsibility and commitment has only a brief appeal and, in practice, quickly becomes sterile and empty. The notion that the sexual revolution is an accomplished fact, that Masters and Johnson now govern our mores, is denied by the tendency of the young to rediscover monogamy, or be trapped into it by the initial blandishments of casual sex.

Even interest in the culture of the 1950's enjoyed a brief resurgence. A year after the greatest wave of student radicalism throughout the nation, political apathy achieved new heights. Campy nostalgia for the good old days was in. From New England to California, college students jammed old-style rock-and-roll concerts, and paid five dollars to see Howdy Dowdy kinescopes and festivals of Hop-a-long Cassidy. At Harvard, Buffalo Bob drew 2,300 students. The Black Panther trial at New Haven was still in progress, but it was impossible to get more than a few dozen people to rally on their behalf while at the same time thousands turned out for a Yale revival of *The Lone Ranger* and *Sergeant Preston of the Yukon*. In November of 1970, Yale radicals called for a massive demonstration. The rally was attended by 500 persons; 60,000 gathered to watch Yale and Dartmouth vie for the Ivy League football championship. "Football is the opiate of the people," the radicals rumbled. The annual prom was revived in 1971 by popular demand, after having been cancelled in response to student revolutionary demands the preceding year. One student reported, "I grew up with Howdy Doody and that show shaped my life in many ways. I cried when it went off the air in 1960. It was great to see Buffalo Bob again. But I got mugged on the way home."

In the period between 1910 and 1920, a cultural revolution was led by literary figures and artists. Their targets were the life and character of the small town. In the realm of culture and ideas, intellectuals mounted a withering attack. Harold Stearns, H. L. Mencken, Sherwood Anderson, and Sinclair Lewis were typical of the cultural revolutionaries of that period. It is significant that at the time of their work, the obliteration and eclipse of small town values was already virtually an accomplished fact. Urbanism, national corporations, and centralized government had undermined the traditional power of the small towns which was embodied in the ritual drama and ideology of Civil War Republicanism, Populism, and early Socialism. The young intellectuals were doing the work of the forces of industrial production and centralized power. Yet, they did it in the name of liberating values and culture. The process is an old one: the underlying fact of social power and function moves swiftly away from tradition, creating new tensions of adjustment. Only when the process is near completion does it become self-conscious enough to provide the basis for ritualization and revision of the culture.

LOTS OF LUCK!

All conclusions, no matter who makes them or however they are arrived at, are and should be suspect and open to examination; in contrast, a good question is a menacing jab in the ribs—we are forced to react whether we like it or not. A good question beckons our anxieties into tentative focus and disquiets our emerging cognitions. In Western civilization, it is the permanence of change and innovation that has gained honor for heresy and guaranteed the right of dissent. The intellectual in Western civilization has a heritage of treason. Responsible criticism—the questioning of conclusions—is a public office.

This society does not exile or crucify its critics. It publishes them, televises them, and pays them consulting fees. The task of the intellectual in a brutal age is the preservation of sacred values. Intellectuals are a kind of clergy without ordination.

Science is an instrument of man to improve his human condition. It builds on man's capacity to see beyond himself and to find ordering principles that transcend his own circumstance and self-interest, insofar as that is possible. The ultimate empiricism is life itself, experience and events. Virtually all hypotheses arise in this sphere. All of the traditional methods of inquiry about the nature of man in society are intrinsically empirical. The social sciences are essentially historical, whether the range of study be remote or contemporary. The basic unit of inquiry is the case history or the case study which portrays a sequence of transactions involving individuals, institutions, and a physical setting. Every hypothesis tends to reflect historical and contemporary materials and a judgment about the future. The future itself is the laboratory that continuously tests and refines each paradigm of provisional truth. In the phrase of Jacob Burkhardt, "the logic of events" constitutes the most compelling basis of judgment for those who seek wisdom. Life is a process; each step builds on the one before it. Critics of the earlier steps are not wiser, only later.

Too readily have social scientists accepted the description of their work as "soft," as opposed to the "hard sciences." The sophisticated physicist and the molecular biologist find their "hard" knowledge dissolving into uncertainty as they learn that knowledge reflects less the subject matter than the theories, preconceptions, purposes, instruments, and methods of the scientist. In the wake of the cultural revolution, we must assert the primacy of judgment and the human scale in a world where uncertainty and tentative knowledge must live by provisional truths. The claims made in the name of scientific rationalism no longer pass unchallenged. The softness of the social sciences becomes a scientific value as an end and a means of truth. Soft truth may be the best kind, and soft decisions, flexible and open, able to be revised and extended, like clay pressed by many fingers, are very welcome. More and more it becomes clear that there are no pure science problems, only human problems and political choices. The technological imperative is dead; the God of Newtonian order died with the myths of scientific certainty.

The universities are and should be vulnerable. If there are those who would rape them, let them be raped. They are a religious extension of the whole society. What goes on there is always a continuing revolution of openness and ideas, where social forms may be invented and promoted. The best defense for the university is the legitimacy of its function as a place of universality and pluralism. It is most needed when these qualities are stomped into conformity by the juggernauts of political and cultural change, whether students or governments. Anyone who would kill a university is condemning himself to an ignominious and ignoble fate.

The process is fundamentally moral. Any antagonist who forces escalation by his own action is bound to find himself offset by the defensive reaction of others and his legitimacy weakened. This is as true of all innovators. It is necessary to run risks, and to accept the risks of action by others, but we must respond in kind and in proportion without enacting any self-fulfilling prophecies.

In the soft dawn of a new morning, it behooves us to refuse to be shocked by the future. No more karate chops of tomorrow! There have been too many saviors, too many gimmicks and pitchmen, too many claims on our credulity, too many unfulfilled promises. Keep cool! Find out what is worth saving and stand up for that. Value the ritual aspects of behavior. The dark symbolisms of threat and peril will be enhanced if we pay them too much heed and make them effective. The decade ahead may turn out to be the indeterminancy decade, in which the incorrigible human desire to be left alone in supreme skepticism and recalcitrance is asserted. There is in our time still a place for effort, skill, imagination, and work. There are still things to do and things worth doing. Symbolic disarray is preferable to the exactions of violence and war. The opportunity of change is accomplished. Now what enduring changes await us?

NOTES

1. Interview, *Rolling Stone*, March 4, 1971, p. 35.
2. Konrad Lorenz, *On Aggression* (New York: Grosset & Dunlap, 1967,) p. 76.
3. Quoted in *The New York Times*, January 12, 1971, p. 33.
4. Lewis Mumford, in *ibid.*, October 20, 1970, p. 77.

5. See report on SDS intrapolitics, U.S. House Committee on Internal Security, *Hearings, Investigation of SDS, Part 1–7* (Washington, D.C.: USGPO, 1969–70).

6. *Interview, Rolling Stone,* March 4, 1971, p. 35.

7. See the study by Urban Research Corporation "Student Protests, 1969," Chicago, January 1970, summarized in *The New York Times,* January 14, 1970, p. 51.

8. Melvin Maddocks, "Rituals: The Revolt Against the Fixed Smile," *Time,* October 7, 1970, p. 43.

9. Victor W. Turner, *The Ritual Process: Structure and Anti-Structure* (Chicago: Aldine, 1969), p. 141.

10. William Braden, *The Age of Aquarius* (Chicago: Quadrangle Books, 1970), p. 52.

11. Testifying in U.S. Senate Committee on Government Operations, 1969, *Hearings, Riots and Disorders,* Pt. 16, p. 3071.

12. Peter Marin, "Tripping the Heavy Fantastic," *The New York Times Book Review,* February 21, 1971, p. 7.

13. Albert Goldman, *Freak Show* (New York: Atheneum, 1971), p. 151.

BIBLIOGRAPHY

Aberle, David F. *The Peyote Religion Among the Navaho.* Chicago: Aldine, 1966.

Allee, W. C. *Cooperation Among Animals.* New York: Henry Schuman, 1938, revised 1951.

Altmann, Stuart A., ed. *Social Communication Among Primates.* Chicago: University of Chicago Press, 1967.

Alvarez, A. *The Savage God: A Study of Suicide.* New York: Random House, 1972.

Arnold, Thurman. *The Symbols of Government.* New York: Harcourt Brace Jovanovich, 1962.

Barnes, J. A. *Politics in a Changing Society: A Political History of the Fort Jameson Ngoni.* Manchester, Eng.: Manchester University Press, 1967.

Barnouw, Erik. *A Tower in Babel: A History of Broadcasting in the United States,* Vol. I, *to 1933.* New York: Oxford University Press, 1966.

————. *The Golden Web: A History of Broadcasting in the United States,* Vol. II, *1933–1953.* New York: Oxford University Press, 1968.

————. *The Image Empire: A History of Broadcasting in the United States,* Vol. III, *from 1953.* New York: Oxford University Press, 1970.

Barth, Fredrik. *Political Leadership Among Swat Pathans.* London: London School of Economics, 1970.

Bastock, Margaret. *Courtship: An Ethological Study.* Chicago: Aldine, 1967.

Beattie, John and Middleton, John, eds. *Spirit Membership and Society in Africa.* New York: Africana Publishing, 1969.

Berger, Peter. *The Social Construction of Reality*. Garden City, N.Y.: Doubleday, 1967.

Berne, Eric, *Games People Play*. New York: Grove Press, 1964.

————. *Transactional Analysis in Psychotherapy*. New York: Grove Press, 1961.

Bettelheim, Bruno. *Symbolic Wounds: Puberty Rites and the Envious Male*. London: Thames and Hudson, 1955.

Bohannan, Paul, ed. *Law and Warfare: Studies in the Anthropology of Conflict*. Garden City, N.Y.: Natural History Press, 1967.

Boorstin, Daniel J. *The Image, or What Happened to the American Dream*. New York: Atheneum, 1962.

Borgese, Elizabeth Mann. *The Language Barrier: Beasts and Men*. New York: Holt, Rinehart and Winston, 1968.

Boulding, Kenneth E. *The Image: Knowledge in Life and Society*. Ann Arbor, Mich.: University of Michigan Press, 1961.

Brown, Les. *Television: The Business Behind the Box*. New York: Harcourt Brace Jovanovich, 1972.

Brustein, Robert. *Revolution as Theatre*. New York: Liveright, 1971.

Burke, Kenneth. *Permanence and Change: An Anatomy of Purpose*. Los Altos, Calif.: Hermes Publications, 1954.

————. *Terms for Order*, edited by Stanley Edgar Hyman. Bloomington, Ind.: Indiana University Press, 1964.

Campbell, Joseph. *The Hero with a Thousand Faces*. Princeton, N.J.: Princeton University Press, 1972.

————. *The Masks of God: Primitive Mythology*. New York: Viking Press, 1970.

————, ed. *Myths, Dreams, and Religion*. New York: Dutton, 1970.

Canetti, Elias. *Crowds and Power*. New York: Viking Press, 1963.

Carson, Robert C. *Interaction Concepts of Personality*. Chicago: Aldine, 1969.

Cohen, Abner. *Customs and Politics in Urban Africa*. Berkeley, Calif.: University of California Press, 1971.

————. "Political Anthropology: The Analysis of the Symbolism of Power Relations." *Man*, June 1969, pp. 215–32.

Cohen, Joel E. *Casual Groups of Monkeys and Men: Stochastic Models of Elemental Social Systems*. Cambridge, Mass.: Harvard University Press, 1972.

Cohen, Yehudi A., ed. *Man in Adaptation: The Cultural Present*. Chicago: Aldine, 1968.

Crawford, J. R. *Witchcraft and Society in Rhodesia*. London: Oxford University Press, 1967.

Crook, John H., ed. *Social Behavior in Birds and Mammals, Essays on the Social Ethology of Animals and Man*. New York: Academic Press, 1970.

Dawson, Richard E. and Prewitt, Kenneth. *Political Socialization*. Boston: Little, Brown, 1969.

Desmonde, William Herbert. *Magic, Myth and Money: The Origin of Money in Religious Ritual*. New York: Free Press, 1962.

Edelman, Murray. *The Symbolic Uses of Politics*. Chicago: University of Illinois Press, 1967.

Edman, Irwin. *The Philosophy of Santayana*. New York: Random House, 1936, originally published in 1894.

Egbert, Donald Drew. *Social Radicalism and the Arts: Western Europe*. New York: Knopf, 1970.

Eliade, Mircea. *The Sacred and the Profane: The Nature of Religion*. New York: Harcourt Brace Jovanovich, 1959.

Feuer, Lewis S. *The Conflict of Generations*. New York: Basic Books, 1969.

Firth, Raymond. *The Work of the Gods in Tikopia,* 2nd ed. New York: Humanities Press, 1967.

Fortes, Meyer and Evans-Pritchard, E. E., eds. *African Political Systems.* New York: Oxford University Press, 1940.

Frankenberg, Ronald. *Village on the Border: A Social Study of Religion, Politics and Football in a North Wales Community.* London: Cohen & West, 1957.

Fried, Morton H. *The Evolution of Political Society: An Essay in Political Anthropology.* New York: Random House, 1967.

Gelfand, Michael. *The African Witch: With Particular Reference to Witchcraft Beliefs and Practice Among the Shona of Rhodesia.* London: E. S. Livingstone LTD, 1967.

Gluckman, Max. *Rituals of Rebellion in Southeast Africa.* Manchester, Eng.: Manchester University Press, 1954.

————, ed. *Essays on the Ritual of Social Relations.* Manchester, Eng.: Manchester University Press, 1962.

Goffman, Erving. *Asylums: Essays on the Social Situation of Mental Patients and Other Inmates.* Garden City, N.Y.: Doubleday, 1961.

————. *Behavior in Public Places: Notes on the Social Organization of Gatherings.* New York: Free Press, 1963.

————. *Encounters: Two Studies in the Sociology of Interaction.* Indianapolis: Bobbs-Merrill, 1961.

————. *Interaction Ritual: Essays on Face-to-Face Behavior.* Garden City, N.Y.: Doubleday, 1967.

————. *The Presentation of Self in Everyday Life.* Garden City, N.Y.: Doubleday, 1959.

————. *Strategic Interaction.* Philadelphia: University of Pennsylvania Press, 1969.

Goldman, Albert. *Freak Show.* New York: Atheneum, 1971.

Goldman, Emma. *Living My Life,* 2 vols. New York: Dover Publications, 1970.

Halleck, Seymour C. *The Politics of Therapy.* New York: Science House, 1971.

Hass, Hans. *The Human Animal: The Mystery of Man's Behavior.* New York: Putnam's, 1970.

Hayakawa, S. I. *Symbol, Status, and Personality.* New York: Harcourt Brace Jovanovich, 1963.

Hayden, Tom. *Trial.* New York: Holt, Rinehart and Winston, 1970.

Himmelstrand, Ulf. *Social Pressures, Attitudes and Democratic Processes.* Stockholm: Almquist & Wiksell, 1960.

Hinde, Robert A. *Animal Behavior: A Synthesis of Ethology and Comparative Psychology,* 2nd ed. New York: McGraw-Hill, 1970.

Hitler, Adolf. *Mein Kampf,* translated by Ralph Manheim. Boston: Houghton Mifflin, 1943, originally published in 1925.

Hobbes, Thomas. *Leviathan.* New York: Dutton, 1950.

Huxley, Aldous. *On Art and Artists.* New York: World Publishing, 1962.

Key, V. O., Jr. *Public Opinion and American Democracy.* New York: Knopf, 1964.

Lasswell, Harold D. and Arora, Satish K. *Political Communication: The Public Language of Political Elites in India and the United States.* New York: Holt, Rinehart and Winston, 1969.

Lawrence, Peter. *Road Belong Cargo: A Study of the Cargo Movement in the Southern Madang District of New Guinea.* Manchester, Eng.: Manchester University Press, 1964.

Leach, Edmund R. *Political Systems of Highland Burma: A Study of Kachin Social Structure.* Cambridge, Mass.: Harvard University Press, 1954.

Le Bon, Gustave. *The Crowd.* New York: Viking Press, 1968, originally published in 1895.

Lee, Richard B. and Devore, Irven, eds. *Man the Hunter.* Chicago: Aldine, 1968.

Levi, Mario Attilio. *Political Power in the Ancient World.* New York: New American Library, 1968.

Lewis, Arthur H. *Carnival.* New York: Trident Press, 1970.

Lorenz, Konrad. *On Aggression.* New York: Grosset & Dunlap, 1967.

Luckmann, Thomas. *The Invisible Religion.* New York: Macmillan, 1967.

Lupo, Alan, Colcord, Frank, and Fowler, Edmund P. *Rites of Way: The Politics of Transportation in Boston and the U.S. City.* Boston: Little, Brown, 1971.

Malinowski, Bronislau. *Magic, Science, and Religion and Other Essays.* New York: Doubleday, 1954.

McLuhan, Marshall. *Culture Is Our Business.* New York: McGraw-Hill, 1970.

————. *The Gutenberg Galaxy.* Toronto: University of Toronto Press, 1962.

————. *Understanding Media: The Extension of Man.* New York: New American Library, 1964.

———— and Fiore, Quentin. *War and Peace in the Global Village.* New York: Bantam Books, 1968.

Middleton, John, ed. *Magic, Witchcraft, and Curing.* Garden City, N.Y.: Natural History Press, 1967.

Morgenstern, Julian. *Rites of Birth, Marriage, Death and Kindred Occasions Among the Semites.* Chicago: Quadrangle Books, 1966.

Mumford, Lewis. *The Myth of the Machine: The Pentagon of Power.* New York: Harcourt Brace Jovanovich, 1969.

Mungo, Raymond. *Total Loss Farm: A Year in the Life.* New York: Dutton, 1970.

Nordhoff, Charles. *The Communistic Societies of the United States.* New York: Schocken Books, 1965, originally published in 1875.

O'Neill, William L. *Coming Apart: An Informal History of America in the 1960's.* Chicago: Quadrangle Books, 1971.

Peacock, James L. *Rites of Modernization: Symbolic and Social Aspects of Indonesian Proletarian Drama.* Chicago: University of Chicago Press, 1968.

Pelton, Robert W. *The Complete Book of Voodoo.* New York: Putnam's, 1972.

Read, Herbert. *Icon and Idea: The Function of Art in the Development of Human Consciousness.* New York: Schocken Books, 1965.

Reik, Theodor. *Ritual: Psycho-Analytic Studies.* New York: International University Press, 1931.

Rolling Stone Editors. *The Age of Paranoia: How the Sixties Ended.* San Francisco: Straight Arrow Books, 1972.

Rosenbaum, Peter C. *The Meaning of Madness.* New York: Science House, 1970.

Rubin, Bernard. *Political Television.* Belmont, Calif.: Wadsworth Publishing, 1967.

Schmookler, Jacob. *Invention and Economic Growth.* Cambridge, Mass.: Harvard University Press, 1966.

Schomp, Gerald. *Birchism Was My Business.* New York: Macmillan, 1970.

Schramm, Wilbur. *Mass Media and National Development: The Role of Information in the Developing Countries.* Stanford, Calif.: Stanford University Press, 1964.

————, ed. *Mass Communications,* 2nd ed. Chicago: University of Illinois Press, 1960.

Schultz, Duane P. *Panic Behavior.* New York: Random House, 1964.

Shamberg, Michael. *Guerrilla Television.* New York: Holt, Rinehart and Winston, 1971.

Slochower, Harry. *Mythopoesis*. Detroit: Wayne State University Press, 1970.

Skornia, Harry J. *Television and Society*. New York: McGraw-Hill, 1965.

Smelser, Neil. *Theory of Collective Behavior*. New York: Free Press, 1962.

Southwick, Charles H. *Primate Social Behavior*. Princeton, N.J.: Van Nostrand Reinhold, 1963.

Spiegel, John. *Transactions: The Interplay Between Individual, Family, and Society*. New York: Science House, 1971.

Stearn, Gerald Emanuel, ed. *McLuhan: Hot and Cool*. New York: New American Library, 1967.

Sumner, William Graham. *Folkways: A Study of the Sociological Importance of Usages, Manners, Customs, Mores, and Morals*. New York: New American Library, 1940.

Suttles, Gerald D. *The Social Order of the Slum: Ethnicity and Territory in the Inner City*. Chicago: University of Chicago Press, 1968.

Swartz, Marc J., ed. *Local-Level Politics: Social and Cultural Perspectives*. Chicago: Aldine, 1968.

Thompson, J. Eric S. *The Rise and Fall of Maya Civilization*. Norman, Okla.: University of Oklahoma Press, 1966.

Tiger, Lionel and Fox, Robin. *The Imperial Animal*. New York: Holt, Rinehart and Winston, 1972.

Turner, R. H. and Killian, L. M. *Collective Behavior*. Englewood Cliffs, N.J.: Prentice-Hall, 1967.

Turner, Victor W. *The Ritual Process: Structure and Anti-Structure*. Chicago: Aldine, 1969.

Van der Kloot, William G. *Behavior*. New York: Holt, Rinehart and Winston, 1968.

Van Gennep, Arnold. *The Rites of Passage*, translated by Monika B. Vizedom and Gabrielle L. Caffee. Chicago: University of Chicago Press, 1960.

White, David Manning, ed. *Pop Culture in America*. Chicago: Quadrangle Books, 1970.

Wickler, Wolfgang. *Mimicry in Plants and Animals*. New York: McGraw-Hill, 1968.

Wills, Garry. *Nixon Agonistes*. Boston: Houghton Mifflin, 1970.

Wilson, Monica. *Communal Rituals of the Nyakyusa*. New York: Oxford University Press, 1959.

Wisse, Ruth. *The Schlemiel as Modern Hero*. Chicago: University of Chicago Press, 1972.

Wolfe, Tom. *The Electric Kool-Aid Acid Test*. New York: Bantam Books, 1968.

———. *The Kandy-Kolored Tangerine-Flake Streamline Baby*. New York: Simon and Schuster, 1966.

———. *The Pump House Gang*. New York: Bantam Books, 1968.

———. *Radical Chic and Mau-Mauing the Flak Catchers*. New York: Farrar, Straus & Giroux, 1970.

Yablonsky, Lewis. *The Hippie Trip*. New York: Pegasus, 1969.

INDEX

Adaptation, 34, 65, 154, 232; anatomical, 23; as response, 26; creative, 33; biological, 37; loss in culture, 49; mutual, 54; in organized society, 83; and violence, 219

Africa: micropolitics in, 22; political instability of, 39; central, 75; tribal balance of power in, 98, 99; and European rule, 101; and witchcraft cults, 112; and circumcision, 130; and mediums, 141

Alienation, 231; social, 95; deepened, 219; of TV audience, 225

Animals, 6, 89, 91; and myth, 14; behavior patterns of, 23, 66; and orienting response, 26; European, 61; Animism, 65; courting and mating, 28, 75; mass ceremonies of, 125; frog war, 126, 127

Apathy: political, 135; and public crime, 160

Art, 31, 51, 67, 131, 137, 169, 175-197, 215, 221, 231, 248; as catalyst for change, 1-3; and reality, 13; primitive, 14; as pseudo-event, 18; and conflict, 38; and artistic imagination, 41, 46; and subconscious forecasting, 52; photography 72; pornography, 75; as exploration, 77; plausibility and immediacy of, 97; public, 202

Assassinations, 70, 88, 166, 215, 217; in U.S., 2; of political leaders, 10

Assimilation, 90; cultural, 42, 208; of ritual, 52; of natural events, 53; gypsy resistance to, 102; of form, 221

Bargaining: in interpersonal and intergroup transactions, 29, 31, 45, 49, 97; and rationality, 6; information as tool in, 43; and separation, 85, 94; and status, 117; informal, 212; high-risk, 218

Blacks, 43, 146, 203, 224, 235, 236, 237; and revolution, 4, 112, 113; status of, 21; Panthers, 54, 86, 87; and sacralization, 77, 90; power of, 114-116; leaders of, 155

Bureaucracies, 110, 156; in the "movement," 116

Caste system, 34, 153; and definition of art, 182

Catharsis, 21, 124, 128, 129, 141, 154, 188, 189, 205, 225, 238; social, 101; of tension, 127

Causality, 30, 207; and fantasy, 52; and history, 73

Ceremony, 17, 21, 24, 101; as pseudo-event, 18; formal behavior in, 19, 52; social meaning of, 23; and mating, 28; and repetition, 46; apotheosis in,

71; increase of, 76; social, 84; and common values, 130; and behavior norms, 150; rebellion against, 153; and art, 180; and mass assembly, 182; and multi-media, 244

Children, 6, 185, 235, 247; and legitimacy, 43; and models, 51; black, 70; initiation of, 84; delinquents, 109; flower, 132; students, 159; and sacrifice, 169

China: and cultural revolution, 2; and feudalism, 33; identity of, 101; Peiping rebellion in, 112; students in, 118, 238

Christianity, 61, 63, 142, 217; and gospel, 32; anti-, 62; Pauline, 153; and suicide, 166

Church, 170, 217, 247; and cult of the Potomac, 63; conscience of, 114; and reparation to blacks, 115, 116

Communications, 23, 47, 77, 204, 210; electronic, 5; interpersonal, 7; process of, 44; maximizing, 85; and media crowding, 160; and feedback, 188; informal, 220

Communism, 2, 96, 204, 206, 230; Communist Party, 111; Chinese students, 118; era of, 160; anti-, 236

Competition, 77, 85, 93, 112, 118, 205, 213, 243; in signals, 29; and value experimentation, 42, 44; and support, 46; and conflict, 57; collaborative, 110, 111, 118, 176; for attention, 216

Conflict, 91, 93, 100, 170, 204, 220, 242; internal and external, 18, 149; and ritual modification, 23; and collaborative competition, 57; over drugs, 73; and status, 84, 130; display, 87; reduction of, 95; unresolved, 96; personality, 97; ritual, 111; suspension of, 124; and crisis, 154; and growth, 81, 231

Constitution: and formalization of institutions, 94; and separation of powers, 98; and authority, 101; Bill of Rights, 219

Creativity, 17, 240; in ritual, 19; in adaptation, 33; in displacement, 88

Credibility: loss of, 43, 208; in crisis, 101; of communication, 202, 205; and problem solving, 233

Crisis, 20, 88, 204; and ritual, 22-23; international, 39, 236, 243; and reaction to new things, 66; resolution of, 91; social, 102; and unprogrammed coercion, 129; and external conflict, 154; and isolation, 162; life and death, 166; in Western culture, 191, 231; in Mid-East, 224